SKINNING OUT

MY TIME AT SEA AND JUMPING SHIP IN NEW ZEALAND

PHILIP SAUL

Published by Elizabeth St Publishing
Contact: elizabeth.st.publishing@gmail.com

ISBN 978-0-473-64832-9 (paperback)
ISBN 978-0-473-64833-6 (EPUB)

A catalogue record for this book is available from the National Library of New Zealand.

Credits: All images collection of author or public domain unless otherwise noted.

CONTENTS

To the ships' crews I sailed with, in every department. You certainly made life entertaining!

And to Kenneth Owen Kirkaldie, my best mate, without whom this story would not have been possible.

CHAPTER 1

IT WAS FREEZING COLD AND THERE WERE A COUPLE OF INCHES of frozen snow on the pavement as my mate Kerry and I attempted to thumb a lift to Birkenhead with the intention of joining the Blue Funnel shipping company as stewards.

We had met early that morning on Chester Square in front of the Town Hall, having skipped our respective technical colleges for the day, and not having enough money for a return bus fare to Birkenhead, we decided to hitchhike there and get the bus back.

We had been walking for quite some time by now, making it as far as Backford, on the A41, and were becoming somewhat disheartened, when a truck pulled over ahead of us and the driver indicated for us to get in.

We were both relieved to get out of the cold and clamber into the warmth of the cab, where the driver asked us where we were heading. As we were both feeling guilty about 'bonking off' college and had an uneasy feeling that running away to sea without telling our parents was vaguely unlawful, we had agreed that if anyone asked us where we were going, we would tell them that we were art students, and going to visit an exhibition which was currently running at the Liverpool Art Gallery.

For some weird reason we were convinced that if whoever offered us a lift found out the real reason we were travelling to Birkenhead, they would take us to the nearest police station and hand us in.

Despite neither of us being in the least interested in art and both doing general courses at tech, being an art student was deemed to be pretty cool at the time, and as we were both wearing our college scarves, we thought we looked the part and thought it was a good cover story.

Unfortunately for us, the truck driver had a genuine interest in art and even knew of the exhibition we were claiming to be interested in, and as he was headed into Liverpool through the Mersey Tunnel, he offered to drop us off outside the gallery.

I managed to convince him that we were really keen to cross the Mersey on the ferry, and after some awkward conversation about art, and a few questions that we were totally unable to answer, he finally dropped us off at Hamilton Square, in Birkenhead, much to our relief and no doubt to his. The poor guy must have thought he had picked up a pair of complete nutters.

After thanking the truck driver for the lift, we headed off in the direction of the docks. As we turned left out of Cathcart Street on to Corporation Road, I caught my first glimpse of the famous blue funnels towering over the cargo sheds at Vittoria Dock — and what a sight they were. I had seen numerous postcards and photographs of Blue Funnel ships, but this was my first sighting of the real thing, and the fact that there were three ships alongside in the dock was a bonus and a great thrill.

Those three tall, pale blue funnels with the broad black band around the top were instantly recognisable anywhere and I couldn't take my eyes off them.

We made our way along Corporation Road to Odyssey Works and after making enquiries at the gate, were directed to the office, where we explained that we were both keen to join the Blue Funnel Line as stewards. We were shown to the office of an elderly gentleman, who explained that the procedure for going to sea as a steward wasn't quite so straightforward as we had assumed, that there was a period of training at the catering school, that positions at the school were much sought after and, moreover, the minimum age for going to sea was 16. As we were both only 15 and a half, this was a major setback to our plans and not something that we had considered, although, in hindsight, it should have been.

That this revelation took the wind out of our sails would be an understatement, but the gentleman who was interviewing us advised us that we could apply to work at Odyssey Works until such time as we were old enough to enter the catering training programme.

We were offered application forms to take away and complete, have signed by our parents and returned to Odyssey Works.

Rather dejectedly, we retraced our steps to the bus terminal adjacent to the ferry terminal and Cammell Laird shipyard and caught the green Crosville bus back to Chester.

While I hadn't been expecting to sign on a ship immediately, I had been hoping that a job offer would have been forthcoming. After all, how hard could it be to become a ship's steward? I was eventually to find out just how hard, but in the meantime I had the task of obtaining the permission of my parents to go to sea in the catering department.

I had enrolled at Chester Technical College in September 1963, having just turned 15 years of age, with a view to applying to Alfred Holt's Blue Funnel Line as an apprentice deck officer at age 17. I had two years ahead of me to secure the required O and

A level certificates to enable me to apply to Holts for a position at Aulis, the training facility in Liverpool.

Unfortunately for me, due to the vagaries of the British education system, if you had not reached your twelfth birthday by 31 July, you were held back a year at primary school and did not sit the 11-plus exam with all your mates but had to join the class below you and take the exam the following year.

As my birthday fell on 9 August, I and a couple of other guys in the same boat had to say goodbye to our mates who were heading off to grammar or secondary school and endure another year at primary.

This was the reason that after only three years of secondary education, I was heading off to tech to join a class who had each had four years of secondary education.

My form teacher at St David's secondary school, Saltney, Flintshire had assured my father that I was quite capable of catching up, and keeping up with the class at technical college, but I'm not sure which planet this guy was on, or how I'd managed to convey the impression that I was some sort of genius.

However, by the end of the first term, it was obvious to me that I was in trouble and seriously out of my depth. I was fine with subjects such as English, History, Geography, and the like, but the really important subjects such as Maths and Physics were becoming a real struggle and simply beyond my capability to catch up.

To cap things off, one afternoon I was at the back of the classroom and the lecturer was writing stuff on the chalkboard which we were expected to copy into our notebooks. The guy sitting at the desk next to me was scribbling away like crazy. I turned to him and said, 'Can you read that from here?'

His reply of 'course I can' nearly floored me and made me realise that I was in deep, deep shit.

When I got home from college that afternoon, I told Mum, who arranged an appointment with an optician who soon confirmed that I was short-sighted and required glasses. I was devastated that my dream of going to sea as a deck officer was over, but in a way, I was quite relieved to have another excuse for failing, as I knew that achieving the required standard to gain a place at Aulis was totally beyond me.

When I did eventually get to sea and found out what an apprenticeship with Holts truly cost, I was even more relieved, as I knew my parents would have sacrificed everything to help me achieve my ambition, and gone into deep debt, but being from a working-class family it would have been a real struggle for them and an unfair burden.

It had been my ambition to join the Merchant Navy for some time and even when I joined Sea Cadets it was only with the intention of eventually joining the Merch and not the Royal Navy like all the other kids.

Sea Cadets was obviously more orientated towards training for the Royal Navy and I didn't mind all the drill and discipline that went with it, but there wasn't much scope for using your initiative, and everything was done by rote.

Whenever a visiting high-ranking naval officer came around on a tour of inspection of the establishment, and he asked us what we intended to be, the answer was always signaller, gunner or quartermaster, even from me, as I was too embarrassed to say that I wanted to be a deck officer on a cargo ship.

No-one, ever, wanted to be a steward or a cook.

I stuck at it for about 18 months, until one horrendous weekend of exercises. Early one Saturday morning, we were issued with rifles, loaded onto a launch, taken up the river Dee and disembarked at Eaton Hall, the Duke of Westminster's place just outside Chester.

The Royal Marine cadets all had battle dress with all the proper kit, but the Sea Cadets just wore any old clothes, and a right sight we looked.

We all split into small groups for the exercise, which involved finding our way to camp at Kinnerton without being detected by the other groups.

The petty officer in charge of our group was an engine driver for British Rail in real life and couldn't read a map or use a compass to save his life.

Despite finding ourselves on the edge of a disused wartime airfield which was clearly marked on the map, and only a short distance from the campsite, this dickhead decided we had to head off in the opposite direction, in spite of our protestations.

This guy decided that he wasn't going to be given advice by a bunch of 12 and 13-year-olds, so we spent the entire Saturday afternoon wandering about the Cheshire–Wales border, scaring the shit out of the locals with our rifles, when we had to go knocking on doors to beg for water. (The rifles had the bolts removed, but the locals weren't aware of this until we pointed it out.)

At one point we found a pub and the PO went inside to ask for directions, and have a couple of pints, while the rest of us sat on the roadside with our rifles.

We eventually reached camp about 1900 hrs and this clown had us all come to attention and then marched us down the farm track while the rest of the crowd, who had been in camp for hours, fell about laughing and giving us some right stick.

The officers and POs then headed off to the pub for the night and left us in the charge of the senior cadets, who decided that they wanted to practise their judo, so we spent the rest of the evening being body slammed into the paddock.

When we did finally get to bed, four of us were settled down in a tent, when one of the officers who wasn't meant to be on the exercise decided to turn up after all and we were turfed out of the tent and sent to sleep on top of a haystack in the barn, where we endured a very uncomfortable night and one of the guys fell off the haystack in his sleep. Luckily, he landed in a pile of loose hay, which broke his fall, but it gave all of us a fright.

Next morning, we were told to pack up all our gear, making sure we did not forget anything, and then stack it on the truck for the return to HQ where we would pick it up later in the day.

When it came time for breakfast and we realised that all our kit including plates, cups and cutlery had gone back to Chester, the Marine Captain took great delight in telling us Sea Cadets that there would be no breakfast, as we had nothing to eat off.

The Marine Cadets, on the other hand, had all their mess gear with them in their backpacks so got to eat.

It turned out to be a long, long day making our way back to TS Deva, in Chester, on foot, through the Welsh and English countryside, having had nothing to eat all day, and at one stage we were within about a mile of my home in Saltney and I just resisted the urge to desert.

When I finally got home that Sunday evening, I ate everything that Mum put in front of me and then fell asleep in the bath.

During the rest of that week, I washed and pressed all my kit and on the following Friday turned up to drill, handed it back and told them I quit.

The weekend exercise had been totally pointless and taught us nothing, but it could have been an opportunity to improve our map-reading, cross-country navigation and field craft.

Instead, I found out that I could go all day without eating and that the majority of the people in charge couldn't give a stuff about us junior members of the organisation and were only there on a power-trip and for what they could get out of it.

Undoubtedly, there were a number of senior members of the organisation who were dedicated and professional and gave fully of their time for not much reward, but, unfortunately, they were not much in evidence on that particular weekend.

The mess kit that the Sea Cadets had was stuff borrowed from home, not proper field kit, and couldn't be carried without a pack. There were a number of private cars belonging to officers who could have taken our mess kit back to Chester with them so that we could have had breakfast, but they just didn't care.

The one thing I did miss about Cadets was that I was a member of the band and had to take my bugle home with me every Friday night.

My mate and I used to call in at the fish and chip shop where all the local yobs hung out and they always insisted on trying out the bugle. I always hid the mouthpiece in my uniform, so I was quite happy to let them have a go and watch guys who were three or four years older than us busting a gut to try to get a sound out of the thing. They were too thick to realise that a mouthpiece was required, but, regrettably, we had to give the place a swerve once someone had cottoned on.

I never told Dad why I packed Cadets in, as I reckon he would have kicked up a fuss, as he always drummed it into me when I joined that if I ever found myself in charge of a group of men, I must always put their welfare first before thinking about my own welfare or comfort. That would have been his army training I suppose and, secretly, I think he held high hopes that I would consider a career in the army.

Anyway, I didn't let that episode diminish my interest in ships and shipping.

My mate Kerry and I bought ship-spotting books and from the

age of 12 we used to catch the bus to Birkenhead and then ride the Mersey Ferry for as long as we could, trying to record the names of passing ships. Not that we ever saw many that far up the Mersey, so we resorted to recording the names of the tugs pushing the shit-barges down river.

On one memorable occasion we managed to wander onto Liverpool's Canning Dock and right up to the stern of the Palm Line boat, *Andoni Palm*, before a policeman spotted us and kicked us out of the dock. He wasn't the friendliest copper, but I think he was just pissed off that we had managed to get into the dock without him seeing us.

I don't remember where this interest in the sea came from, as although my grandfather had been at sea, on deck, all his life until an injury ended his seagoing career, Dad never, ever spoke about him to me.

Dad had been a regimental sergeant major in an engineering regiment during the war. Growing up, our toys were mainly military, although, as Dad worked for British Rail after the war, train sets became more popular as we got older.

My grandfather had joined Blue Funnel in 1900, sailing as able seaman (AB) in the *Achilles* and eventually making bosun in the *Keemun*, a Straits boat, in 1913. During the First World War he was AB and then bosun's mate in the HMAT *Nestor* and made bosun again in 1919.

I knew none of this until recently when my youngest sister, Nic, did some research and came up with the record of his voyages from 1900 to 1925.

It was only after I had expressed interest in going to sea that Dad had contacted Holts and obtained the brochures regarding a career at sea as a deck officer and the requirements for gaining a place at Aulis, the Blue Funnel training school for mates in Liverpool.

Apart from my obvious educational failings at technical college, there was another, more personal reason for not being too happy there and that was that I was terribly naïve when it came to matters of sex and not very worldly at all.

Mum was pretty strait-laced and bad language wasn't tolerated in any way whatsoever.

I never heard my father, uncles or maternal grandfather ever swear, apart from the odd 'bugger' and even that was met with horror from my mother if she happened to be present.

When I was about 10 years old, Mum happened to walk into the room as I used the word 'shag' in front of my seven-year-old brother, Roger. I knew it was a naughty word but didn't have a clue what it meant. Mum gave me a real thrashing for using it.

I was so pissed off that I told Roger there was no such thing as Father Xmas, and that it was my dad that left the presents. (This was the middle of summer, by the way.) He went running to Mum to tell her what I had told him, and she gave me another thrashing.

Anyway. The point of this is that talking about sexual matters to my parents was definitely not something I would have contemplated, so all my sexual knowledge came from my mates at school, and it was fairly basic and confused.

There was a guy in my class at tech named Geoff who was quite a few months older than me and very much a 'man of the world'. He was part Scottish and part Nepalese, and his father was an officer in a Gurkha regiment, stationed in Chester, and attached to Western Command.

Geoff was one of the nicest blokes you could wish to meet, but very mature for his age, as he had been all around the world with the army, stationed in exotic places like Singapore and Hong Kong, and his experiences with girls made me extremely envious.

If he hadn't actually 'done it' with a girl, he had come very,

very close. I was fascinated by his experiences and hung on every word, as did most of the other guys in the class.

One lunchtime, the two of us were talking about sex (what else?) when something I must have said gave him reason to pause. He looked at me and said, 'Do you know where babies come from, Philip?' and waited for my answer.

Well, of course I knew where babies came from!

When out riding my bike when I was about 11, I came across a cow in the lane by our house. It had just given birth to a calf and the farmer was driving his van with the calf in it back to the farm, while the cow trotted behind with the afterbirth still hanging out of its backside.

I had also watched numerous Sunday lunchtime farming programmes featuring sheep giving birth to lambs and the screen always gave close-up shots of the lambs sliding out of the sheep's backside, so of course I knew where babies came from! What a stupid question.

When I said to Geoff that babies come out of a woman's arse, he cracked up. When he had finished falling about laughing, he couldn't wait to tell the rest of the class, and as a quarter of the class were girls, my 'class cred' was shot to pieces.

When they told me where babies really came from, I couldn't believe it and thought they were having me on, but I still couldn't pluck up the courage to go home to Mum and ask.

I had also figured out that to engage in sex, you either had to get married or go with a prostitute, and as there were no prostitutes in Chester, or so I thought, then you had to go abroad.

I had a paper-round for a couple of years and the *News of the World* regularly printed exposés of red-light districts, which were always located in exotic places like Hong Kong, Singapore, Paris, Hamburg or Amsterdam.

I used to devour these stories, along with all the lurid details of the Profumo Affair, which seemed to go on forever, and figured that if I wanted to get laid, I had to get abroad somehow.

And so there were a number of reasons that I, along with my mate Kerry, had set out on that icy February morning to hitchhike to Birkenhead to try to become a steward with Alfred Holt's Blue Funnel Line.

CHAPTER 2

WELL, I HAD THE APPLICATION FORM AND NOW I HAD TO GET my parents to sign it. Dad came around after a couple of days, but he definitely wasn't happy that I had decided to apply to Holts as a steward. Mum was adamant that there was no way that I was going away to sea in the Merchant Navy as crew. She kept coming up with ideas for jobs ashore, which meant carrying on at tech and trying to pass some exams, but I was determined to go to sea and stuck to my guns.

The pack that Dad had received from Holts, regarding cadet training, also contained brochures about the deck training school at Odyssey Works in addition to the catering training school. The deck school was obviously out, due to my poor eyesight. I had no mechanical inclination whatsoever, so the engine room was also out, and that just left catering.

I wasn't the least interested in catering either, but the photos on the catering brochures showed guys in white jackets running around carrying silver trays, and I thought, 'How hard can that be?'

I told Mum that if I had to continue at tech I wasn't going to try, so it would be a complete waste of time and eventually she very reluctantly gave in and signed the form.

I was to regret having painted myself into a corner, when after my first trip I found it so different to anything I had imagined and wanted to pack it in, but couldn't, after all the fuss I had made, and just had to stick it out and make the best of things.

My mate, Kerry, showed the application form to his parents who ripped it up and told him that there was no way he was going into the Merchant Navy and that he was going to carry on at tech. I don't really think he had his heart in it and was only doing it because I was. Anyway, he went back to tech and eventually ended up joining the Royal Navy.

Once my application form was signed, I caught the bus back to Birkenhead, made my way to Odyssey Works and handed the form to the elderly gentleman who had interviewed us the first time.

He told me to carry on at tech and as soon as a vacancy occurred at the works, they would be in touch with me.

As I was leaving, he asked me a question and when replying I omitted to call him sir.

For such a little guy he couldn't half shout and the whole of Odyssey Works must have heard him bollocking me. His final words to me were 'Don't ever forget, lad, that Jack's never as good as his master!'

I really thought I had blown it and walked out never expecting to hear from them again and cursing the teachers at technical college, who dissuaded us from calling them sir or miss and insisted on being called by their names.

After a few weeks of going through the motions at college, I finally received a very formal-looking letter, which advised me that I had been accepted for catering training at Odyssey Works and gave a commencement date and time.

At this time, Dad was employed on shift work at Associated Octel in Ellesmere Port, and on the day I was due to start, he was on nights, which finished at 6 a.m. As I had to catch the first bus to Birkenhead which left Chester at 7 and he arrived home at 6.30, he told me to wait for him and he would come to Birkenhead and accompany me to Odyssey Works.

Well, what self-respecting 15-year-old wants his Dad turning up with him on his first day of work?

Not me anyway, so at 6.15 I headed out the door on the 25-minute walk into Chester.

I was standing on Chester Square in the cold and the dark, waiting for the bus and congratulating myself on having gotten away with it, when striding across the square came my old man in a very agitated state, and wanting to know why I hadn't waited for him.

I made some excuse about 'making sure that I didn't miss the bus', and just had to accept the fact that he was going to come with me, whether I wanted him to or not.

On the hour-long trip he told me quite a bit about the Blue Funnel Line and its history, which he'd never mentioned previously, so the journey turned out to be rather more interesting than I had anticipated. Looking back, I think that the problem had been that he wasn't particularly close to his father who had been away at sea a lot of the time when Dad was young, and reading between the lines, I think his father had had a bit of a drinking problem.

Dad and his two brothers never drank, at all, and when my brothers and I grew up and took Dad out for a drink, he was 'as pissed as a fart' after a couple of pints.

When we arrived at the Works, we were met by the old gent, whose name I can't remember, who had given me such a powerful bollocking for not calling him sir. He and Dad got on like a house on fire, talking about Blue Funnel, and the fact that my grandfather had been the shore bosun at Odyssey Works following his injury at sea, which had put paid to his seagoing career.

After some time, Dad left and I was taken across to the staff canteen and introduced to the husband and wife couple in charge and an old ex-seagoing cook. They were three really nice people who were great to work for, and despite the mountains of dirty dishes, pots and pans and cutlery I was to wash over the coming months, I really enjoyed working there.

I was going to be working in the canteen until I was old enough to move into the catering training school, a bit closer to my sixteenth birthday.

Odyssey Works was the big workshop complex on Corporation Road opposite the Vittoria Docks that serviced all the Blue Funnel ships before they departed Birkenhead for deep sea, and it also housed the Deck Boys training school, the Catering training school and Radio training.

It was also the base for a group of women and girls who repaired all the soft furnishings for the ships, and what a hard-case lot they were. I really fancied one or two of them, but they weren't the least bit interested in some spotty 15-year-old and just took the piss.

One of the guys who worked with me was a Liverpool Chinese steward named Tony Chan. Tony was 19 and was one of the Chinese catering crowd that used to coast (work coastal trips) for Blue Funnel.

He was due to get married and was working at the Works while waiting for the big day. He was a good-looking guy and the women were all over him while I could only look on in envy, but he wasn't interested and if you'd seen the photo of his fiancée, you'd understand why.

Tony was a really nice bloke who never tired of answering all my dumb questions about ships and life at sea, and he had a really great sense of humour.

From the window by the big sink, where I washed dishes, I could see the Clan boats, and others, coming down through the Duke Street bridge from the West Float and used to daydream about being in one of them and heading out deep sea. I couldn't wait to get the training out of the way and head to sea.

My pay was £3 per week, and out of that I gave Mum a pound, my bus fare to Birkenhead cost 15 shillings per week, so that left me with 25 bob a week, which was the same amount I used to make on my old paper round. Still, at that time I didn't drink — well, not legally anyway — so it was enough to go to the movies occasionally and buy a few records, and I was happy enough.

The first bus from Chester didn't arrive in Birkenhead until about 8 a.m. and as clocking-on time was at 8, I was given dispensation to start work a little later, and this carried on over to when I worked on the shore gang later in life. I could normally make it to work by 8.15, but no-one seemed worried if the bus was delayed and I was a bit later.

I loved the hustle and bustle of Odyssey Works, with lifeboats turning up for repair on the back of a truck, or engine parts going to the workshops for service and the occasional person turning up in seagoing uniform. It felt great to be part of this marine environment, albeit an extremely minor part of it.

After a few months working in the canteen, I was finally accepted into the Catering Training school and joined about a dozen other boys in the class.

The first thing we had to do was go to the chandlers adjacent to the works and purchase our kit, which consisted of a couple of T-shirts, a couple of pairs of khaki dungarees, a couple of white mess jackets, silver buttons, with the AH (Alfred Holt) monogram, for the jackets and a pair of blues.

I think my parents must have helped me out with the purchase of my kit as I don't think I could have afforded it out of my wages.

The jackets and blues were sort of 'one size fits all' so they required a bit of work in order to make them fit and look reasonably fashionable. The waist of the jackets had to be brought in to give them some shape and the blues made a little tighter around the arse, although not too tight as they still had to pass muster in the classroom. That had to wait until we went deep sea.

The person in charge of the classroom was an ex-2nd steward named Mr Mackie and his offsider was a huge ex-saloon steward, Jim McIntyre, who used to be in the *Gunung Djati*, the ex-Blue Funnel pilgrim ship which was on the Far East to Jeddah run carrying Muslim passengers.

They were both reasonably nice guys and the atmosphere in the classroom wasn't too onerous as long as you did what was expected of you.

The class was made up almost exclusively of local guys from Birkenhead, Wallasey and various parts of Liverpool, with me being classed as the only outsider, coming from Chester. It just goes to show you how parochial people were in those days, as although Chester is only about 18 miles away from Merseyside, I was made to feel as though it was the other side of the world.

The other thing that I quickly became aware of was that, although I had only had three years of secondary education and a couple of months at tech, I was the most educated person in the class by a country mile, and that was already beginning to be an issue.

I seriously needed to dumb down a bit and also start using some serious swear words if I was going to fit in and not stand out like a sore thumb.

I think I was beginning to understand why Mum made such a

fuss about me going to sea. She obviously knew a few things that I didn't.

The first item on the classroom agenda was hygiene, which was quite comprehensive and at the end of the first week we were told to write an essay on it over the weekend.

The author during coastal training

Come Monday morning, I turned up to class with my two foolscap pages of essay and found out that I was the only one in the class to have bothered. Mr Mackie was totally impressed and read my work out to the rest of the class. Boy, was I in the shit!

The other issue was religion and although I knew my family was C of E, that was about as far as it went. The only times I had attended church was when I was in the Cub Scouts and the Sea Cadets and perhaps the odd family christening.

Religion was not a big thing in our family, and at the age of 12 I was beginning to have my doubts about it.

One day I asked Dad whether there any such thing as God. He 'ummed' and 'ahhed' for about a minute and then changed the subject. I decided at that point that if Dad couldn't tell me that there was a God, then there probably wasn't.

I asked Mum to write a letter to school to excuse me religious instruction as I would rather spend my time in the school library.

Mum said, 'Of course not. What do you think the neighbours would think?'

She wasn't worried that I was agnostic, but worried about the neighbours, which says something about the importance of religion in our family.

Anyway, it was approaching July and all the guys in class were going on about the Orange and The Green, which I had never even heard of, and didn't know what they were on about, so that was something else to beat me over the head with.

The leader of the class was a ginger-haired bloke who was a bit of a smart-arse and I didn't get on too well with him.

Every Thursday we used to go to the local Guinea Gap baths for swimming and life-saving lessons, and on one occasion there was a class from the local girls' school sharing the pool with us.

This guy jumped into the pool beside one of these girls and splashed her, so she said something to him. He told her to fuck off, as you do, and she complained to the mistress who was in charge of the class.

The mistress knew who we were and she also knew someone in Holts management, and complained about this guy's behaviour and language. As the only one with ginger hair, he was easily identifiable, and the following morning he was called up before the class, told to collect his gear and dismissed on the spot.

While I didn't have too much sympathy for the guy and wasn't too unhappy to see him go, I was a little unsettled by the ruthlessness of the dismissal and the fact he wasn't given the chance to apologise or make amends, or even given the chance to give his side of the story.

My essay on hygiene had made me a bit of a favourite of Mr Mackie, who kept referring to my class effort, but I very nearly managed to stuff up all of my good work on one occasion.

He was giving a demonstration on hand-washing, and using a bar of soap, he would wash his hands, let the water out of the basin, refill it and wash his hands again, and repeat this a number of times.

The scum from the soap would float on the surface each time and he would use this to prove that you could never, ever get your hands properly clean.

I was about to blurt out the obvious, that the scum wasn't dirt, but the residue of what the soap was comprised of. Fortunately for me, a little voice perched on my shoulder urged me not to be so stupid and keep my mouth shut, which I did.

I can just imagine the reaction if I had been dumb enough to have embarrassed him in front of the class. My seagoing career would have been over before I knew it.

It was the summer of '64 and I had only been in the training class a few weeks when another member of the class and I were called out and told that we were being sent up to Glasgow to join the company ship SS *Pyrrhus*.

Pyrrhus was one of the four famous Blue Funnel P-boats, fast cargo-liners of 10,000 tons with a single screw giving a service speed of 18 knots and having accommodation for 35 first-class passengers.

Her sister ships were the *Perseus*, *Peleus* and *Patroclus*, which between them carried out a three-monthly regular express service to the Far East, via the Suez Canal.

Peleus was the favourite ship to obtain a berth in, as she was always home for Xmas and New Year.

When the P-boats arrived in Gladstone Dock from deep sea, they were met by the catering boys who had completed their training at Odyssey Works, and under the supervision of a chief and 2nd steward, they coasted the ship, up to Glasgow usually, and then back to Vittoria Dock in Birkenhead, where she prepared for her next voyage to the Far East.

The catering boys usually did three of these coastal voyages before being allocated a berth in a Blue Funnel ship which was about to go deep sea.

Now, this other kid and I were off to join a ship partway through a coastal voyage and I had only had minimal training, so I was a bit apprehensive, to say the least.

The other guy had done the full training previously, but had suffered some sort of illness, and had been held back in training until something came up, and he also knew most of the catering crowd aboard the *Pyrrhus*, who he had trained with.

We found out that we were replacements for a boy who had fallen down a companionway and broken a leg, and another boy who had gotten into some sort of shit, but I can't recall what it was about now.

My training hadn't even gotten as far as table service, or silver service, and I voiced my concerns to Mr Mackie, but he assured me that I would be able to pick all of that up during my coastal training.

We were told to be at Liverpool Lime Street Station in time for the 17:30 train to Glasgow, and Mr Mackie met us there and saw us off on the three-and-a-half-hour trip to Glasgow. There we were met by the 2nd steward, Ted McKain, and the baker, who were both a bit grumpy, as they had had to interrupt their night's drinking to meet us.

We hadn't had anything to eat so they bought us a pie each and then we made our way to the docks to board *Pyrrhus*.

She happened to be in dry-dock at the time and I was blown away by the sight of this ship sitting on the stocks. She looked huge, and the contours of her hull made her look sleek and very impressive.

We boarded via a temporary gangway from the quay, and I was met for the first time with that smell unique to ships: fuel oil intermingled with the smell from the galley and odours from the hold. It was a smell I came to love over the years, but at that time I was just feeling homesick and sorry for myself as it was the first time in my life I had been so far away from home, and I was not enjoying myself. Things were to get a lot worse.

The author's first ship, SS Pyrrhus, *was one of the four famous Blue Funnel P-boats*

We were allocated a double berth in the stewards' alleyway and the following morning we hit the deck running. Well, the other guys did, but as the two of us who had just joined didn't have a clue what we were supposed to be doing, we just stood around like a couple of spare pricks until the 2nd steward got around to us.

I was detailed to join another couple of guys at the pantry sink and prepared to start washing all the breakfast dishes which were beginning to pile up. Partway through this operation, I was approached by some dude in uniform with two wavy bands on his sleeve, who told us guys on sink duty to stop what we were doing and follow him.

He led us down a companionway, along an alleyway, to a locker with a pile of boxes of spirits and told us to pick up one each and take it up to the bar on the second deck, which we duly did.

Now, when we were taught about badges of rank and insignia when I was in Sea Cadets, I couldn't have been paying attention, because I thought this guy was the radio officer.

After dropping the case of liquor off at the bar, I came back down to the pantry, noticed that the dirty dishes had piled up and proceeded to deal with them. This dude came down with the other boys and noticed me back at the sink washing dishes. He asked me who the hell had told me to carry on washing dishes when he had other work for me.

He then proceeded to rip me another arsehole, to the great amusement of everyone else.

Turned out that this was the chief steward, a guy named Charlie Griffiths, and definitely not someone you wanted to be offside with.

A little later that morning, the 2nd steward took me and the other guy ashore to the shipping office to sign on, and while returning to the ship we saw the Blue Funnel Victory ship, *Talthybius*, with the woodbine funnel, gliding past on the Clyde at the bottom of the street. She was quite a sight with her distinctive funnel and there weren't too many Victory ships still around at this stage so the scene remains etched in my memory.

We were in Glasgow for a further five days, and during that time I did not set foot ashore, apart from the trip to the shipping office, as I was flat broke.

I was also a little depressed, as washing dishes, cleaning

shithouses (heads) and scrubbing alleyways on my hands and knees was not what I had signed up for, and if the truth were known I wanted to pack it in big time, and just wished that I had not made such a fuss about going to sea and could find a face-saving way out.

We departed Glasgow and made our way around to the Mersey and up to Birkenhead, arriving at Vittoria Dock mid-afternoon. Steaming up the Mersey, I had the most euphoric 'channels' experience – a feeling of great excitement – I ever had in the entire time I was at sea, which did not bode well considering that I had only been away five days.

Those of us who lived local, and Chester was classed as local, were allowed home each night and weekend, and that night I caught the bus to Chester. I was accompanied as far as Bebington by one of the other catering boys, a guy called Ken, who had already done a couple of coastal trips and was due to go deep sea. He was a really nice bloke and easy to talk to. Unfortunately, he was tragically killed in a motorbike accident a couple of years later.

We worked by the *Pyrrhus* until she was ready for sea, when we handed over to the deep-sea crowd and then went over to join the *Peleus*, which had just docked in Gladstone Dock.

Fortunately, it was high summer and the good weather helped to keep me in a cheerful mood, plus the fact that I now knew the rest of the crowd, which helped enormously.

The chief steward on this coastal trip was a guy named Bob Shakeshaft, who was a bit of a sarcastic bastard and forever pulling guys up about something and taking the piss.

He took me into the pantry and introduced me to the pantry-man and told him I was to be the pantry-boy for the first week. We changed jobs each week so that we experienced all the different aspects of training.

The pantry-man was an old bloke who no longer went deep sea and was permanently on the coast, as was the chief cook.

The pantry-man seemed like an okay bloke and pleasant enough but did not say much except issue instructions to me. During the first day's dinner service he told me to go to the cook and ask him for another tray of baked fish, which was the main course.

What I wasn't aware of was that the pantry-man and the cook had a long-standing feud going on and couldn't stand the sight of each other. When I brought the tray of fish over to the hot-press, the pantry-man said, 'What the fuck's that?'

'It's the tray of fish you told me to get, pants,' I replied.

He said, 'Well, you can take it back and tell that fat bastard I'm not serving that, 'cos it's as dry as a nun's cunt.'

Well, I know I was agnostic, but some things were off limits as far as I was concerned, and that included profane language in relation to any religion or religious person. I was just gob-smacked and couldn't believe I had just heard this from some old guy who was old enough to be my grandad.

I sure had some growing up and hardening up to do, because things carried on in the same vein for the rest of the week, and I was stuck in the middle.

Fortunately, the week finally came to an end, and I was able to move to another position and let some other poor bastard put up with their juvenile crap.

One morning, after we had completed our scrub-outs, Ted McKain, the 2nd steward, made us all assemble with our buckets, scrubbing brushes and cloths.

He had one of the boys standing beside him, with a supercilious grin on his face, holding a bucket, over the side of which was draped an immaculate scrub-out cloth, which was almost the same colour as when it was first issued.

The rest of us looked down at the dirty, slimy cloth lying at the bottom of our buckets and realised that this guy had been 'dhobying' his cloth every morning after scrub-out and this was the result.

McKain didn't do this guy any favours, as we gave him shit for weeks and we never did get around to laundering our cloths.

When it became my turn to do a stint in the saloon, I explained to the powers that be that I hadn't done any training on table service or silver service and was out of my depth. I was told that I had 'better fuck'n learn then, and make sure you don't fuck up'.

As all the lunch and dinner service was silver service, I just had to watch the other boys and copy what they did. Fortunately, they were all sympathetic and helped me out as much as they could, so that I got through the ordeal without too many mishaps.

Silver service is now a thing of the past, but if anyone is under the illusion that it is easy and that anyone can do it, they should give it a go and find out just how difficult it really is.

Some guys made it look really easy, but that just showed how skilled they were, and I always envied the way some of them made it look so effortless.

Glasgow, back in 1964, wasn't much of a run ashore, especially as we couldn't go into the pubs, and had to make do with local coffee bars to listen to music.

By this time, I was hating the place and couldn't wait to get back to Birkenhead, and then home, as I was really homesick again and hating the job and the people.

The two songs at the top of the charts were The Beatles' 'Hard Day's Night' and The Animals' 'House of the Rising Sun', and to this day I can't listen to those two songs without being reminded of one of the most depressing times of my life.

When we arrived back in Vittoria Dock, I was advised by Mr Mackie that I was going deep sea in *Peleus* as catering-boy.

Having only had a couple of weeks at the training school, and only one and a bit coastal trips, I was a little unsure that I was up to it, to say the least, but Mr Mackie told me that my reports had been very positive and that he felt that he felt that I was up to it.

Well, I knew that I could handle most of the work, the cabin cleaning, the scrub-outs, the pantry work and the like, as they were arduous but straightforward. But the saloon service was another matter and required experience and skill, which was a bit of a worry.

I put on a brave face when I informed my parents that I was going deep sea and made out that I was really excited at the prospect. I would have given anything to find an excuse not to go, but it was too late now. I'd shouted my big mouth off once too often for my own good.

The day I had my bags packed and was about to leave home, my elder sister Sandra said, 'Aren't you excited that you're going to Japan?'

I just replied, 'Not really.'

Anyway, before that happened, I had to continue working by *Peleus* in Vittoria Dock, visiting the medical centre in Odyssey Works for all my check-ups and injections, including smallpox vaccination, and purchasing additional white mess-jackets.

There were three of us first-trip catering boys and we would be joining the galley-boy and a couple of senior boys from the previous trip.

CHAPTER 3

WE JOINED THE SHIP THE DAY BEFORE WE SAILED FROM Birkenhead, at the beginning of September, and became fully involved in the madhouse that is a Blue Funnel ship preparing to depart on a deep-sea voyage.

We were sailing the following morning, so there was an inspection by all the shoreside big-wigs, and the huge amount of work that went into preparing for that, with it having to be spotless all over and everything in place.

People were running everywhere, and no sooner had we boys been allocated one job than we were instructed to 'fuck'n leave that and come with me' and given another task to carry out.

We were at the beck and call of everyone, which got pretty confusing at times and resulted in plenty of bollockings for leaving one task unfinished and embarking on another.

Being at the very bottom of the 'food chain', it was a bit difficult to refuse the request of, say, the saloon-bobby or similar, when he told you to do something.

Stating that the 2nd steward allocated you this job was just met with the response 'Fuck the 2nd steward, I need you to do this right now.'

When the 2nd steward turned up and bawled you out for not having completed the original task, there was no point blaming the saloon-bobby, or whoever, as it was easier just to give you shit.

I just had to accept the fact that this was the way it was going to be for the next two years, until I made rating.

I was cleaning the engineers' heads when Ken Kirkaldie appeared at the door with some guy in tow that I had never seen before.

Ken was on his fourth trip as catering-boy in the *Peleus*, and he was to become a good mate for most of my life, but at that point I hardly knew him. He had a sort of sly smile on his face as he introduced me to this guy, who turned out to be the engineer's assistant steward, while I was the engineer's-boy.

This meant that this guy was my immediate boss and there was something about him that I just could not put my finger on.

Turned out that he was gay, which was what Ken found so amusing, but as I had never knowingly come across a gay person before and had absolutely no knowledge of homosexuality, I just found him to be a little unusual.

He turned out to be a nice enough person and wasn't too bad to work for, but as the voyage progressed and I became a little more worldly-wise, his 'camping it up' used to piss me off and I began to give him a bit of cheek.

It progressed to such a stage that when we called into Dublin at the end of the trip, prior to arriving at Liverpool, the pantry toaster had broken down and there was no toast available for breakfast.

I was pantry-boy at that stage and when he minced up to the hot-press and asked for a rack of toast, I replied that 'you know there's no toast this morning, you stupid fuckin' bitch'. He understandably chased me around the pantry and would have given me a good thrashing if he had managed to catch me.

I pulled my head in after that for a while.

It took me a while to realise that it wasn't the gay 'queens' who 'came out' that you had to worry about, but the blokes in all departments who tried to hide the fact that they were gay. And there were plenty of those at sea!

SS *Peleus*

A full complement of passengers embarked that afternoon, and we were scheduled to sail late the next morning.

We were 'put on the shake' by the 2nd steward at 05:30 the following morning, and I was out of my bunk instantly and hit the deck running. After a quick wash and cleaning of teeth, I was in the pantry preparing the morning tea for the engineers who weren't on watch. I was responsible for all the engineers' cabins from the third to the ninth and for the senior and junior electricians, plus the engineers' bathroom and heads and the recreation room. The alleyways were also my responsibility, so there was a lot to do, and I was always chasing the clock.

After delivering the morning tea and clearing the previous night's supper dishes, I began on the watch keepers' cabins and managed to complete them before heading down to the saloon to prepare for breakfast.

I was responsible for one of the long tables at either side of the saloon, known as 'aircraft carriers', which seated nine engineers. The one opposite seated the junior mates and radio officers, while the rest of the saloon was taken up with five round tables for the passengers.

These round tables were headed by the Old Man, Captain 'Bronco' Lane, the mate, the chief engineer, the 2nd engineer and the doctor.

The doctor was an elderly Irish lady with a no-nonsense attitude, but once you got to know her you found that her bark was a lot worse than her bite. We carried a doctor as we had 35 passengers on board.

I set a table up under the eagle eye of the saloon-bobby, and everything had to be perfectly clean and in the right place. I then headed down to my cabin to change into mess-jacket and blues.

When I made my way back to the saloon in time for the first sitting, I found to my horror that all my breakfast cups and teaspoons had vanished. The saucers were still sitting there but no cups or spoons. I was in a panic and went running to the saloon-steward. He didn't give a shit and just told me that I 'should have fuckin' looked after them a bit better'.

What I wasn't aware of was that breakfast cups and teaspoons were like 'hen's teeth' and all the other stewards took their cups and spoons down to their cabins with them and never let them out of their sight, but no -one had told me this.

Afternoon tea cups, on the other hand, which only held half as much as the breakfast cup, were 'ten a penny' so I had to use those and share a couple of teaspoons, which I had managed to get hold of, around the table. The engineers were not impressed and moaned like fuck, so I was off to a really bad start.

I never did discover who had stolen them, but it was a lesson well learnt, and over the course of the voyage as I managed to build up a collection of cups, I kept them stashed in my cabin and never out of my sight.

We left Vittoria Dock and locked out into the Mersey late morning and by lunchtime were steaming across Liverpool Bay towards Point Lynas, where we would drop the pilot. It was a beautiful day and the sea was like glass, but *Peleus* had developed a slow, steady roll as she built up speed.

I was in the saloon, at my station, with three portholes opposite me, waiting for the engineers to come into lunch, when I noticed that the horizon was slowly sliding up and down the ports.

I was mesmerised by this for a few minutes and then had to make a dash into the pantry where I threw up into the 'gash-bucket', much to the delight and amusement of the rest of the crowd.

It was to be 12 months before I finally overcame sea sickness and until then, I only had to have a warning that 'heavy weather' was on the way to start feeling ill.

We steamed south, down St George's Channel, and then up the English Channel to Rotterdam. We were in Rotterdam for three days topping up with general cargo, and then sailed down the Channel, through the Bay of Biscay, which was nowhere near as rough as everyone told me it was going to be, and after three days we turned to port and entered the Mediterranean. A day later we responded to an emergency call from a homeward-bound Ben Line ship, which was requesting a doctor, and when we came up with her, the motor-lifeboat was sent away with the doctor on board.

It transpired that the crew, including the apprentices, were working on one of the MacGregor hatches when the mechanism was activated while a crowbar was lodged in the rollers. The crowbar had hit a first-trip apprentice in the back of the head, killing him instantly, and the doctor was needed to issue a death certificate.

The doctor was a bit subdued when she returned, and as the Ben boat parted from us to continue her voyage home, I could only think about the poor sod getting killed on his first trip, only four days from home.

It rather unsettled me at the time and didn't help with my chronic case of homesickness either.

Three days later we arrived at Port Said and I was excited at the thought of transiting the Suez Canal.

It was a bit of a bind having to make sure your cabin was locked, ports dogged, leaving nothing lying around that could be nicked and putting up with the 'bum-boat men', Rifle-eye, George Robey and the 'gully-gully men' and the Port Said 'bibles', but eventually we were off as part of the south-bound convoy.

What a major disappointment it turned out to be, as there was nothing to see apart from the sand banks of the canal, and the only interesting part was passing the north-bound convoy in the Bitter Lakes.

We exited the canal at Port Tewfik, dropped the pilot and entered the Gulf of Suez, where we picked up speed and proceeded to overtake all those ships in the convoy that had been ahead of us.

With a service speed of 18 knots, and usually doing nearer 19 knots, the P-boats were ocean greyhounds in their day, and made short work of overtaking the other ships. In my two years and six trips in *Peleus*, I can only recall one ship ever overtaking her and that was the liner *Canberra*.

There may have been others during the night, but you would

usually hear of it in the mess or the saloon, next morning, so I'm presuming there weren't. On one memorable occasion, we even overtook a Royal Navy frigate in the Med and we had a couple of knots on her cruising speed. It must have really galled the navy boys to see a big fat merchantman go steaming past them.

Leaving the gulf, we steamed down the Red Sea for three days before turning the corner into Aden for bunkers.

The Red Sea had been extremely hot for someone who was unacclimatised to the heat, and working in the pantry or doing scrub-outs was hard work and very enervating, so it was a bit of a relief to get into the Indian Ocean where it was marginally cooler and there was some breeze.

Being a boy-rating, I couldn't get beer, which would have been heaven, but I was going through Coca-Cola like it was going out of fashion, as the weather was so hot.

A couple of weeks out and I was beginning to get used to the routine of shipboard life and not finding it quite so frantic.

Inspections took place every day at sea at 10:30 hours, except Sundays, and the inspection party consisted of the captain, mate, chief engineer, doctor, chief steward and 2nd steward.

I had to stand to in the engineers' accommodation with my white mess-jacket on and dirty dungarees while this group passed by inspecting my work.

I was always expecting someone to tell me what a great job I was doing, but that never happened and all I got was the 2nd steward coming back with a long list of things I had overlooked or not achieved to the required standard.

It took me a long time to finally realise that Blue Funnel expectations were way above any standard that I could possibly achieve. Life would have been a lot easier if I had been able to accept that fact from the beginning.

To be running down the alleyway a few yards in advance of

the inspection party and find a big engineer's boot mark on the brass step which you had just minutes ago buffed to a high shine would have been so much easier to bear with a more laid-back attitude.

Crossing the Indian Ocean on the way to Singapore, the flying-fish were a bit of a novelty, and I was amazed at just how far they could skip across the surface of the ocean. My afternoon break was spent sunbathing (on the bronzie, as it was known) down aft on the poop deck at the stern of the ship, in an attempt to get as brown as the rest of the crew. It took a couple of trips but, eventually, my milk bottle-white body gradually began to develop a healthy-looking tan.

The Chinese engine-room ratings were located in the poop-deck accommodation. It always amazed me how they managed to put up with the noise and vibration of the ship's propellor going day and night, but I suppose you can get used to anything over time.

I did not see much of the passengers as I was not permitted on the passenger deck without a reason and had to be properly dressed in mess-jacket and blues if I did go up there. I tried to avoid it if possible, and when they came into the saloon, it was always the sitting following the mates and engineers, so I was on the pantry sink washing dishes with the rest of the boys.

There was, however, one passenger that all the crew were breaking their necks to see, and that was a young woman of about 17 years of age who was extremely attractive.

She, along with her family, was emigrating to Australia and on the way to Singapore to join *Centaur*, the Blue Funnel ship that was permanently on the Singapore–Australia run.

Not only was she very attractive but she was also pleasant and down to earth and even gave me the time of day once or twice. She gave her address in Australia to one of the ABs, but I didn't give much for his chances, as with her looks I didn't think she would still be unattached by the time he got down to Aussie. Still, he was over the moon to know that she was interested.

We entered the Malacca Strait and were soon surrounded by ships and boats of every size and description, heading up and down the Strait and across from side to side, so we were forever changing course and changing speed.

When we arrived at Singapore, I couldn't believe the number of ships anchored in the roads waiting for a berth or loading from lighters.

We went alongside straight away and my first impression was how green the place was, but I didn't get to see too much of the entry into Keppel Harbour as I was too busy in the accommodation.

Most of the passengers disembarked in Singapore, but we still had some who were travelling on to Hong Kong.

There were a number of other Blue Funnel ships alongside, and I was to find that this was not an unusual occurrence, as Singapore was a major hub for Holts, and on subsequent trips I have counted as many as nine Bluies alongside at the one time.

It was always a place for reunions with guys that you had been working alongside on the shore-gang back in Birkenhead.

I ended up not seeing too much of Singapore as I had promised all the family, including aunts and uncles and cousins, a souvenir, so most of my money went on presents and there wasn't much left over for anything else.

It was a similar situation in Hong Kong, where we were alongside at Holts Wharf, Kowloon and disembarked the remaining few passengers. I only went ashore to buy souvenirs and didn't even make it over to Hong Kong Island on the Star Ferry.

The Chinese traders came aboard and set up shop on deck, where you could buy just about anything at ridiculously cheap prices. I bought my first pair of flip-flops, which were to become my footwear of choice over the coming years, in addition to white T-shirts and underpants (skiddies) of which I came to own untold dozens of sets over the coming years. You could never have too many of either, as the hot, humid weather had you changing your underwear a number of times a day.

There were also the ubiquitous car-coats which all the lads on the shore-gang used to wear. Although I could not afford to buy one that first trip, the following trip I was to purchase my first of many.

Hong Kong was also the place to buy your suits and after I had purchased my first one, I tried to buy a new one every other trip so that over the years I built up quite a collection of three-piece suits of extremely good quality.

The Chinese tailors would come aboard on the outward leg of the voyage and take your measurements and do a fitting and the suit would be ready for you on your return to Hong Kong on the homeward leg, and they were always a perfect fit.

The crews of Blue Funnel ships had excellent, long-standing relationships with the Chinese traders who were thoroughly honest and reliable and always remembered you from a previous trip.

Now that the passengers were no longer aboard, things were a little more relaxed as we steamed up to Japan and there was just one sitting for meals, so life was a bit easier.

We came across huge fleets of Chinese fishing junks, which stretched from horizon to horizon, and we had to slow right down and weave our way through them. Some of the junks barely scraped along the side of the ship and you had to wonder how many, over the years, had been struck during the night and left to their own devices.

As a month had now gone by since we sailed, we junior boy ratings switched jobs and I was now crew Peggy for a month.

Crew Peggy was the guy who looked after the crew and petty officers' mess rooms, and what a shit job that was. It was definitely the worst job in the ship, and everyone hated it and tried to avoid it at all costs.

Looking after the mates and engineers was a piece of piss compared to looking after the crew.

The stewards were okay as they normally ate on the run, here, there and everywhere, and mostly cleaned up after themselves, but the deckies and petty officers were a bunch of prima donnas. If you believed the constant whingeing, they were used to having four-course meals served at home in the Merseyside suburbs or the wilds of Wales.

I was forever getting a boot up the arse or threatened with having my teeth pushed down my throat, if I didn't 'pull my fuckin' finger out'.

One big Scouse prick even picked me up by my T-shirt (I weighed about 9 stone or 57 kg, wringing wet) then picked up the gash-bucket and took me out on deck to the rail, where I really believed he was going to throw me overboard. To my immense relief he threw the gash-bucket overboard and me onto the deck, just because I had not had time to clean it out before he came in to breakfast and objected to eating in a mess room with a dirty rubbish bin.

I then had to go to the 2nd steward to ask him for another gash-bucket and tell him that I had dropped the old one overboard, so that was another huge song and dance and a lecture on looking after company property.

The other downside to being Peggy was that at dinner I had to serve the chief steward and the 2nd steward dinner in the chief steward's cabin and that was a bit of a nightmare.

The chief steward was okay and a bit of a gentleman, but the 2nd steward was a bloke named Tommy Connell, who was built like a brick shithouse and was rumoured to work as a bouncer at some Liverpool night club when he was on leave.

He was always smiling, and the smile might have been on his lips but it never reached his eyes, and he scared the shit out of me.

He was always picking up on my mistakes during service and complaining about the standard of my training. When I tried to explain that I hadn't actually had any proper training, he didn't want to know and just moaned about me constantly. I got the impression that he didn't like me too much. Surprise, surprise.

The chief steward was much gentler on me when reminding me that it was time I changed my dungarees for a clean pair, as the pair I was wearing were almost standing up on their own, or that the peach-fuzz on my chin was in need of the attention of a razor.

The term Peggy is said to have originated in warships during the age of sail, when crew who had lost a leg in battle and wore a wooden peg-leg, being unable to work on deck or aloft, were allocated to work on the mess-deck looking after the crew.

Anyway, it was a term I detested and a job I absolutely hated, as did all the other boys.

We arrived in Kobe, Japan, on the main island of Honshu, and again I only went ashore to shop for gifts for the family. The main shopping street in Kobe was the Motomachi, which was a long, covered street of shops and bars, and you could pick up all sorts of bargains. I had promised my sister and my cousin a kimono each, but when I discovered that the cost was around 12,000 yen each, which was about three weeks' wages, they had to settle for something a little cheaper.

From Kobe, we went up the coast to Nagoya, and then on to Shimizu, where you got a fantastic view of Mt Fuji, and then around to Yokohama, where we tied up to the buoys and did not go alongside.

I did not get ashore in Yokohama as I was flat broke, but the 1964 Olympics were on in Tokyo at that time and the newspapers were full of it.

Boy ratings from Peleus ashore in Japan

CHAPTER 4

So, I had been halfway around the world but had actually seen very little of it. I had managed to avoid the bars, though, and was still drinking Coke. The Seamen's Missions were still my main hangout and as they never tried to ram religion down your throat, I was quite happy.

From Yokohama, the magic words 'homeward bound' suddenly became a reality as we retraced our route back down the coast, and then down to Hong Kong where we tied up to buoys and cargo was worked from junks and sampans.

A number of passengers were embarked and we were back to double sittings at meal times, so the easier times were over.

The ship's hull was painted by Chinese painters, and we left Hong Kong looking very smart.

The number and variety of ships in Hong Kong harbour was amazing and the place was a ship enthusiast's dream.

As the Vietnam War was escalating, the US Navy was well represented, both on the water and ashore.

As the second month of the voyage ticked over it was time for us boys to rotate jobs again and I found myself working as pantry-boy, under the pantry-man, Jimmy Blower, an ex-Royal Navy destroyer division boxing champion.

Jimmy was a hard man, but he took care of the boys who worked for him, and he wouldn't let the stewards and cooks fuck us about or anyone fuck with him. When I had started out as engineers-boy, I had served the 3rd engineer a deep-fried doughnut-type dessert for lunch, and when he saw it, he told me to take it back to the pantry-man and tell him to stick it back up his arse, where it came from.

He then said 'no, no' he was only joking!

I didn't tell Jimmy, but I did make the mistake of sharing the joke with another of the boys, who did tell Jimmy, and the shit really hit the fan.

Jimmy wanted to take this guy out on deck and sort him out, but the chief steward managed to calm him down. The 3rd was forced to apologise and I ended up not being the flavour of the month with either the 3rd or Jimmy.

Pantry-boy wasn't the most glamourous of jobs either, but it sure beat Peggy, and there was lots of variety in the work and not so much dish washing (pearl diving, as it was known), but it was a long way from the coveted saloon work.

The hardest part of the pantry-boy's job was scrubbing out the main working-alleyway on hands and knees every morning. As it was the main alleyway for the crew there was constant coming and going even as you were scrubbing, and some guys tried to stand on your hands as a 'joke' or kick the soap or scrubbing brush along the alleyway, which was about 20 metres long, so you had to keep constantly getting up off your knees to retrieve them.

One morning I was in the bakehouse picking up some fresh rolls from the baker, Paul Maddrell, who was putting suet through the mincer, and for some reason I thought it was preparation for a dessert and would be sweet. Paul nipped out of the bakehouse for a second and I popped some of this in my mouth before he returned.

When he came back, he was speaking to me and I was trying not to gag as I answered him. It taught me a lesson not to nick anything unless I knew precisely what it was.

Paul was a guy with a huge belly and his favourite trick, if you pissed him off, was to bump you up against the bulkhead with his belly and just keep bouncing off you until you begged for mercy. Not a guy to be trifled with but a nice enough bloke when you got to know him.

Paul was a fantastic baker, and made many memorable desserts while in *Peleus*, my favourite being a Bombe Vesuvius. This was a version of Bombe Alaska, with a half eggshell full of brandy set in the top, which was set on fire prior to being taken into the saloon where the lights had been dimmed. I can still recall the 'oohs and aahs' as it was carried in and served. Very impressive.

On the occasion that I took one into the saloon, my assistant steward insisted on the right to serve it as he didn't think I had the expertise to do it justice, and when he had finished serving the table, he had butchered it. The remains of the dish, of which there was half left, looked as though some little kid had been playing in it.

When I returned it to the galley, Paul went berserk and threatened me with all sorts of shit.

I couldn't blame the A/S as it was my responsibility, but I think the saloon-bobby had a quiet word with Paul later and sorted it out for me.

Before leaving Singapore, there was a bit of an unsettling incident when a couple of the older boy ratings returned from a run ashore after a few beers and started fighting on the wharf. The 2nd steward, Tommy Connell, instead of stopping the fight, was actively encouraging them to get stuck into one another, and it got a lot worse than it needed to be.

Getting the boys to fight one another was a popular pastime with the cooks and stewards, who would keep shit-stirring between two guys until you went on deck. Not fighting wasn't an option if you didn't want to spend all voyage being picked on.

Although neither of you really wanted to fight, as the other guy was either a cabin-mate or the person you went ashore with, it was a matter of status and not wanting to look like a coward.

During my first few trips, I won a few and lost a lot, and the sight of a bit of claret was usually enough for things to be brought to an honourable conclusion and the crowd kept happy.

One morning, another boy and I were out on the foredeck fighting, surrounded by a group of cooks and stewards, when the bosun, Paddy Proctor, came by.

He told me and the other guy to get off his deck and get back to work, which we both did with a sigh of relief. The bosun then climbed into the crowd who were encouraging us and gave them a right verballing, until they all slunk away.

We ended up not having to fight so often after that and I was always grateful to Paddy Proctor for his intervention.

We now picked up our full complement of passengers prior to departing Singapore and sailed for Port Swettenham (now known as Port Klang) and then Penang.

The passengers were mainly armed forces and their dependants and government workers and empire builders. I doubt if any of them paid their own fares, and most of them would have been travelling courtesy of the British, Singaporean or Hong Kong governments or their employers.

On one trip, the *Peleus* was slightly ahead of schedule by a day or two, and had to put into Gibraltar, where the agent's launch came out to meet us and a passenger was transferred ashore to stay in a hotel for a few days at Holts' expense and then flown to the UK.

The reason was that if he had arrived aboard *Peleus*, he would have had to pay his taxes and Holts had guaranteed that he would not arrive in the UK before a certain date, so they had come up with a way around the problem. I later found out that this was not an unusual occurrence and had happened on a number of occasions.

Now that we were well and truly homeward bound, the deckies were kept busy, greasing the gear, painting the decks, housing and derricks and the like, and the catering crowd began painting the interior alleyways, storerooms and bulkheads, so that the overwhelming smell was of fresh paint.

From Penang, we recrossed the Indian Ocean to Aden for bunkers, and then up the Red Sea to Suez for the canal transit, which was no more interesting going north than it had been travelling south.

Departing Port Said, it was 'four to the rock, three to the dock', being four days steaming to Gibraltar and three days from Gibraltar to Liverpool, which meant that we were a week from Liverpool. The temperature in the Med was noticeably cooler, as it was the end of November, and it felt good to be back in a temperate climate after the rigours of the tropics.

Everyone was in a cheerful mood as we got closer to home, and even a couple of adverse experiences couldn't diminish my excitement and yearning to be home and off this ship.

The first hiccup was when one of the old bedroom stewards talked me into buying a Swiss watch off him for 30 'bob'. It was a nice-looking watch, but the bloody thing never ran for more than an hour at a time before stopping, and when I took it back to him, he just said that 'it was working okay when I sold it to you' and wouldn't refund my money.

I persevered with it until midway through the following trip, when, in frustration, I gave it the 'deep six' in the Indian Ocean, where I suppose it sat on the ocean floor ticking away quite merrily.

I bought a new watch in Japan, which cost me the better part of a week's wages, but this one didn't survive too much longer either, as I ended up giving it to a girl in Manila in exchange for the taxi-fare back to the ship. But that's another story.

The other incident occurred a couple of days from home, when the 2nd steward had me cleaning out the passengers' bar fridge one morning. He and I were in the bar, which was a really tiny enclosed space, and I had my head in the fridge with the motor running. He kept asking me questions, which, because of the noise from the motor, I could not hear, and kept saying pardon.

After about the fourth time, he said, 'If you say fucking pardon to me once more, I'm going to stuff you in that fucking fridge.'

Well, I was terrified, and if you'd seen the size of this guy, you would understand why. I paid very close attention to his every word after that, not that he spoke much after that outburst, and I knew that I just couldn't do another trip with this bloke, as he'd had it in for me all trip.

We called into Dublin for a couple of days prior to arriving at Liverpool, to unload a small amount of cargo, and while we were there I went ashore with a couple of the other boys and had my first ever meal in a 'proper' restaurant. We ended up having steak and chips. What else!

Arriving at Gladstone Dock, Liverpool, I had that most amazing feeling of 'the channels', which is absolutely the best feeling in the world and hard to describe if you have never experienced it.

It's the gradual build-up of excitement over the days as you get closer to home and the people you miss most. It can't be replicated by air or rail travel as both those experiences are over so fast, but travel by sea is a steady build-up of anticipation, and you never get used to it, no matter how many trips you've done.

Docking day was just as frantic as sailing day, with the boy-ratings in hot demand and being chased up on jobs all over the place. One of the junior engineers kept pestering me to go up to his cabin to empty his rubbish bin, which I had already emptied earlier in the day when I cleaned his cabin, so it wasn't a job very high up on my to-do list and which I never got around to doing, much to my regret.

It turned out that he wanted me to come up to his cabin so that he could tip me for looking after him on the voyage and when I turned to on the shore-gang at the completion of my leave, he had left an envelope addressed to me, with Mr Mackie, which contained a £1 note. As I was only on about £3 a week at that time, this was a substantial amount of money and as I never saw him again, I deeply regretted ignoring his request to empty his bin so that I could have thanked him properly. This was the only tip I ever received from anyone while I was at sea, apart from when I was in the Holyhead ferries.

We eventually managed to get away after being cleared by Customs and I shared one of the big private taxis with some of the guys who were going in my direction.

We all had to give the driver half a crown each for the copper on the gate, to prevent him searching our baggage for contraband.

Later, I was tempted not to bother bribing them, but the thought of having all my gear spread across the docks and having to repack it got the better of me, and I decided that discretion was the better part of valour.

The guys who owned these big Fords and Vauxhalls charged each person as he dropped them off, and as they weren't metered, it was a quid or two quid depending upon distance.

These limousine drivers met every Blue Funnel ship that docked in Gladstone Dock, so they had a very lucrative business going.

They were earning probably four or five times the amount that a metered Black Cab would charge, but what the hell, it was docking day, and we just wanted to get home, and it always felt great turning up on your council housing estate in a ruddy big limo, with all the neighbours wondering 'who the fuck's this noter'.

It was good to catch up with family again and although I had only been away three months, it felt like a lot longer.

The following morning, I had to head back into Birkenhead, to the shipping office in Hamilton Square to pay off, and Dad insisted on going with me again.

All the crew were there and we lined up to sign off, and then settled our debts with the Chinese laundryman.

All the P, H and M boats, which carried passengers, also carried a Chinese laundryman, and what an asset these guys were. For a very small amount of money they would launder, starch and press your white mess-jackets, so that they looked immaculate.

They always put so much starch in that the jackets would stand up on their own, and you had to punch your arms down the sleeve the first time you put them on.

I think my first account for three months' laundry came to about 12 shillings, so it was well worth it.

In all the trips that I did with laundrymen, I only came across one steward who refused to pay his full account and would only pay half. He was a guy from Wrexham and a bit of a lazy fuck, who had the laundryman do all his laundry, including his underwear, which was how he came to rack up such a big laundry bill.

He wasn't coming back next trip, so I suppose he thought he could get away with it, although I always held out the hope that he would end up sailing with the laundryman again, sometime in the future, and the laundryman would refuse to do his washing for him.

On top of a £1 per week allotment being paid to my mother out of my wages, I was only permitted to sub a percentage of my wages each week as an advance so that you always had money in the ship.

You could not sub on your overtime and as turn-to was at 06:00 every day of the voyage and we worked until 20:30 or 21:00 each night with a couple of hours off in the afternoon. This meant that there was quite a bit of overtime for the catering department.

Although the hourly overtime rate for a boy rating would not even buy you a pint of mild in the pub, the hours accumulated over the course of the voyage, and combined with what was left of your pay after advances, meant that I had a fairly healthy amount coming to me.

Well, it was healthy for me and far more money than I had ever seen before in my life. Looking back, I just wish that someone could have sat me down and taught me to spend it wisely or invest it, but Mum and Dad must have thought that as I had earned it, it was mine to do with as I liked.

Over the coming years, what the ladies didn't get out of me, I donated to the breweries.

With my pay-off in my back pocket, it was around to Birkenhead Markets to purchase The Beatles' latest album, and then catch the bus back to Chester and enjoy 12 days' leave.

One noticeable innovation introduced while we had been away was the advent of the mini-skirt, which was all the rage, and the sight of girls' knees was very exciting and salacious, although in those early days only an inch or so above the knee, and not yet mid-thigh as came later. But they were still a turn-on.

I had no girlfriend so leave was spent catching up with old

school mates from tech and secondary school, and as I was still too young to get away with drinking in most pubs, alcohol was out of the question. Most of our time was spent at the bowling alley or the movies.

Leave flew by and before I knew it, it was time to report to the shore-gang at Vittoria Dock, Birkenhead, a few days prior to Xmas '64, and the ritual early morning Crosville bus ride from Chester every day.

We clocked on the shore-gang with Eric, the timekeeper, every morning and were then allocated our ships for the day, or perhaps a trip over to India Buildings, Holts main office in Liverpool, to spend a day in the staff restaurant.

The catering shore-gang were used to stow all the Bluies with stores for a deep-sea voyage. The stores were usually stowed over a period of two to four days, but occasionally, a one-day stow came along, which was bloody hard work and non-stop all day.

As the name implies it was a complete stow in one day and meant that the shore-gang took delivery of meat, vegetables, dry stores, liquor, cleaning materials and so on all within the course of one day.

It was hard yakka, broken only by the lunchtime trip over to the Wheatsheaf pub on Corporation Road, where the catering crowd took over the snug.

Fran, the barmaid, didn't give a shit how old you were as long as you were spending money, so we boy-ratings got stuck into some serious drinking, and as long as you didn't turn to after lunch looking the worse for wear, no-one said a word.

It was advisable to stay on side with the time-keeper and try not to piss him off as he could make life difficult for you and give you some crap jobs, one of them being India Buildings.

Over time I grew to hate the place and dreaded going over there. You were dealing with 'suits' who wouldn't give you the time of day, getting bossed about by the most junior typist and getting past the doorman was a mission in itself.

I didn't mind kissing Eric's arse if it meant not going across the river.

On one occasion, when I had made rating, and was working by, I got on the piss one night and decided to sleep over on the ship rather than catch the bus home, and back the next morning.

I had no toilet gear with me and when I clocked on, Eric noticed that I had not shaved so he informed me that I was doing a special lunch aboard one of the ships.

I said, 'Sorry Eric, I can't do it as I haven't got any shaving gear and haven't had a shave.'

Eric said, 'I can fuckin see that. That's why you're doing the lunch.'

Well, I knew that if I had turned up to do a special without having had a shave, my arse was going to be in a sling, so during 'smoko' I shot up to the old barbers on Duke Street and talked him into giving me a shave. He didn't normally do them, but he got his old cut-throat razor out and gave me the best shave I've ever had.

Whenever Eric gave you a shit job and you asked 'Why me Eric?', his standard reply was always 'They asked for my best man, and that's you.'

The morning ritual on the shore-gang was to clock on, then scoot round to the dockers canteen on Vittoria Dock, for a big mug of tea and a bacon sarnie, before reporting to the ship you had been assigned to for the day.

The atmosphere on the shore-gang so close to Xmas was upbeat and lunchtime sessions in the Wheatsheaf very jovial, but the thought of having to sail deep sea in the *Peleus* again was getting me down and a big black cloud was hanging over me. I was desperately hoping something would come up to prevent me going, but I still didn't have the balls to tell Mum and Dad that I had made a huge mistake and didn't want to go to sea again.

One morning I arrived at the time-office and was instructed to report to the medical centre at Odyssey Works for my seagoing medical, prior to rejoining *Peleus*.

I was sitting in the waiting room when two of the assistant stewards from the *Peleus* walked in and I overheard them saying that Tommy Connell, the 2nd steward, had been made up to chief steward and was joining *Ulysses*.

Once I had confirmed that the information was genuine, even the thought of having to have another injection did not get me down, and a huge weight was lifted from my shoulders.

Suddenly, I was not dreading the thought of another trip in the *Peleus*. I hadn't realised just how much the attitude and actions of one person had affected my outlook.

To cap things off, the news going around the docks was that when Tommy Connell had joined *Ulysses*, which was berthed in the West Float, the dockers had broken into his bond store and stolen the spirits. Couldn't have happened to a nicer guy.

CHAPTER 5

PELEUS DEPARTED BIRKENHEAD EARLY JANUARY '65 FOR THE one-and-a-half-day passage around to Rotterdam, and we left behind the usual chaos of sailing day.

There had been a number of changes to the crew for this voyage, and most pleasing for me apart from the 2nd steward was a wholesale clearing out of the deck crowd, apart from the petty officers and one of the leading hands.

The new crowd of ABs and EDHs were a much friendlier bunch of guys and a lot easier to get on with.

In the catering department the new 2nd steward was a good bloke and popular with the crowd. The new Captains Tiger, a guy named Charlie, was as gay as, and introduced himself as 'Charlotte, the Harlot'.

He was a great laugh and used to camp it up, especially when he was on the piss, which was most of the time.

During lunch and dinner, and occasionally breakfast, he had a breakfast cup in the drawer of his dummy, or dumb waiter, his work station in the saloon. Everyone at first assumed that it was black coffee, but it was, in fact, Guinness, which he quaffed at a prodigious rate, and seemingly none the worse for wear.

His favourite watering hole was the Magic Clock in Liverpool, to which he was always inviting me, and one trip I did think about catching up with him there until I found out it was a well-known gay pub.

Charlie fancied me and was always having me on, which used to really piss me off.

One day he was carrying on and giving me a hard time when I yelled at him: 'Charlie, I'm not a fucking queer, so leave me alone.'

His reply was 'I don't know what you're getting so upset about. I only want to suck your cock. And just remember, if the queens fancy you, then so will the women,' which at the time wasn't too much of a consolation.

The other newbie was the engineers steward, a 19-year-old guy from Bradford who was my working boss a little later in the voyage when I became engineers-boy. He was engaged to a girl back in Bradford that he never stopped raving on about. He had made the huge mistake of opening a joint bank account with her, into which he was depositing his weekly allotment.

Partway through the voyage he got a letter from his mother telling him that this fiancée had spent all the money in the account, so he called off the wedding but still kept moaning about her.

Having seen numerous photographs of her, I considered him bloody lucky to have gotten off so lightly, but I couldn't tell him that of course.

The weather in Rotterdam was freezing, and I envied the security people in their full-length leather coats, looking a bit like the Gestapo.

We had only been there a day or so when tragedy occurred. The leading-hand from the previous trip, a nice old guy in his sixties, was found dead in his bunk early one morning, from natural causes. The body was taken ashore that morning, but we found out later that his only relative, a sister, couldn't afford the money to have his body repatriated, and he was buried in Rotterdam.

It was a sad time and put a real dampener on everyone's spirits.

I was pantry-boy again to start the voyage, and about this time I started to suffer from severe stomach pains, which the pantry-man, Jimmy Blower, put down to my feeling homesick.

Well, I was feeling homesick, but that wasn't the reason for the pains. It turned out that I had not sat on the toilet since leaving home the morning I joined *Peleus*. I had been so busy chasing my tail during the day, and so tired when I knocked off at night, that I just didn't get around to going.

It was now three-and-a-half to four days later, and I really needed to go. The trouble was I had held it for so long that getting rid of it was a major problem. I nearly passed out from the pain and at one point was on the verge of calling for the doctor but managed to finally get rid of it. It would have had to have been the closest a male could come to experiencing the pain of childbirth and I made bloody sure in future that I never let things get to that stage again.

It was the most eye-watering moment of my entire life.

I had a couple of runs ashore in Rotterdam, and then we departed for warmer climes. The Bay of Biscay and the Med were rough enough to make me seasick, but not too rough and there was no excitement in approaching the Suez Canal this time.

There was an inordinate amount of interest in my sex life, or lack of, to be more precise, and guys were forever quizzing me about it. I suppose they were trying to confirm which side of the fence I was on, for their own peace of mind.

Never having had a proper girlfriend and being too shy to

realistically ever find one was a bit of a challenge to some of these guys, who seemed to think that if you didn't carry a photo of some girl with you, you were seriously suspect.

One steward, who was quite a few years older than me, asked me one day whether I had ever been 'muff-diving'.

When I replied that I didn't know, as I didn't know what it meant, he described it for me and I was almost physically ill. I couldn't believe that anyone could indulge in that kind of behaviour and really believed that he was making it up. Turned out he wasn't making it up, and the term was slang for cunnilingus, as we all now know.

Anyway, this was the type of thing that the other boys and I had to contend with until we had proven ourselves.

One afternoon, I had just commenced my pantry-watch, which consisted of me being on duty in the pantry and galley while the rest of the crew took their afternoon break.

The work during the watch consisted of melting milk blocks in a large pot on the stove, which I decanted into a milk churn and placed in the chiller, plus any other odd jobs that the chief cook and the pantry-man left for me.

Suddenly, Jimmy Blower, the pantry-man, appeared back in the pantry, handed me a book which he told me to read, and took off again.

In between the odd jobs, I commenced reading this book, which turned out to be a well-thumbed Port Said Bible, or pornographic literature. There were no photographs, but the stories more than made up for that and I couldn't put the thing down.

By the time I was relieved for my afternoon break, I was well into it and took it down to my cabin to continue reading it, which I did for the rest of the afternoon.

I learned more about sex in that one afternoon than I had known about in my entire 16 years.

One major problem for me, though, was that I had never experienced masturbation, and in fact I actually had real sex on numerous occasions before I discovered the pleasure of masturbation.

I just wish that I had known about it that afternoon.

After Suez, we were back in the hot weather again, calling into Aden for bunkers and then across to Singapore, where we disembarked some of the passengers.

It was the run-up to Chinese New Year and one night the 4th mate, Paddy, was with a group of guys up Bugis Street, where all the transvestites hang out, and it was not uncommon for you to be standing at a urinal, when some gorgeous-looking lady came and stood beside you, pulled up her skirt and began taking a piss.

Anyway, Paddy, wearing shorts, was sitting at a table, very intoxicated, and with a string of Chinese fire crackers on the table. He leant forward with a cigarette in his mouth and lit the crackers which went off with such a bang it made him push back from the table, the crackers shot off the table and up the leg of his shorts, where they continued to explode.

The poor bastard had to go to hospital and spent the next few days hobbling around the ship in great pain. Obviously, everyone thought it was the funniest thing and gave him plenty of stick, but he was extremely lucky it didn't result in much more serious burns, or damage to his crown jewels.

It was then on to Manila in the Philippines, and then Hong Kong, where we disembarked the remaining passengers.

This time in Hong Kong, though, we actually took on board a single passenger who was going to travel with us around the Japanese coast and back to Hong Kong.

She was an extremely attractive young lieutenant, or captain, in the British Army who was using some of her leave to see Japan.

There was no separate passenger sitting in the saloon for meals, so she joined the Old Man's table for the single sitting.

Although she was very attractive with a nice figure, she was a bit strange and hardly ever spoke to anyone. She almost always went ashore alone and although most of the junior mates and engineers tried it on, none of them seemed to have any luck.

I passed her in the passengers' alleyway on a couple of occasions and she would barely acknowledge me.

One morning, I was talking to one of the old bedroom stewards who looked after the passengers, in the passengers' alleyway, when she walked by. The bedroom steward, who had been in Japanese captivity during the war and was a slightly strange geezer, said to me 'Jeez! What would you like to do to that?'

I replied, practising my newfound sexual expression, 'that I would like to rip her kecks off, and give her one!'

The bedroom steward turned to me and said, 'You dirty little bastard. I'm going to tell her what you just said,' and ran down the alleyway after her, calling 'Miss, miss.'

Well, I just about shit myself and ran and hid in the gents' passenger heads, thinking I was safe in there. However, this guy brought her into the heads and said to me, 'Now tell her what you just said.'

I was almost in tears and denying I had said anything, but this prick went and told her what I had said and then let her go.

For the next few weeks, I was expecting to be called to the captain's cabin and logged, and right up to the beginning of the following trip I was expecting to be dismissed from Holts.

If the powers that be could sack some guy for telling a girl to fuck off at Guinea Gap Baths, what were they going to do to someone who had made sexual comments about a first-class passenger.

That was another hard lesson learned, and I was always wary about what I said about anyone, and to whom, in future.

We proceeded up the Japanese coast via Kobe, Nagoya and Shimizu to Yokohama.

I was on watch in the pantry one afternoon, along with the galley-boy who was doing some prep. He was almost a year older than me, and a bit of a suave-looking bastard and much more worldly-wise. He fancied himself as a bit of a trend-setter and a fashion aficionado. One time in Rotterdam, when a group of us boys went ashore to a night club, he insisted on wearing a full-length, silver pac-a-mac, done up to the neck, which he refused to take off all night.

The girls refused to dance with him because he looked so ridiculous, so he was up on the dance floor, dancing on his own all evening and looked like a freakin' condom.

His older brother had been an EDH in Bluies but was now a ladies' hairdresser, which may have gone some way towards explaining his flamboyance.

He did introduce me to Bob Dylan music though, so I shouldn't be too hard on him.

Anyway, next minute, the chief steward stepped into the pantry accompanied by the most beautiful part-Japanese, part-American girl of about my age. He introduced me to her and we chatted for a while, but I was too tongue-tied to do much chatting and embarrassed about the way I was dressed, which was dirty khaki dungarees, minty, sweaty T-shirt and pantry-cloth around my waist for an apron.

Turned out that she was the daughter of the ship's provedore, an American who was married to a Japanese lady.

They then moved on to the galley-boy and had a few words with him and then departed.

About 20 minutes later the chief steward returned alone and said to me that the young lady wanted to invite me out to her father's country club for an afternoon by the pool.

I said to the chief steward, 'Boss, you've got the wrong guy. She must mean the galley-boy.'

He replied that, no, he had the right guy, it was me she had invited out, but I could invite the galley-boy as well and he was giving both of us the following afternoon and evening off work to go.

He warned us against drinking any alcohol and threatened that if we stepped out of line, there would be hell to pay.

I now had another problem, as at the start of the trip I had two pairs of swimming togs, one new pair and one very old pair that I had when I was about 13 years old.

Going through the Suez Canal, I had left the new pair in the drying room and they had been nicked. I now only had the old pair that I had not worn for quite some time and no time to buy a new pair.

When we got to the country club, my worst fears were realised when we got changed, and I found that my togs could not fully contain my tackle, and bits and pieces were poking out all over the place. Not that I was overly well endowed, but these old togs were really, really tiny.

The young lady, whose name I can no longer recall, had brought along two girlfriends for company and both were Japanese American and equally as beautiful.

I can honestly state that they were the three most beautiful young women I have ever been in the company of, and I was wondering what the fuck I was doing there.

I spent the entire afternoon squirming in embarrassment and

trying to discreetly push back in the bits that kept escaping from my togs, and a couple of young American kids even took the piss out of how skimpy my togs were.

The girls were too well mannered to let on and just kept chatting away and laughing with us all afternoon as if there was nothing wrong.

The only consolation for me was when the galley-boy climbed to the top of the high diving platform, dithered around for ages threatening to dive off, but chickened out and had to come down to a lower level and jump off feet first. Watching him squirm meant that my afternoon wasn't a total disaster.

That evening, they took us for pizza and Coke to the PX on an American base, which was packed with American teenagers, whose parents were in the services.

These kids were a complete pain in the arse, arrogant, racist and looking for trouble.

The galley-boy and me kind of stood out so we had to be careful, and if the girls hadn't been with us, we would have been in the shit.

I've been to the States on numerous occasions and always found Americans to be among the politest and friendliest people on the planet, but these kids were something else.

We parted from the girls and made our way back to the ship. The next morning the chief steward wanted to know how it had gone and we said 'great', but really it wasn't. There had been too much stress for me, and I still wondered why such good-looking and well-educated young women had taken an interest in us.

I thought about it a lot and came to the conclusion that they must have been similar to the girls who turned up at Seamen's Mission dances, where it didn't mean anything romantically; they were just being nice to people they considered to be lonely and far from home.

Anyway, I forgot about it for the time being, but when the ship left the Japanese coast and returned to Hong Kong, there was a letter waiting for me from the girl who had invited me out. It was a long, chatty letter and obviously not written just out of duty. To my everlasting shame I did not reply and thought that that was the end of it.

As she had not heard from me by the time we returned to Liverpool, she wrote to the chief steward enquiring about me and whether I was okay.

When I joined *Peleus* in Vittoria Dock for my third trip, the chief steward was waiting for me and asked me whether I had received a letter from her. When I answered in the affirmative, he asked me why I hadn't replied. My answer sounded a bit lame, even to me, and he just exploded.

He gave me the biggest dressing down I have ever experienced in my life and then he dismissed me from his office with a look of utter contempt.

My relationship with him never really did recover from that, and although he didn't prove to be vindictive, which he had every right to be, our relationship was somewhat strained and he didn't joke around any more.

I couldn't feel sorry for myself, as I deserved everything I got and if I could have turned the clock back, I would have dealt with things a lot differently and treated her with the respect she deserved. The incident was just further confirmation of my immaturity and total lack of confidence.

Things on the shore-gang were more of the same, with sessions in the mess playing poker when things were quiet, and long, lunchtime sessions in the Wheatsheaf, drinking pints of bitter and playing records on the jukebox. One morning, during 'smoko', a crowd of us were playing poker in the mess and there was a large amount of money in the pot, when Mr Sparrow, one of the catering superintendents, walked in, observed the pile of notes and coins on the table, took off his bowler hat, swept the cash off the table into the hat and declared that it was all going to the lifeboat fund. We were all highly pissed off, but none of us had the balls to ask for it back.

There could be anything up to about 25 guys stowing ship, and on cold wet days when the ports in the mess were dogged and everyone was smoking it was like a London fog. I didn't smoke but was so used to it that it didn't worry me. Looking back, though, it's hard to believe I actually put up with it.

I was about the only non-smoker I can recall, and when stowing ship guys were always coming up to me and asking me to cover for them while they went for a smoke, which wasn't a problem.

One particular day, when I had covered just about everyone on the gang, I decided I needed a break and asked someone to cover me. As I was heading up the companionway, the working boss, a guy I had sailed with as chief cook and who had just been made up to chief steward, said, 'Where are you going? You don't fuckin smoke. Get back to work.'

I told him I had to go for a piss and made sure I was away a while.

I was really enjoying the shore-gang, as every day was different, the camaraderie was good and time passed relatively quickly.

I was also looking forward to the next trip and really beginning to feel that I was part of the system and enjoying life in the Merchant Navy, and my language was beginning to reflect that, with my sentences peppered with plenty of expletives.

I was hanging out with Ken, who had been boy in *Peleus* for three trips before I joined her and had done his training at Gravesend prior to joining Bluies. Ken was from Valley, just outside Holyhead in Anglesey, and was much more a 'man of the world' than I was.

Before going to Gravesend, he had worked as a waiter at the Trearddur Bay Hotel, outside Holyhead, and had silver-service experience, which he taught me and helped me out with.

He was to become my best mate for most of my life, and the reason we got on so well was that we were similar in outlook when it came to having a good time.

At a time when every cabin in *Peleus* could boast a huge Akai reel-to-reel tape recorder secured to the bulkhead, and blasting out country and western music, neither Ken nor I ever owned such a thing. In fact, neither of us even owned a transistor radio.

Every single yen we subbed on the Japanese coast was to be spent on beer and women, but that was all in the future.

First of all, I had to lose my cherry.

CHAPTER 6

WE HAD A NEW SKIPPER FOR THIS TRIP AND HIS NAME WAS
Captain Charlie Collett. Captain Collett had been 2nd mate of a
Blue Funnel ship which was captured and then sunk by the
Admiral Graf Spee in the South Atlantic, during the Second
World War, and had spent the rest of the war as a POW.

He was a nice guy and a gentleman, and he had a habit when
approaching a companionway to a lower deck of turning with his
back to the ladder and descending backwards, which looked rather
peculiar, but it must have been a safer way of getting down the
ladder.

Departing Birkenhead early May, we steamed around to
Rotterdam where Ken and I enjoyed a few runs ashore.

We got talking to an attractive blonde barmaid in one bar who
we started chatting up over pints of Oranjeboom. She was friendly
enough but had a boyfriend, which I wasn't surprised about, with
her looks, and wasn't interested in a couple of kids. Still, we turned
up a couple of nights in a row thinking we had a chance, but we
were dreaming.

I had now discovered that once you left the UK, no-one gave a shit about under-age drinking, and we could always get a beer almost anywhere in the world without being challenged. The only exceptions were Aussie, New Zealand and the States where the drinking age was higher.

On the last night in Rotterdam, Ken and I were in a bar in the red-light district, and I had seen a few women hanging about on the street.

It must have been one of the quiet nights early in the week because the place was deserted. I put a guilder in the jukebox and selected five records, and as I was walking back to the table, I made a decision.

I said to Ken, 'I'm going to do it.'

Ken said, 'Do what?'

I replied, 'Go with a woman. Wait here for me,' and before he could reply I had shot out of the door.

I walked around the corner and could see a lady silhouetted against a streetlight. I couldn't see her face, but I could see she was wearing a short skirt, so I approached her and asked her how much for a 'short time'.

She replied '12 guilders', which was about £1-10 shillings in real money.

I said okay, and she led me up some stairs to her apartment, where, when she turned the light on, I could see that she was almost old enough to be my mother. I was too embarrassed to back out and tell her I had changed my mind, so she pulled down my trousers and underpants, put a condom on me, lay back on her bed and pulled me on top of her.

She put me inside her and it was all over in less than 10 seconds.

She pushed me off, stood up, grabbed me by my now flaccid tackle and dragged me across the room to the wash-basin, with me following behind taking penguin steps with my gear around my ankles.

She ran some water in the sink, removed the condom, plunged my tackle in, patted me dry with a towel, pulled my pants and trousers up, patted me on the head and said, 'Good, ja?'

I said yes and then scuttled down the stairs thinking to myself, 'Well, I'm not doing that again.'

When I got back to the bar, Ken didn't believe I had done it as I had been away such a short time that my records were still playing on the jukebox. It was only when I showed him my wallet, with my money gone, that he believed me.

Ken couldn't wait to get back to the ship and tell everyone that I had had sex with a woman, and next morning everyone was coming up to me and slapping me on the back and congratulating me. My status on board had suddenly changed and I was now 'one of the boys'.

Little did they all know that that was the first and last time I intended having sex with a woman. I knew I wasn't gay, as the thought of having sex with a bloke was nauseating, but I thought I must belong to a group of people who didn't do sex.

At the catering training school at Odyssey Works, it had been drummed into us that if we ever slept with a woman, we were going to get VD and nasty things would happen to our private bits. As I had now slept with a woman, even though wearing a condom, I was scared I might have caught something so opted to visit the VD clinic in Singapore when we finally arrived in that port.

I entered a small office where a man in a white coat sat behind the desk. After asking me a few questions, he told me to drop my trousers and expose my tackle.

After staring at it for a few moments he told me to pull my pants up and said, 'The doctor will be here in a moment,' and left the room.

Another guy came in and took blood for a test and I gave the Hong Kong agent's address for the results to be sent to. This became a pattern for quite a time, as once I had had sex with a woman, I would go for a blood test and receive the results at some port later in the voyage. The problem was that by the time I received the results of the test, I had invariably slept with another woman so the result was meaningless and my arm was beginning to look like that of a junkie.

I gave away the blood tests eventually and just relied on close observation!

A week or so later, I was in a bar in Manila with a girl in her early thirties and it was closing time. She asked me if I wanted to go home with her, but I told her that I had no money. She told me that that was okay and I could come home with her for nothing.

Well, since Rotterdam I had spent time in a ship where the testosterone-charged air was in abundance and was feeling horny again. We said goodnight to the mama-san of the bar and walked back to her room, where I stripped off and lay on the bed.

She took ages getting ready for bed but eventually she had stripped to her bra and knickers, showing she had a very attractive figure and wasn't bad looking. I was lying there with a rock-hard erection in anticipation, when she reached under the bed, pulled out a piss-pot and hoiked up a huge green gob of phlegm and spat it into the pot.

At that point, my erection lost its rod of steel and went somewhat limp.

However, it soon recovered when she lay on the bed beside me, but she had no intention of allowing me to have sex with her, and I realised that the only reason she had invited me home was to prove to the mama-san that she still had it and could attract the younger guys.

Well, I wrestled with her for ages, but she wasn't going to give in and kept telling me to go to sleep. As if!

Something had to give, and although she still had her knickers on, in my excitement, I lay on top of her and ejaculated all over her belly. She got quite irate at that and gave me a bollocking, but I had now calmed down.

I lay beside her in the dark, thinking to myself that this was definitely the last time I indulged in sex, as it obviously wasn't for me.

The following morning, I made my way back to the ship in time for turn-to and because I had been ashore all night, the crowd knew I had been with a woman, and were all over me again and congratulating me. Little did they know.

Thinking about the incident, I began to realise how lucky I'd been, and what a risk I'd taken.

A few nights previously, Ken had ended up going with a girl to her room and had been accosted by a gang of Filipinos who had made him swap his good jeans and shirt for a manky pair of shorts and a dirty, torn Hawaiian shirt. They had also made him exchange his Filipino pesos for Japanese occupation pesos, so he was in a pretty foul mood when he returned to the ship for turn-to.

We had all fallen about laughing at the sight of him, but on reflection he was lucky not to have been knifed and if he'd put up any sort of resistance, he probably would have been.

From Manila we steamed the short distance to Hong Kong, where I received the results of my Singapore blood test, and then on to Japan, the first port being Kobe. It was in Kobe that I finally found out what sex was all about and how fantastic it could really be if you did it with the right person.

I was in a bar up the Motomachi one night when one of the bar-girls asked me was I going to spend the night with her. She was young and attractive, so I said that I would like to. She spoke to the mama-san and then took me by the hand and led me out of the bar to a small hotel a short distance away.

It cost me 1000 yen for the hotel room, and 1000 yen for the girl to stay all night, with the exchange rate being 1000 yen to the pound.

The hotel room came with a deep sunken bath, filled to the brim with very hot, steaming water. We both undressed and then she made me hunker down on the edge of the bath while she used a dipper to ladle the hot water over me. The bath was too hot to get straight into so by ladling the water over you it helped you to adjust to the heat. We then both eased into the bath, where we soaked for a few minutes before she led me out of the bath and dried me off with a huge towel.

We climbed onto the bed, where I finally discovered just how good sex could be, and I was hooked.

The bath must have been heated, as it remained at the same temperature all night, and we repeated the bathing process after each session of sex until 05:00 when I had to return to the ship for turn-to.

Heading back to *Peleus*, I felt like I was walking on air, and although I was tired, I felt wonderfully relaxed.

I couldn't wait to get back there and spent the rest of my time in Kobe with the same bar-girl.

Obviously, this was an expensive exercise, and on my boy-ratings wages, unsustainable for very long, but on one night, when I was short of money, she spoke to the mama-san and I only had to pay for the hotel.

It was amazing just how well the bar-girls looked after you and seemed to genuinely care about you and what you were doing. I know money was involved, but on many occasions when I was in Japan, money did not enter the equation. I had quite a few nights when going out for a few drinks, a meal and back to the girl's place where no money changed hands wasn't uncommon, and I know that that was the experience of other seamen I knew. It was part of the reason that Japan was such a popular destination in the 60s and 70s.

We departed Kobe and headed to Nagoya at 08:00 one morning and had just exited the breakwater and were steaming slowly through the roads, surrounded by dozens of anchored ships of all shapes and sizes, waiting for a berth, when suddenly a thick fog descended. From amidships you could not even make out the bow, so the anchor was dropped immediately, and we sat there sounding the foghorn and listening to the dismal moaning of the other ships' horns.

I had occasion to go up to the bridge to remove a breakfast tray I had taken up earlier, and as I climbed the companionways through the four levels of deck from the main-deck to the bridge-deck, it got lighter and lighter. When I stepped onto the bridge-deck it was bright sunshine and the fog was spread out around the ship like a flat white tablecloth, with the masts and funnels of the surrounding ships poking out of the fog.

It was an amazing sight and I was wishing that I had the time to dash down to my cabin for my camera and return to take a picture, as it was a sight that has stayed with me all these years. But the moment passed, the fog soon lifted and we were under way again.

From Kobe we proceeded on our regular run to Nagoya and Shimizu and then on to Yokohama, where we went alongside.

The berth we were on had an elevated walkway along the top of the cargo sheds, and on Sundays when cargo wasn't being worked, this was open to the public.

Sunday afternoons always saw hordes of young Japanese, male and female, practising their English on us. As Liverpool was our port of registration, and appeared under the ship's name on the stern, questions about The Beatles were the most popular, as the group was huge in Japan. Any band, in any bar, at that time were always playing the latest Beatles releases and the group was almost as big in Japan as they were in the UK.

Of course, we had all been to school with The Beatles, or lived in the next street, or went to the Cavern on a regular basis, and these Japanese kids were fascinated with this Liverpool connection.

There was always a huge crowd clustered on the walkway adjacent to *Peleus*, compared to the other ships tied up on the wharf.

It was amazing just how gullible they were and how shameless we were, with our claims to know John, Paul, George or Ringo personally.

When we tried to chat the girls up and arrange a date, they just dissolved into fits of giggles, and we never got anywhere. When they translated what we had asked them to the people around them, the whole crowd broke into gales of laughter, so it lost its attraction in the end and we got a bit fed up answering the same questions over and over.

Ken and I had a couple of runs ashore until our money ran out, and then we were confined to the ship.

One night, at about 22:00 hrs, I was lying on my bunk reading a book, and things were pretty quiet, as most of the crew were ashore. Suddenly, there was a thump on the bulkhead from Ken who was in the next cabin, and a shout of 'How many yen have you got?'

I replied that I had about 300 yen. Ken said he had about 400, so we decided to club it together and then went around any of the crew still aboard, begging for spare yen and offering to repay it when we got our next sub.

We even went up to the mates and engineers who were still on board, and ended up accumulating about 1800 yen, which was enough to purchase about three of the large quart bottles of Japanese Kirin or Sapporo beer.

We showered and changed and headed ashore. Not having enough money to waste on taxi fares, we decided to walk into the centre of Yokohama to the Peanuts Bar. Peanuts was a bar that stayed open all night and had live bands playing right through and was very popular. When all the other bars closed at about 01:00hrs, the girls who had not managed to score a client descended on Peanuts in droves to drink and dance the night away until 05:00 when it closed.

Well, it was a bloody long walk and gone 01:00 when we arrived.

The first person we saw as soon as we walked through the door was John McLoughlin, the saloon-bobby from *Peleus*. John must have been well pissed, because he shouted us each a beer before heading back to the ship.

Ken and I sat at a table with these two large bottles of beer and proceeded to sip away and make them last as long as possible. On the next table to us was a Japanese bloke who was so far gone that when he tried to speak to us in English, neither of us could understand a word he was saying, so we just nodded and smiled.

He had one-and-a-half large bottles of beer in front of him, and when he got up to stagger out, he plonked both bottles on our table, uttered something completely unintelligible, and disappeared into the night. We were over the moon, as we had all this beer and hadn't spent a single yen of our own money.

Peanuts was spread over two levels, with a circular gallery of tables looking down onto a central stage on the ground-floor level, where the live band played the latest Beatles music.

By this time the place was beginning to fill up, and the next thing we knew, we had a group of girls sitting with us and chatting.

We explained that we could not afford to buy them a drink, as we didn't have enough money, and they said they were quite happy to buy their own, and most of them were only drinking water anyway.

We were getting on well with them, and they asked us where we were from. We replied that we were from one of the ships in the port, and then either Ken or I asked them whether they would like to come back with us and see the ship.

To our complete surprise, three of the group said they would like to go back with us, so we finished our beers and got them out of the door before they could change their minds. As we hadn't had to buy any beer, we had enough for a taxi back to the ship, and the five of us jumped into the first available cab.

We got the cab driver to drop us behind the sheds on the wharf, and Ken climbed the accommodation ladder to distract the Japanese nightwatchman who was on duty on the main deck. As soon as he had the watchman distracted, I shot the girls aboard and into our cabins.

I had one girl in my cabin, and there were two in Ken's. I was all for jumping into my bunk with the girl in my cabin as she was quite keen and already stripped off and lying in the bunk, but next minute Ken was knocking on my door and telling me that the girls in his cabin weren't too keen on him jumping into bed with one of them while the other one watched on.

Bugger! It was now about 03:30 and only a couple of hours before turn-to so time was of the essence. We had to offload one of the girls in Ken's cabin pretty smartly.

We started off in the cooks and stewards' accommodation to begin with, and I didn't think for one minute that we would have a problem, but everyone we put on the 'shake' either thought we were joking or didn't appreciate being woken at that ungodly hour, and told us to fuck off!

When we had exhausted the catering crowd, we started on the deck crowd, but received similar responses from everyone we woke up. I couldn't believe it, as if someone had woken me in the middle of the night with the offer of a willing woman, I would have been there like a shot.

Having exhausted the search for a willing partner in the catering and deck crowds, we were stumped, as we could hardly go searching among the mates and engineers, since the girls shouldn't have been aboard, and if the chief steward, mate or skipper were to find out we would have been in deep shit.

By this time, it was getting really late, and close to turn-to, so I did the only decent thing and left Ken to it, while I jumped into my bunk with my very willing partner.

When I turned to, Ken still hadn't had any luck and still had the two girls in his cabin, while the galley and pantry were full of stewards, moaning that we hadn't tried hard enough to convince them that the offer was genuine.

These guys had really gone down in our estimation, as Ken and I thought most of them were just too scared of what might happen to them if the authorities found out, and were using the excuse that we hadn't tried hard enough, to cover their arses.

We didn't have much free time during the working day, but every chance I got to get back to my cabin saw me jumping into my bunk for a 'quickie', while Ken was still fuming about no-one helping him out.

We took the girls breakfast and lunch, which we had to forego in order to feed them, although we could fill up on cheese rolls.

I was now looking forward to the finish of the day so we could get them back ashore in the evening, as word had started to get around the ship on the upper decks and the chief steward was beginning to get wind of it.

I also needed some serious sleep, as it had been a hectic and exhausting 24 hours.

We called a cab and just walked the girls down the ladder, past the nightwatchman, who did not appear too bothered about them. We just had to ensure that there were no mates about. We put the girls in the cab and gave them the money we had from the night before, which was enough for the cab fare with a bit left over, and sent them on their way.

Ken and I had achieved some sort of notoriety, as bringing girls back to a Blue Funnel ship was unheard of, and we enjoyed a period of celebrity.

We both had unusual surnames and as we were hanging together a great deal of the time, we were becoming known and linked together.

A few months later I was drinking in the snug of the Wheatsheaf, in Birkenhead, when someone used my surname. One of the assistant stewards from another Bluie who was drinking there as well said, 'Are you one of those guys who got the women on board in Japan?'

I modestly admitted that I was.

When we had first arrived in Kobe, I bought a pair of contact lens, which back in the day were a lot different to the ones you get now.

I had been persevering with these things around the Japanese coast by wearing them for a couple of hours a day, but they weren't getting any easier to wear and were very uncomfortable.

On the run from Hong Kong to Singapore, it was very humid and I was wearing them in the pantry one night during dinner, when I tried to rub the sweat out of my eyes and overdid things. When I opened my eyes, the right eye was blurry so I thought I had rubbed one out and it had fallen on the deck. I told Jimmy

Blower, the pantry-man, who got everyone searching the deck on hands and knees, but they couldn't find anything.

After a bit of searching with no result, he looked in my eye and spotted the top of the lens poking out above the muscle at the bottom of my eye. The doctor was called and she took me to the sick-bay where she made me stand on my head against the bulkhead. Gradually, the lens slid back down until the doctor could remove it from my eye.

She suggested that I not wear them for a few days, but the incident had given me such a fright that I never wore them again, even though they had cost a small fortune.

One night ashore in Singapore, Ken and I were in Toby's Paradise Bar on Anson Road when we met a couple of local girls. They asked us if we wanted to go sightseeing with them and we jumped at the chance. We left Toby's and jumped in a cab which took us up to Mt Faber Park where you could get views over the city, and from there we did another couple of spots before dropping the girls at home and heading back to the ship.

They had let us take just enough liberty with them to keep us interested but not let us go too far, and when we dropped them home, they arranged to meet us in Toby's the following evening.

When the cab dropped us off at the wharf gate and we went to pay the driver, he asked us if we were seeing the girls again, and when we said we were, he told us we didn't have to pay, as he would see us again the next night.

Ken and I thought we had a right sucker here, as with the thousands of cabs in Singapore, the odds of seeing this guy again were zilch.

When we met the girls in Toby's and they again suggested going for a drive, we were all for it. It was only when we went out to the taxi, and found the same driver, that we began to suspect that it was a stitch-up, and things were not kosher.

After a repeat of the previous night, when we again got nowhere with the girls, we dropped them home and then headed back to the ship, where the driver demanded $60 for the two nights' fares. We offered him $20, but he got a bit upset at this and started making a scene, so the policeman on the gate came over to see what was going on, and I thought we were in the shit.

The cab driver was Indian, while the cop was a Malay, so there was no love lost there then.

We told the cop that we only had $20 on us, as we had spent the rest of our money on the cab driver's girls. The cop took our $20, gave it to the driver, and effectively told him to fuck off.

Ken and I thanked the cop and shot through the gate back to the ship before he could change his mind.

The Singapore wharf police were not always so friendly, and understanding, as on another trip I had gone ashore to shop and was returning to the ship when the policeman on the gate started to close it when I was about 30 metres away. I called out to him to hang on a sec, but he shut the gate in my face. I knew the gate closed at 22:00, but this was just being spiteful when he knew how close I was, and the ship was berthed only 50 or so metres away.

I was now faced with a walk of a few hundred metres down to the next gate and then a return of the same distance to get to the ship, and as it was a hot night, I wasn't too happy. I let him have a few choice words, and was going to have him on when I got onto the wharf, but by the time I made it, he had called for back-up and a couple of jeeps were waiting for me.

At that point I decided that discretion was the better part of valour and high-tailed it back to the ship.

CHAPTER 7

In Singapore we embarked the remainder of the passengers on the morning of the day we were to leave, and during the afternoon, a large group of the local 'gin & tonic brigade' expats turned up to see someone off. They were all fairly intoxicated, loud and obnoxious.

We were used to seeing them up Orchard Road when we were shopping, but they'd never give you the time of day, as they knew precisely what, and who, you were and didn't want to know.

The ship was singled up, ready to pull away from the wharf, and the deck crowd had pulled up the shit-chutes in readiness for going to sea. The shit-chutes were large wooden boards which hung down over the side of the ship to cover the waste outlets from the heads when the vessel was alongside at the wharf. The crap would shoot out of the outlet when the toilet was flushed, hit the board and fall straight down into the water, instead of arcing out and falling on the wharf.

One of these expats strolled over to the ship and leant on the hull while talking to someone on the passenger deck.

As it was mid-afternoon and not yet turn-to time, a few of the catering crowd were standing on the main deck taking all this in, when Paul Maddrell, the baker, ducked into the accommodation, and the next second a cascade of water shot out of the side of the ship all over the gent who was leaning on the ship.

As if that wasn't enough entertainment, one of the women passengers started using toilet rolls as streamers and began throwing them to her friends on the wharf. The captain, Charlie Collett, spotted this and roared down from the bridge to cease immediately. The poor lady got such a fright that she fainted or, at least, made out that she had.

It was quite a send-off.

Among the new set of passengers embarked in Singapore were a mother and daughter, the wife and daughter of a British Army officer, who was remaining in Singapore. The mother was in her early forties, quite attractive with a good figure, and the daughter was about my age, approaching 17, and fairly attractive.

I hadn't seen the passengers come aboard, but that first evening in the saloon I was still clearing and setting up my 'aircraft carrier' from the mates and engineers' sitting when the passengers came in for the second sitting.

I was vaguely aware of this teenage girl but didn't pay her much attention as I was racing to get finished in the saloon, get changed and get back to 'pearl-diving' in the pantry sink, before the saloon-bobby got on my tail.

Partway through dinner, one of the assistant stewards came into the pantry and told everyone that she had been enquiring about me, asking my name and age. Of course, everyone began taking the piss and giving me some stick, which I tried to ignore.

In Port Swettenham and Penang, I saw her ashore once or twice, and also saw her in the saloon briefly during the change of sittings each mealtime. We never spoke, and after my experience with the female army officer the previous trip, I had no intention of ever speaking to her, and definitely no intention of becoming romantically involved.

Not that I ever thought it would be feasible for one second, as we carried a full complement of cadets, a number of junior mates and engineers, and a young, bronzed and fit deck crowd, all of whom were sniffing around and showing a keen interest.

The day we departed Penang for the run across the Indian Ocean to Aden, I was approached by an assistant steward named 'Flash'. He was a tall, blond version of Johnny Cash, aged about 22 and a bit of a big mouth who used to give me a bit of a hard time, until I lost my cherry, when his attitude towards me mellowed a bit.

He told me that he wanted me to entertain the teenage passenger in the crew recreation room for a couple of hours each night, at the end of service, while he was up in the passenger cabin screwing her mother.

As the girl and her mother shared the cabin, there was no way he was going to get anywhere with the mother without first side-tracking the daughter. Apparently, the mother was very willing, and complicit in the attempt to get me to keep the daughter occupied.

I told him no way, I was not interested, as I could only see me getting into trouble, and asked him how the hell he thought that I could get away with spending the night in the crew recreation room with a girl, without the rest of the crowd finding out, and told him he was fucking nuts.

However, he had done his homework and told me that the mother had already spoken to the daughter, who was agreeable, though what she thought her mother and 'Flash' would be doing while she and I were in the rec room was beyond me, and he had also approached the crew, who had agreed to steer clear while we were in there.

To clinch the deal, he informed me that if I didn't agree to go along with it, he was going to knock my fucking head off.

Well, I was horrified to find that the arrangement wasn't even going to be a secret, and that half the crew already knew about what was proposed, so I still declined to get involved and was willing to accept whatever retribution was coming my way.

'Flash' then got the 2nd steward to talk to me and assure me that the deal was fine and for me not to worry about getting into trouble.

Long story short, a couple of nights later, Flash showed the young lady to the rec room, introduced me, and left while I locked the door from the inside.

Conversation was awkward for a while, and I only had my collection of Bob Dylan albums for entertainment. She hated Bob Dylan.

After a while, the atmosphere improved and things thawed a bit, but every time I heard a set of footsteps approaching down the alleyway, I froze, expecting the captain or chief steward to be knocking on the door, and me ending up on the bridge.

However, the allotted time soon passed, and once I had given Flash enough time to get clear, I escorted her back to the passenger accommodation and wished her a good night.

The next night was a repeat of the first, but the conversation was easier, and things got a little more romantic. I had made sure that the rec-room ports were dogged and the curtains pulled, but the movement of the ship meant that the curtains swung away from the ports at times, and I knew that despite the crew offering to give us privacy, there would be prying eyes.

I was perfectly happy to maintain the status quo, listening to records and engaging in conversation, as she had a few stories to tell about expat life in Singapore and was interesting to talk to. I also held onto the belief that as long as I stuck to that, I couldn't get into too much trouble.

However, it was becoming clear, by words and actions, that she was expecting much more than just listening to music and conversation and it was also obvious that she knew precisely what Flash and her mother were getting up to while she was with me.

Accordingly, the following night I turned off the rec-room lights and we got down to it on one of the settees, although it wasn't very satisfactory for either of us, as I had no condoms and had to get off at Edge-hill.

That gave us both a bit of a fright, and for the future, we just engaged in very heavy petting.

The following morning one of the boys asked me why the fuck I had turned the lights off, which only confirmed my suspicions.

After a few days, it was obvious that the mates and engineers, in addition to the crew, were well aware of what was going on and made a few crude comments, but the main topic of conversation was about Flash and the mother, and even the other passengers were aware of what was going down.

I was still pretty uncomfortable about the whole thing, and worried that I was still going to find myself in trouble, but now that I had had a taste of what was on offer, I was reluctant to call it quits, so despite all the gossip, we kept at it.

Mid Indian Ocean, we had 'Board of Trade Sports', being weekly lifeboat drill, but in this instance one of the boats was called away and lowered into the ocean. As luck would have it, it was the boat I was allocated to, and once in the water, we cast off the falls, shipped the oars, and rowed away, or to be more precise, the ship steamed away from us until out of sight, while we floundered around, clashing oars and 'catching crabs'.

Eventually, *Peleus* reappeared over the horizon and we

managed to come alongside, to a lot of clapping and heckling from the passengers and rest of the crew.

Once we had managed to hook the falls on, one of the ABs who had worked in the fishing fleet previously ran up the ladder hanging over the side of the ship, like a monkey, to a warm round of applause from all those watching. Luckily for me, the boat was lifted out of the water with the rest of us in it and raised to the boat deck, as there was no way I could have handled that ladder.

That evening, my girlfriend had a laugh at my expense and told me that if they had to rely on us in an emergency, they were going to end up going down with the ship, as she reckoned the boat looked like a beetle with legs going in all directions.

So much for our oarsmanship.

Unlike some companies, Blue Funnel took 'Board of Trade Sports' seriously and on one voyage I was assigned to a party of engineers, deckies and stewards to complete a rescue exercise. *Peleus* was brought to a stop in the middle of the Indian Ocean and our party, along with a Neil Robertson stretcher, descended a shaft from the main deck, via a steel ladder, down into the bowels of the ship, into the cofferdam and then along and into the propellor-shaft tunnel where I was instructed to lie in the stretcher. I was then secured in the stretcher so that I resembled an Egyptian mummy and completely immobilised, and if you were prone to claustrophobia, which I am, then this was not the place to be. I had obviously been chosen for the part of the casualty as I was the lightest person in the crew at under 9 stone and you would have found more meat on a butcher's pencil than was attached to my skinny frame.

The rescue party hauled me out of the shaft tunnel, along the cofferdam, to the base of the vertical shaft, where after some manoeuvring, it was discovered that there was only room on the steel ladder for one person at the head of the stretcher and one person at the foot of the stretcher, so the plan to haul me up the shaft to the main deck was abandoned as too dangerous, much to my relief. Thankfully, I was released from the stretcher to make my own way up the shaft and back to the safety of the main deck. I secretly vowed that I would not be going back down below if I could possibly avoid it, as the experience had scared the shit out of me and I had nightmares for some time afterwards.

The only thing I learned from that exercise was that if you became incapacitated in the propellor-shaft tunnel and you weighed over 9 stone, you were probably doomed, because there was no way they were going to be able to get you out.

Upon arrival in Aden for bunkers, most of the passengers went ashore shopping, although security was tight, due to the troubles kicking off, which made it a dangerous place to visit, and only got worse as time went by.

We continued our liaison for the rest of the trip home, but at one stage we did have a bit of a bust-up and stopped seeing one another for a while, but Flash's frustration soon put an end to that interlude and we carried on as usual.

Captain Collett had been off side with the passengers ever since the incident which happened departing Singapore, and quite often ate his meals with the early sitting to avoid them. Steaming up the Mersey on docking-day, being a Friday, and the official Board of Trade Sports Day, he decided to call a lifeboat drill, which didn't endear him to the passengers or crew.

Docking-day was busy and hectic enough without the hassle of boat drill, and no-one was amused, with the exception of Charlie Collett, as he extracted his revenge on the passengers.

I only got to see my girlfriend briefly, once we had docked, but she managed to slip me her address in London and her telephone number, and invited me to visit for a weekend, while I was on leave. She and her mother were going to be staying with her maternal grandmother, who lived in Kingston-upon-Thames, out Wimbledon way, and her mother and grandmother were quite happy for me to visit for a weekend.

A week into my leave, on the Friday afternoon, I caught the train to London and she met me at Euston Station and then we caught the train out to Kingston-upon-Thames, where I was introduced to her grandmother. There was no grandfather, so I presumed he had passed away, although I never clarified the situation.

The suburb was pretty up-market and the grandmother's home was a large detached house with beautiful gardens and quite secluded. The grandmother spoke with a very refined accent and managed to disguise her horror at having to host me in her house for the weekend.

Judging by the photographs and artefacts scattered about the house, they were obviously a family of empire builders, very well established and comfortably off.

The following day, being a Saturday, we caught the train back in to central London and spent the day and the evening sightseeing and having dinner.

On the Sunday, we had lunch at the house, which was a bit of a nerve-wracking experience for me, as I was trying very hard not to embarrass myself by making too many gaffes.

After lunch, she took me into a quiet room of the house to say goodbye as I was going to catch the train back into London and then back to Chester. Our petting started to get a bit heavy, when we were interrupted by the grandmother who was going out and had come to say goodbye. Unfortunately, I had an erection, and was attempting to hide the bulge in my trousers when she shook my hand, which was an awkward moment, to say the least.

Her mother then took me aside before I left and let me know, in a roundabout way, that there was not much future for me with her daughter, as when she finished school, she was bound for university and I didn't figure in their plans for her. She was very nice about it, but she needn't have bothered, as I definitely had no long-term plans for her daughter, wasn't the least interested in a long-term relationship, and was only keen on getting back to the bar-girls in Kobe.

I had the hots for the mother, and I think she knew it, as she always had a half-smile on her face when she looked at me, and her knowing that I knew about her activities in *Peleus* just made it that more lascivious.

Partway through the following trip I received a 'Dear John' letter from the daughter but wasn't in the least concerned and didn't bother replying. It had been a pleasant and exciting experience, and my only regret was that I had not managed to seduce her mother.

When leave was up, it was back on the shore-gang while I waited for *Peleus* to return to Birkenhead from her coastal voyage.

Upon her returning to Vittoria Dock, we found that she had been de-passengerised, or DP'd, and eventually, would no longer carry passengers, just cargo. In the meantime, though, some of the passenger accommodation had been converted into state rooms for a Japanese princess and her entourage.

This was Princess Chichibu, who was going to launch one of the company's new ships being built at the shipyards in Nagasaki and would board *Peleus* when we reached Kobe.

Because of the princess and the number of people who would accompany her in Japan, the catering crowd had not been reduced, and she still carried the two bedroom stewards who would look after those people when they embarked.

We also had a new chief steward, who had a reputation as a bit of a 'hard' man, as, in his youth, he used to prize-fight for beer-money on the Australian coast and had recorded a string of wins.

Although now in his late forties or early fifties, he looked the part, with a broken nose and solid shoulders. Even Flash, who fancied himself as a bit of a 'hard' man, backed down when this guy offered him out on deck one time, after they had a bit of an argument.

He turned out to be okay, as long as you didn't try to have him on, as I found out to my cost a couple of trips later.

We locked out into the Mersey that trip in the early hours of the morning and I was still awake and reading in my bunk when I heard the blast of a ship's horn sounding in the night. The sound was so mournful, but beautiful, that it made the hair on the back of my neck stand up, and I had to stick my head out of the port to see where it came from.

Slowly steaming up the river was a Japanese Maru boat, which must have been signalling for tugs, and that sound has lived with me to this day. There is no sound so plaintive, or more beautiful, than the sound of a ship's horn, or a foghorn, at night when you are wrapped up warm in your bunk.

The trip out East was uneventful, apart from my Dear John letter, and when we had finished discharging cargo in Japan, we berthed in Kobe to await the arrival of the Japanese princess. Three of us boy-ratings were detailed to carry her baggage aboard, and on the day of her arrival were standing to attention in our blues and mess-jackets at the foot of the accommodation ladder.

We were so excited at the thought of being so close to a beautiful young, real-life princess that when a huge limousine pulled up on the wharf and a short, frumpy, middle-aged woman stepped out, we thought she was one of the entourage and were waiting for the princess to appear.

Our disappointment was intense when we found out that she was, in fact, the princess and she had a huge pile of baggage to be brought aboard. It was a cold day, but we soon warmed up carrying all that luggage up the ladder.

As soon as the party was embarked, we left the berth and steamed slowly through the Inland Sea, towards Nagasaki. The sea was full of small craft and numerous islands, and it would have been a pleasant cruise had the weather been better.

On the way to Nagasaki, the princess wanted to stop off and visit Miyajima Island, a sacred island off Hiroshima with a shrine situated on it, so we dropped anchor off the island, and the party went ashore in a launch.

Unfortunately, when it came time to return to the ship, the weather had deteriorated even more and the launch couldn't make it back. *Peleus* then had to steam about looking for a suitably sheltered spot, to enable the launch to make a safe return, which it eventually did.

Following the launching of the company vessel, we retraced our path to Kobe, where we disembarked the royal party, and commenced loading cargo. *Peleus*'s brief sojourn as a royal yacht was over, and we reverted to the mundane job of being a freighter.

Headed home, I had encounters with bar-girls in Hong Kong and Singapore, but the experience was nowhere near the same standard as the women in Japan, and I vowed to save my money for the girls of Kobe, Nagoya and Yokohama.

By now, I was consuming beer on a regular basis and beginning to get the taste for it. Although I was still too young to purchase beer on the ship, it was easy to pay the ratings to buy beer for me or exchange Coca-Cola for those who didn't drink. Purchasing beer ashore was now no problem either, even in the UK, and although I looked closer to 15 than 18, I had no problem getting served in pubs and was rarely denied service.

On our approach to Liverpool at the end of the trip, we were steaming up St George's Channel, between Wales and Ireland,

and it was a really wet, stormy night. We would be docking in Liverpool early the next morning and I had been working late.

I had left my dhobi until the last minute and had a pile of underwear to wash and dry prior to leaving the ship. When I went to hang my dhobi in the drying room I found that everyone else had beaten me to it and there was no more room, so I had to rig a line in the alleyway to hang my washing. The breeze blowing down the alleyway was laden with moisture from the storm, and I could see that there was no way it was going to dry by morning.

At that moment, the Chinese laundry-man came down the alleyway and saw what I was trying to achieve. He told me 'No, no, never dry' and took all my washing down and took it away with him. When I turned to at 05:30 the next morning, a brown-paper parcel tied with string and containing all my underwear, dried and pressed, had been shoved through my door and was lying on the deck, and he didn't charge me a penny for doing it. I just loved those guys and wondered what we would do without them.

Leave dragged a bit, as I was growing away from my schoolmates and we didn't have too much in common any more. Mum was forever moaning about me constantly playing Bob Dylan albums on the record player all morning and being in the way when she was trying to clean up.

The novelty of being away soon grows old, and I tended to wear out my welcome, and I was still far too shy to get myself a girlfriend.

I was glad to get back on the shore-gang again and couldn't wait to get out to Japan and back to the bar-girls.

CHAPTER 8

When I eventually rejoined *Peleus* in Vittoria Dock, the passenger accommodation had been converted to cabins for the junior mates, engineers and petty officers, while the accommodation on the deck above had been enlarged for the senior officers and engineers. This meant that now even the junior officers could take their wives away with them and this was happening more and more often.

Wives on board were a bit of a contentious issue, as some of them were okay, while some of them tended to adopt their husband's rank and could be a bit of a pain in the arse. With nothing to do and all bloody day to do it, some of them could be a bit of a trial, plus, you had to constantly be aware of your language as you never knew who was just around the next corner.

The catering crowd had been much reduced with the loss of the passengers, but one of the positives was that we all had single-berth cabins, which made a nice change, and meals were down to one sitting which made for an earlier finish in the evening.

The end of day routine in the galley and pantry was much the same, despite not having passengers, and after service for the engineers in the saloon, I had to make a quick change and get on the pantry sink as soon as possible. Jake Finn, the saloon-bobby, was soon on our cases if we tried to skive off and wasted time getting changed.

Jake was a good guy, but if he thought you were being a smart-arse, he had plenty of ways to get back at you. One of his favourites was to go through the racks of plates we boys had just washed and find one with a speck of food on it. When he did, we had to take all the plates out of the racks and wash them all again, even if they were clean.

Another killer was that just as you thought you had completed washing and drying everything, he would pull out the zinc bath, fill it with boiling water, add soda crystals and silver foil, and we would have to dip all of the silverware until it was bright and shiny again.

On completion of the 'pearl-diving' the pantry and galley sinks were filled up with hot, soapy water which was then slung by the bucketful over the deck, and all hands set to scrubbing everything down, after which the deck was rinsed off with fresh water.

This was the routine at the finish of every single day, and the standard of hygiene was extremely high and never compromised.

When we had finished work, it was down to the accommodation for a shower and then maybe a few beers and listening to music or just bullshitting.

The main type of music was country & western, with Johnny Cash, Hank Snow, Hank Williams, Roy Orbison, et al., which wasn't my cup of tea, as I was into Bob Dylan, and surprisingly, considering *Peleus* was a Liverpool ship, The Beatles didn't feature much either and definitely no Rolling Stones.

The trips in *Peleus* were by now becoming routine, with the ports slipping by as regular as clockwork and the express schedule being maintained, despite no longer carrying passengers.

One event which did stand out on this trip occurred in Hong Kong, when two of the ABs, returning from ashore late one night, came across the chief steward and the chief cook lowering cartons of eggs over the side of the ship to a sampan below and selling them to the Chinese.

This was classed as a perk of the job, and went on in all the departments, from deck to engine room, where all sorts of ship's stores were flogged off to the locals. The secret was not to get caught.

Where they got all these spare eggs from was beyond me, as no-one went short of eggs on any trip, and although I never ate eggs and bacon for breakfast, making do with toast and coffee, if anyone wanted two eggs for breakfast, they got them. And that was completely across the board.

However, these ABs decided to make something of it and had the chief steward on.

As mentioned previously, the guy had been a prize-fighter, and these two ABs spent most of the following week looking like a couple of pandas, with huge black eyes, and probably wishing that they had turned a blind eye to what was going on.

At this time, the British Army was gradually pulling out of Singapore, now that that country had achieved independence, and we carried a lot of army equipment as deck cargo. The ship swarmed with 'squaddies' who were delivering the trucks and other gear to the wharf, and they were forever trying to bum beer, spirits or cigarettes off us. These same 'squaddies' didn't return the favour, as a couple of trips later in another ship, most of the catering crowd decided to visit the bar in the Tanglin army barracks. One of them got a bit boisterous and broke a glass, which pissed off the army boys, who, with all that fitness training and nowhere to vent, got stuck into them.

When they turned to next morning, every one of them was sporting a black eye, missing teeth, or cuts and bruises.

Luckily, I hadn't been with them for some reason, but this incident put me off going ashore in large groups, as it was too easy to get into trouble and much preferred to go ashore in the company of one or two people. It was easier to stay out of trouble that way.

We were alongside in Port Swettenham and the lads were all going to the bar in the kampong, the jungle village, situated just off the main highway to Kuala Lumpur. I had to call at the Seamen's Mission to purchase some stamps and post some mail, so I said I would meet them in the bar a bit later.

Having posted my mail, I headed down the road and then veered off onto a path into the jungle which led to the kampong. It was dark but the path was lit, and as I reached the outskirts of the village, I met a good-looking woman in a long gown who asked me if I wanted sex.

The way she looked and dressed made me think that she was some rich lady from Kuala Lumpur looking for 'rough trade' as she was so out of place in the jungle village, and I was keen to oblige. There was no money involved, so she took me into a hut, where it was pitch dark, lay on a bed and hiked her dress up. She then pulled me on top and I climaxed in about 10 seconds flat.

When it was over, I headed off to the bar, where I couldn't wait to tell the lads about my amazing experience. When I tried to tell them about this gorgeous woman I had just met, they called me a lying little bastard, and accused me of making the story up, so I let it go and forgot all about it.

It wasn't until a few years later when the memory came bubbling up from the dark recesses of my mind that the penny finally dropped and I froze in horror. However, it was far too late to change anything so I prefer to believe that she was the beautiful lady I thought she was, and not what she might have been!

On my last trip in *Peleus*, my sixth voyage, we sailed from Birkenhead early in May 1966, just a few days before the start of the Seamen's Strike.

Getting away when we did meant that we missed the strike, and when we later heard about the hardship the strike caused so many seamen, we were grateful for that, even though there were constant rumours around the ship that we were going to tie up in the first port we visited and walk off the ship.

Being a boy rating, I would have just followed the ratings, and at that time had no understanding of the issues behind the strike. All I kept hearing was guys going on about the 1960 unofficial strike, which many of them had taken part in, but could not grasp the significance of one or the other. There were so many sides to the argument, that most nights this topic took up most of the conversation and I found it somewhat confusing, and downright boring after a while.

The strike lasted six weeks, and every ship with a British crew that entered a British port during that time saw the crew walk off and the ship tied up for the duration. The ports became clogged with all these idle ships, and the seamen who were out of work for the duration suffered extreme hardship, especially the married men.

I wasn't at all sure about what had been achieved when the strike was called off, as some were calling it a major success, while others declared it a major disaster and a sell-out.

My only experience had been of Holts, and conditions on Blue Funnel ships were excellent, and not something I could complain about. They were excellent feeders, with good accommodation and the company looked after its crews. I heard a few horror stories from people who had sailed with other companies but considered that some of this was exaggerated for effect, or maybe I was just lucky in having been employed by Holts.

About the only positive outcome of the strike that I can recall was that we no longer had to turn to on Saturday mornings when working on the shore-gang. This may not sound like much, but to me it meant not only a saving on bus-fare but that we got a full weekend off and, most importantly, it meant no more broken journeys on the way home to empty my bladder.

The trouble with working Saturday mornings on the shore-gang was that we only worked until 12 midday, and then it was straight into the pub for a session of three or four pints of bitter, and then onto the bus for Chester. The bus trip took an hour, but unfortunately my bladder was only good for half that time, and I always found myself having to get off the bus at Great Sutton to duck into the White Swan for a pee.

I then had to wait for the next bus, and as they only ran every hour, it meant I just got on the piss again while waiting. By the time I finally got to Chester, I was 'three sheets to the wind' and Saturday night was usually a write-off.

I got into a spot of bother in Singapore when I went ashore with one of the other A/Ss and we ended up in a bar on Orchard Road, where we met a couple of New Zealand girls who were with a group of British Navy guys. We got talking and dancing with these girls, and when it came time to return to the ship, I was so sure I was getting somewhere with one of them that I decided not to turn to for dinner but stayed in the bar.

The other A/S returned to *Peleus* and left me in the bar.

It turned out I was kidding myself, as a couple of hours later the navy guys took off and so did the Kiwi girls. I was well pissed by this stage, so caught a cab back to the ship, where the chief steward was waiting at the head of the gangway. He took one look at me and told me he would deal with me next day.

In the morning, he bailed me up in the saloon just before breakfast and gave me a right bollocking, and I was very contrite. He then walked out of the saloon through one door but a minute later came in the other door and caught me laughing my head off at something one of the other guys had said to me.

He immediately assumed that I was laughing about him and flew into a right paddy. He ordered me to get out of my blues and jacket, change into working gear and get on the pantry sink, where I remained for the next day and a half, with everyone giving me a hard time and taking the piss.

Fortunately, a few of the engineers requested that I be reinstated, as the boy-rating who had taken over from me wasn't quite up to speed and the chief steward relented.

He didn't log me though, for which I was grateful, as I thoroughly deserved to be docked pay for my behaviour.

We arrived back at Gladstone Dock, Liverpool in early August 1966, just a few days before my eighteenth birthday. This meant that I now made rating to A/S but found that there were no berths in *Peleus* for A/S, so was bound for the shore-gang until a berth became available in another ship.

I spent most of my leave in my local, the Dee Miller in Newton, on the outskirts of Chester, but was glad to get back on the shore-gang and with the guys I knew. Girls were still a problem, as I was far too shy to chat them up, so my mind was always on the other side of the world in some bar down the Motomachi.

I think my not having a girlfriend was becoming something of an issue with Mum, and I'm sure she thought I might be gay.

I was sitting on the couch one evening watching TV and waiting for the pub to open. Mum and my older sister were talking when a well-known pianist appeared on the telly and Mum said, 'I really like him.' My sister replied, 'Oh no, he was in the navy and he's one of those.'

Out of the corner of my eye, I then saw Mum put her finger to her lips to shush my sister and point at me.

I took off for the pub.

It wasn't until a good while later, when she came across my collection of Japanese bar-girl photos, which the mama-sans used to hand out to clients, and found some condoms in my jeans pocket when she was doing some washing, that she realised she was barking up the wrong tree.

Still, she sent Dad up to my room to complain about me carrying condoms around with me.

I was ever hopeful.

I was on the shore-gang for a while, when one morning Ken turned up having just finished leave off the A-boat, so we started knocking about together.

To save him having to sleep on the ship, as he couldn't travel home to Holyhead every night, I invited him home to Chester, where he slept on the couch, and this became a regular occurrence. We did a pub crawl round Chester just about every night, and as it was the sixties and there were 32 pubs within the city walls, plus all the pubs outside the walls, we could choose a different direction and combination every night. It was great.

Come the weekend and he invited me back to his place in Holyhead for the weekend.

On Friday afternoon, we picked up rail passes from the Seamen's Union office in Hamilton Square, Birkenhead, and then caught the train from Hamilton Square, changing at Chester, to Holyhead.

At least we were getting something in return for our union dues, and when I used to do this journey on a regular basis, and told the old union guy that I lived in Holyhead, he was too fuckin lazy to check up, so I always got away with it.

When we arrived in Holyhead at about 20:00 that night, Ken

took me around to his girlfriend's place, and she had a couple of her friends with her. Both her mates were attractive, but I liked the look of one in particular. Of course, I was too shy to do anything about it, apart from keep giving her looks, but I did tell Ken I fancied her and he arranged for his girl to bring her along on a date the following night.

When I finally managed to untie my tongue, I found out that she fancied me as well, and it was the beginning of a relationship that lasted a while or, at least, a lot longer than I deserved it to last.

The only fly in the ointment was that she was still only 17, and Holyhead being such a small place, everyone knew everyone else, and as Holyhead barmaids were very protective of their space, there was no way that she could drink in the local pubs. If we wanted a drink, we had to travel outside of Holyhead where she was less well known, and the same applied to Ken's girl as well.

The other issue for me was that her father, who was a very big man, and an ex-matelot in the Royal Navy, gave me the impression that he could read my mind and anticipate my every move, so I was very reluctant to try anything on with her, as he was very protective.

Ken bought a mini-van, which ran okay most of the time but occasionally caused a few headaches. Not many of the lads in those days owned a car, so when we were on the shore-gang, he was always being sent to out of the way places and I usually ended up going with him.

One morning, we were sent to the dock in Bromborough, to work by the *Oti*, one of Elder-Dempster's ships. Elder-Dempster had been taken over by Holts, and all their ships were on the West African run.

When we went aboard her and opened the galley door to start cleaning, the whole space moved. The place was alive with cockroaches from deck to deck-head, and I had never seen so many in one place.

We told the working boss that there was no way we would be cleaning the galley until they fumigated for cockroaches as it would just be a waste of time. Whether they did or not we never knew, as we were recalled to Vittoria Dock and given other work.

When I stayed at Ken's place in Valley, he had a double bed in his room which we both slept in. The mattress on his bed had the worst case of roll-together I have ever come across, and you went to sleep desperately hanging onto the edge of the mattress, but when we woke up in the morning, we would both have rolled together in the middle and lying face to face. Needless to say, we were both out of bed straight away, and didn't bother having a lie-in.

One Friday, just after lunch, we were working by an A-boat up in Bidston when the working boss told us that the time-keeper, Eric, wanted both of us to report to the time-office in Vittoria Dock straight away.

We had been on the ale the night before, and before we left the A-boat, Ken decided he needed to go to the heads for a crap. I waited for him by the car, but he was quite some time doing the business, and at least 15 minutes had elapsed before he got into the car.

When we got to the time-office, Eric was doing his nut, saying, 'Where the hell have you two been? I sent for you over half an hour ago!'

I said, 'It wasn't my fault, Eric. Ken had to go for a crap!'

Eric said, 'Jesus Christ! Do you two fuckers sleep together as well?'

Ken and I looked at one another and said, 'Well, as a matter of fact, Eric...'

All he wanted was for us to take one of his mates, a chief steward, home and drop him off at Speke, in Liverpool. Eric told us that when we had dropped him off, we would be finished for the day and could go straight home. Unfortunately for us, after we dropped the bloke home, we missed the Runcorn Bridge across the ship canal and ended up almost at Salford before realising our mistake and turning around.

It was quite late by the time we finally got on the road for Holyhead, and after stopping for a few pints at Conway, in North Wales, we arrived in Holyhead after closing time and that was the end of Friday night.

I paid regular visits to Holyhead most weekends, staying at Ken's until he shipped out and then I stayed at my girlfriend's house. I remained on the shore-gang for a couple of months and was then assigned a berth in the MV *Melampus*, as engineers' assistant steward. *Melampus* was one of six sisters, of around 8500 tons and 17 knots, the others being *Maron, Machaon, Menestheus, Menelaus,* and *Memnon.*

They carried 12 passengers but were in the process of being de-passengerised, and this was to be *Melampus*'s last voyage carrying passengers.

On the voyage out, we were carrying a group of young missionaries, male and female, who spoke with very refined southern accents, and seemed to spend all their time in the bar. They were a bit obnoxious at times and created a bit of a scandal ashore in Manila, returning to the ship well inebriated and receiving a bit of a telling off, but I'm not sure what the problem had been.

I can only remember thinking, 'God help the people they were going out to save.'

We dropped them off in Hong Kong and then proceeded up to Japan, with Kobe again being the first port of call.

As I now had a girlfriend in the UK, I was trying to be a good boy and remain faithful, so when I went up the Motomachi I now tended to drink in Clancy's Bar.

Clancy was a big Aussie guy, an ex-squaddie, who had married a local girl and opened the bar. It was not a 'girlie' bar, so you weren't pestered by women, but a lot of Aussie visitors and expats drank there, and almost all Blue Flue guys had visited at some time.

Clancy wasn't a particularly welcoming guy, well, not unless you were an Ocker, but I suppose he must have had a fair few run-ins with drunken British seamen, which may have accounted for his attitude.

By the time we got to Yokohama, my resolve to remain celibate was beginning to crumble, and one night I ended up in the Peanuts Bar. I got talking to one of the girls but had no intention of inviting her back to the ship, as I just couldn't be bothered with the hassle.

I bought her a couple of drinks and something to eat and then we caught a cab back to her place. She lived in a tiny apartment, and I ended up staying the night, with no money changing hands.

When I left to return to the ship next morning, she said she would meet me in Peanuts that night, after the bars closed, if she didn't have a client.

As luck would have it, it was the early part of the week and fairly quiet, so she was there again and took me home. We managed to connect a couple more times while *Melampus* was berthed in Yokohama, but I wasn't going to write to her. The arrangement was that I would look her up if I came back to Yokohama next trip.

CHAPTER 9

Back in Hong Kong, we embarked the passengers for the trip home and among them was a family of five: father, mother, two daughters and a boy.

The father was a British officer in the Hong Kong police, married to a petite Chinese lady, and in this day and age someone would have reported him for domestic abuse, but back then, everyone pretended to turn a blind eye.

She was a lovely lady, very polite and friendly, and absolutely terrified of him, but he was a complete arsehole, and spent every minute in the bar.

The eldest daughter, of about 14 or 15, was very attractive and dined with the adults on the second sitting. The younger daughter of about 11 or 12 dined with the young boy, who was about eight years old, at a special children's sitting, at the same time as the junior engineers and mates, and were served by Wally, the passengers' assistant steward.

The boy was spoiled rotten, as the whole family doted on him, and was the most obnoxious little bastard I have ever come across. The engineers were forever complaining about his whingeing and crying while they were dining, but as he was a fare-paying passenger, there wasn't a great deal we could do about it.

The mother used to assist Wally in feeding the kids and was forever cajoling this little prick to eat his food, and Wally had come to hate him.

One lunchtime, I heard a 'bong' and looked over to the children's table. Wally had hit the kid over the head with his waiters' cloth, in which he'd concealed a serving spoon. The kid was rubbing his head and crying, and the mother was wondering what had happened. Wally explained that he had just touched the kid on the head with the waiters' cloth and couldn't understand why he was so upset, so the mother told the kid off for being such a baby.

It may have given Wally some satisfaction, but things didn't change much, and the kid remained a little shit.

Arriving at Point Lynas, Holyhead, to pick up the pilot to take us into Liverpool, I was summoned to the mate's cabin and handed a letter from my girlfriend. I was astounded and asked the mate how on earth a letter had arrived for me.

It turned out that my girlfriend's friend's father was a crewman on the pilot boat and had offered to take a letter from her and give it to the pilot, to give to me. It was a very welcome surprise.

One incident which remains in my memory from this trip was that I had bought my girlfriend's young brother a remote-controlled car in Japan, and when I arrived home and gave it to him, it wouldn't work. We tried new batteries, and his father took it for someone to look at and try to fix, but it was beyond repair.

I was highly embarrassed, and the young brother was extremely upset, so it was not a good look for me.

When I rejoined the *Melampus* for the next trip, the guys let the secret out of the bag. One night when I had gone ashore, a couple of them came across it in my locker and decided to give it a run up the alleyway. They had managed to crash it and wreck it internally, so had repacked it carefully, and placed it back in my locker, and of course, as I had no reason to open it, I had not realised there was anything amiss.

I was totally pissed off when they told me, but everyone thought it was a huge joke at my expense.

The last weekend in Holyhead, prior to going back deep sea in *Melampus*, I got the feeling that my girlfriend was after some sort of commitment from me, but in my ignorance and inexperience, I assumed that girls thought just like guys and were content with just having a good time.

I had absolutely no intention of ever settling down and getting married, and the thought of having children filled me with horror and panic. I was now totally immersed in my life at sea and loving every minute of it.

I just couldn't understand the mind-set of the people I worked with, when they reached the age of 18 or 19, who were breaking their neck to get some sort of job ashore, especially as they had completed the training and had got through the worst part of life at sea as a boy rating. I lost count of the number of times someone told me that their girlfriend's father was going to get them a job at Fords or Vauxhalls on Merseyside.

I should have seen it coming, but I didn't, and when I received my second 'Dear John' letter in Hong Kong, later that trip, I was devastated. She was a very attractive girl, with a lovely figure and a bubbly personality, and although I still had no intention of getting married, I knew I was going to miss her very much. And I was also going to miss her family, who I had become attached to.

I went ashore that night on my own, got blind drunk, and then decided to get my own back by going with a bar-girl.

Unfortunately, I was so drunk that I couldn't manage to 'do the deed', ended up throwing up all over this poor girl's bedroom and had to pay her extra money to compensate for the mess, and ended up with a massive hangover next morning.

When we arrived in Yokohama, we were moored on the buoys in the harbour and had to catch a launch to and from shore, which was a bit of a hassle, as you couldn't just come and go as you pleased and were dependent on the launch schedule.

I managed to reconnect with my girlfriend at Peanuts, and we had a couple of nights at her place, with me leaving early to catch the 05:30 launch back to the ship, arriving at 05:45, in time for 06:00 turn-to.

On the last morning I was with her, I climbed out of the taxi onto the wharf to see the launch disappearing into the early morning mist and had to wait 30 minutes for the next one. This meant that when I reached the *Melampus*, I was 15 minutes late turning to.

I apologised to the chief steward for being late and thought that was the end of it, but mid-morning the chief steward approached me and told me to change into my blues and mess-jacket. I was going up to the bridge to be logged by the mate for being absent without leave.

I couldn't believe it, particularly as I was an arse-licking 'Company Man' who had always made a habit of turning to by 05:45, at the latest, every morning.

The chief steward accompanied me up to the bridge, where the mate logged me 'a day, and a day', being the loss of two days' pay for being 15 minutes late to work.

To say I was pissed off would be an understatement, particularly in view of the fact that had I taken the whole day off, I would still have been logged 'a day and a day'. I resolved there and then that in future, as the catering department never, ever, got a day off, no matter how long the trip lasted, I was going to take a day off every trip, at a time and place of my own choosing.

When the mate asked me whether I had anything to say, I told him that she had been well worth it, but two days' pay for a night in the sack was a bit steep.

From Yokohama, we sailed across to Pusan, or Busan, as it is today, and spent three days anchored off the port until we were redirected to mainland China, where we came to anchor at a port down the coast from Shanghai.

A launch full of uniformed Immigration and Quarantine officers came out to us and made themselves at home in the officers' recreation room. They took it in turns to sleep in the sick-bay, and we had to feed the lot of them during the days they were on board.

They supplied each of the crew with a little cardboard pillbox and a matchstick, which we were supposed to take with us when we went to the toilet, use the matchstick to take a sample of what was in the toilet, and put this in the pillbox. We then had to take this to the Quarantine officers, who would test it for cholera.

This method of testing for cholera had been superseded throughout the rest of world by more up-to-date methods, but China still retained the system.

The entire crew had to have been tested before the ship was allowed to go alongside, so the pressure was on. I had tried to do it, but I was very squeamish and each time had chickened out of using the matchstick, and just flushed the toilet instead.

On the second day, the chief steward told me that they were waiting on me, and to get a move on. I told him that I was constipated, and couldn't do it, but he told me to drink a big mug of black coffee and get the deed done.

I went to the toilet, but when it came to using the matchstick, I just couldn't, and flushed it instead.

Jimmy, the officers steward, was in the next cubicle and said to me, 'Give it here and I'll do it for you.'

I tossed the pillbox under the cubicle door and after a few seconds, he tossed it back.

I wasn't game enough to take the lid off the box to see if he had filled it, so I just had to take his word for it and ran up top, to present the box to the Quarantine people. The Chinese guy accepted it without any expression and ticked my name off the crew list on the table in front of him.

When a couple of hours had passed and no-one had come looking for me, I relaxed, but then started to worry that they were going to test it, find that there were two identical samples and realise what had gone on.

As the scourge of the Red Guard was then at its height, I spent all the time there fretting about being marched off to some unknown fate, and couldn't wait to get out of the place.

The place was a nightmare, with propaganda blaring from loudspeakers on the wharf, dock workers marching to work in squads, like soldiers, and the movies at the Seamen's Mission which we were invited to were all propaganda films about the Chinese atomic bomb.

We all had to remove any world maps from our bulkheads, which showed the British Empire in red, as red was reserved to depict mainland China. All cameras were locked away and photography forbidden.

We were all given a little red book of the sayings of Chairman Mao before we departed, but I gave mine the 'deep six' prior to arriving in Hong Kong.

From Hong Kong, it was down to Singapore, where we lost our captain, H.K. (Hong Kong) Martin.

Captain Martin was a great bloke and everyone liked him, he

always spoke if he met you, smiled a lot, and was always polite, so when he left us it was a pretty sad moment.

The reason we lost him was that another Blue Funnel ship had been departing Singapore and had run aground. It was rumoured that the captain of that ship was intoxicated, so he was removed and flown back to the UK, and Captain Martin replaced him in command.

The mate of *Melampus* was given command and all the mates moved up in rank. Unfortunately, this arrangement only lasted as far as Penang, as a new captain was flown out from the UK to take command and all the mates reverted to their original status, which they weren't happy about.

The new guy was not very popular, as he was anti-drinking, and a wee bit temperance.

At one crew meeting, he went on about the evils of drink and wanted us to cut down, but he was wasting his breath.

From Penang, we made our way to Trincomalee, in Sri Lanka, or Ceylon as it was then. Trincomalee was a beautiful spot, with a nice harbour and lovely sandy beaches.

One afternoon, the motor-lifeboat was lowered and we all headed off across the harbour to the beach for a swim. We were towing a hatch-board with a rope handle which we were using as a surfboard.

Jimmy, the officers' steward, was on the board in the middle of the harbour when a huge ray leapt out of the water and landed with a big splash, a few feet from him. Jimmy was so startled that he took a couple of steps forward, which caused the leading edge of the board to dip into the sea, and as the boat was moving at a few knots, this caused the board to dive straight down. Jimmy had wrapped the steering rope around his arms so he went down with the board.

The towrope went from horizontal to vertical in a matter of

seconds and we thought it was going to get wrapped around the propellor, so stopped the boat. After a lengthy period of time, in which a few of us were preparing to dive over the side to rescue him, Jimmy slowly floated to the surface, with the board, red in the face and coughing and spluttering.

After a great afternoon at the beach, we were back aboard for dinner.

The next port was Aden for bunkers, but we also loaded a few tons of ammunition to ship back to the UK for the British Army. The army was in the process of pulling out of Aden, and in fact pulling out of the Far East altogether. Armed soldiers patrolled the wharf at all times, as the situation in Aden was really dangerous and we were not allowed ashore.

We then steamed up the Red Sea for three days, arriving off Suez on the evening of 4 June, where we dropped anchor for the night.

The following morning, 5 June, at 09:30 hrs we joined the north-bound convoy, in the position of 'arse-end-Charlie', and proceeded into the canal.

A little later, we heard over the radio that hostilities had broken out between Israel and Egypt, but in our naivety, we did not think that it would impact on our transiting the canal, and that we would still be arriving in Liverpool in just over a week's time.

The only war-like activity we observed were groups of Egyptian soldiers digging in on the west bank of the canal. The junior electrician, John Hughes, was descending the foremast after repairing a light and was forced to leap the last few feet to the deck, injuring his ankle, when some of these soldiers aimed their rifles at him.

Later in the morning, as we approached the southern entrance into the Bitter Lakes, we observed a column of thick, black smoke rising from the Egyptian airfield, situated on the shores of the lakes, and this turned out to be coming from a burning tanker-truck.

A group of us were out on deck, adjacent to the saloon, having a coffee, and the ship ahead of us was just drawing level with the airfield, when someone spotted four fighter-bombers approaching from the east and flying a few feet above the water.

They were Israeli planes using the convoy for cover to attack the airfield, and as they swept up and over the ship ahead, they proceeded to plaster the airfield, and Egyptian planes parked there, with bombs.

We were extremely fortunate that the Egyptians had not spotted them coming across the lakes, because we would have been directly in the path of any anti-aircraft fire directed at the Israeli planes.

Some of the Egyptian planes attempted to take off but none made it, and I'm ashamed to say that those of us in *Melampus*, observing all that was going on, were jumping up and down, and cheering like fans at a football match. It wasn't until I saw the tears running down the face of one of the old Egyptian canal-boatmen we carried on board for the transit of the canal that I realised that we were watching people actually die over there.

This was a sobering thought, but as the Egyptians were seen as the aggressors and Israelis as the underdogs, we were rooting for Israel. How times have changed, and now we see Israel as the arrogant aggressors.

The convoy moved a couple of miles into the Bitter Lakes and anchored. The Israeli planes returned a few more times during the day, and there were intermittent artillery duels across the canal, which we stayed up late into the night to watch, but we were still under the illusion that we would proceed with the transit as normal.

The following morning, the Blue Star boat, *Scottish Star*,

entered the canal from the south and joined our convoy, so there were now 14 ships making up the north-bound convoy.

The south-bound convoy passed us in the lakes and proceeded to exit the canal at Suez.

Later we upped anchor and moved closer to the northern entrance to the canal from the lakes, at Ismailia, and dropped anchor again, where on the third day we were notified that the canal was now blocked at both ends. The 14 ships then settled down to wait for, what we thought, was to be a few days, or weeks, at the most, until the canal was cleared.

Although the feeling of being trapped in the canal wasn't very pleasant, we weren't too apprehensive or worried, but we would have been had we been aware of the claims being made by President Nasser of Egypt and King Hussein of Jordan.

In an effort to save face, they both claimed that some of the aircraft that had attacked on 5 June had flown from British and American carriers, as they found it hard to believe that the Israelis had managed to achieve such success on their own.

President Nasser did not back down on this claim until over 12 months later and the claim is still widely believed in much of the Arab world to this day, having been repeated on the Al Jazeera television channel only recently. Fortunately, for our peace of mind, we did not become aware of these false claims until very much later.

We also became aware of the rumour concerning the incredible Israeli attack on the USS *Liberty*, an American electronic surveillance ship, sailing in international waters, which resulted in the killing of 34 of her crew and the wounding of 171 others.

Despite transmitting her position and being clearly defined as an American naval vessel, clearly marked and flying the appropriate ensigns, she was attacked for over an hour by Israeli planes and gunboats. This attack occurred on 8 June and when we first heard rumours of the attack, we assumed that the ship must have been in the canal and attacked by accident, but that was not the case as she was at least 15 miles off the coast of Gaza in international waters and the Israelis had been closely monitoring her for almost eight hours prior to the attack.

One of the Israeli pilots was monitored on radio and overheard declaring that the ship was American but was ordered to attack anyway, which they did, with napalm, cannon and rockets and the gunboats fired five torpedoes, only one of which struck the ship.

The Israeli government has always maintained that it was an accident and a case of mistaken identity, but the overwhelming evidence is that the Israelis deliberately targeted the ship knowing that she was a US naval vessel sailing in international waters.

The supposition is that the ship had picked up evidence of the proposed Israeli attack on the Golan Heights in Syria, scheduled for the following day, and the Israelis were afraid that the Americans would share this intelligence with the British who would then pass it on to the Arabs.

Another reason which was put forward was that the ship had picked up radio messages authorising the murder of Egyptian prisoners of war.

Whatever the reason, the Israelis made a concerted effort to sink the USS *Liberty* and despite numerous attempts by the survivors to call for an official enquiry, this matter has been swept under the carpet by the US government and remains a mystery to this day.

At about 08:00 on the third day, some of the crew, including the lamp-trimmer, were enjoying a breakfast coffee on deck, when shouting was heard and someone could be seen in the water, about 50 or 60 metres away from the ship, and waving for help.

The 'lampy' immediately stripped off his shirt, boots and

knife/spike-belt, leapt onto the bulwark and dived into the lake, while a group of us set about lowering the accommodation ladder. The 'lampy' dragged this guy to the ladder and we got him aboard, where it was found out that he was one of the members of the Egyptian Army who were retreating through the Sinai Desert, and we being the nearest ship to the eastern shore, he had decided to swim out to us.

We then spotted a few more people in the water and the motor-lifeboat was called away to go and pick them up. It was then observed through binoculars that the eastern shore of the lakes was swarming with them, and the soldiers we had rescued advised us that they had no food, water or medical facilities.

Following some discussion between ships, the decision was taken to drop the canal-boats into the lake and tow these by motor-lifeboat to the shore so that these trapped soldiers could make their way across the lake.

The canal-boats were small rowboats, placed on the ships for the duration of the transit of the canal. In the event that a ship should break down while in the canal and hold up the convoy, the boats would take lines from the ships to the canal bank to secure the ships from drifting ashore, or into one another.

There were four boats per ship, and soon the lakes were dotted with lifeboats towing fleets of canal-boats to shore, where they were cast off and left for the soldiers to use.

One of the ships carried a doctor and he went ashore and set up a temporary medical centre, to assist sick and wounded soldiers.

The lakes were soon dotted with these rowboats coming the other way as the troops made their escape, most of the boats being heavily overloaded and containing from 12 to 16 men plus their rifles and other arms.

A few of the boats came alongside *Melampus* and a freshwater hose and baskets of bread and cheese were lowered down to the men.

This went on for some time until one of the soldiers decided to show his appreciation by firing his rifle into the air. That was enough, the hose was drawn up and the crew ordered back into the accommodation, while the boats were sent on their way.

Egyptian soldiers retreating across the canal, receiving food and water from Melampus. *(Note the rifle on the thwart in one of the boats.)*

Things settled down, although there were still occasional

artillery duels across the canal and on one occasion, an Egyptian Mig came roaring up from the south, low across the lakes, with an Israeli Mirage right on his tail and shells from the Mirage whipping up the surface of the lakes.

The Israeli Mirages were not fitted with missiles, but still used cannon, and the tactics were to get up close with the cannon rather than rely on a long shot with a missile.

The waters of the lakes were busy with lifeboats going from ship to ship, swapping stores or taking the crews across for parties or film-shows. A favourite destination was the Port Line ship *Port Invercargill*, which carried a number of passengers, including a group of young, attractive Australian women, who were heading to the UK for their big OE.

Fresh water had now become a major problem, as the ships were too close to shore, and were not permitted to evaporate drinking water, so rationing was introduced and water only used for essential purposes. There had been no contact with the authorities ashore, so we were not yet receiving stores or water from ashore and had to rely on what we carried or what we could swap with other ships.

There were four British ships in the convoy, these being *Scottish Star*, *Port Invercargill*, *Melampus* and another Blue Funnel ship, *Agapenor*.

Agapenor carried a Chinese catering crowd, apart from the chief steward, who was British.

After a couple of weeks, we were informed that all the junior members of each department were about to be repatriated, along with the passengers from the *Port Invercargill* and all the Chinese crews in both Blue Funnel ships.

Blue Funnel employed mainland Chinese in the engine room of all their ships as greasers, firemen and the like, and some ships, such as *Agapenor*, also carried mainland Chinese in the catering department.

The decision to repatriate the Chinese crews was taken to prevent Communist China becoming involved in the conflict, which, although calming down, was still ongoing.

Jimmy and I were the two youngest assistant stewards of the four carried in *Melampus* and were looking forward to going home. However, the chief steward came to see me and said that I would be staying, as he was sending one of the older stewards home.

This older guy, who was in his thirties, had a few years earlier fallen over the side of a ship onto a barge tied up alongside and sustained a head injury, from which he had recovered and been passed medically fit for sea. He did, however, have a serious drinking problem (didn't we all!) and had had numerous run-ins with the chief steward, who was now using his head injury as an excuse to get rid of him.

CHAPTER 10

I HAD MIXED FEELINGS ABOUT STAYING, AS ALTHOUGH I wanted to go home, like we all did, there was still some intermittent action in the canal that made things interesting, and we were now on a special bonus for being in a war zone, so it was worth staying from a financial perspective.

We watched those being repatriated depart with mixed feelings, as we were sad to see some of our mates go and would have liked to have been going with them, but the extra money eased the parting.

As soon as the launches had departed, the 2nd steward, John Morrow, the 2nd cook, John Taylor, and I packed our bags and transferred over to the *Agapenor*, whose crew had been left without any cooks and stewards.

Melampus was our home, and we were sorry to be leaving, but an event had occurred a few nights earlier that had unsettled me and made the transfer a lot easier to bear.

I had been in my cabin, reading, when Jimmy, the officers' steward, had knocked on my door and entered, followed by the Geordie 2nd engineer. I thought it a bit strange that the 2nd engineer would be socialising with the crew, which just didn't happen back then.

Jimmy then ducked out of the cabin and left me with the 2nd engineer, who was well pissed, and proceeded to take his shirt off. The guy grabbed me and tried to kiss me, so I hauled off and punched him in the face as hard as I could.

He shot out of my cabin, leaving his shirt behind, and disappeared, and I was informed by members of the engineering crew many years later that he had gone down to the engine room and was running around naked.

As I stated earlier, it wasn't the 'queens' in the catering department you had to worry about, but those guys, in the so-called 'macho departments' like deck and engine room, who hid their homosexuality, that you had to watch out for, and there were plenty of those, believe me.

I had serious words with Jimmy, who apologised and thought it had been a joke, but from then on, I began to doubt his sexual orientation, and was wary of him.

The 2nd had the good grace to look very sheepish whenever he saw me after that, but the transfer to *Agapenor* gave me peace of mind and was a positive move.

I was allotted the 2nd steward's cabin, which was adjacent to the saloon and rather isolated, but much larger than my cabin in *Melampus*, while John Morrow, and John Taylor, being petty officers, were given junior officers' cabins on the next deck. The chief steward was a Scouse guy named Ron Clarke, and he was easy to get on with.

Although the three people I was working closely with were officers or petty officers, they didn't put on me and we all shared the same work load equally and socialised together. I ran the saloon and looked after the captain's and officers' accommodation, while the three of them shared the galley work, and cooking, and then all of us mucked in for the clean-up.

Turn-to was changed to 07:00 from 06:00, but there was a lot to fit into the day, and time flew by, and even though the crew was much reduced, there was still plenty of cleaning and food preparation to be carried out. Although water was still scarce, I saved as much clean water left over from galley use as I could, for alleyway and saloon scrub-outs, and tried not to let standards slip too much.

MV Agapenor (Credit: Chris Howell)

The skeleton crew that we were now reduced to was just big enough to get us to the nearest port, in the unlikely event that the canal was cleared unexpectedly.

Holts were doing all they could to keep our families informed of our situation, and we received twice-weekly telegrams from home at the company's expense, although there was not much they could put in a telegram, so they became somewhat monotonous after a while.

The company also took one of the crew who had been repatriated around to see our families and give them some idea of the conditions in the lakes, which put their minds at ease, and we were grateful for that. Our own letters were censored, so we had to be careful what we wrote to avoid having them returned.

A few days later the radio-shack was sealed by the authorities, and an armed guard placed aboard each ship to prevent any further incidents of the lifeboats being used to communicate between ships. This was a serious blow, and impacted on morale, as the ship-to-ship exchanges were something to look forward to and kept our spirits up.

However, after a couple of days, the armed police had been bribed with food and drink and turned a blind eye when the boats were again put to use, and the lakes were soon as busy as ever.

One of the policemen aimed his handgun at the chief cook through the galley-door grille on one occasion, following an altercation, and although we didn't believe he actually had any ammunition, the chief steward complained to the authorities and the guy was replaced.

One night, the four of us were drinking out on deck and we were literally scraping the bottom of the barrel, as we had emptied the beer locker, and were down to the last couple of cases of McEwan's Ale.

This was a dark beer, not well suited to a hot climate, and tasted awful. I had decided that if this was the only beer on offer, I was going to have to give up drinking, as I couldn't stand it.

Lo and behold, the very next morning a barge drew alongside, full of stores, and prominent among the stores was a supply of East German lager. This was definitely a moment that stands out.

Among the stores was a side of beef from a beast that had

obviously just been slaughtered. The crew of the barge brought this on board and threw it down the companionway to land outside the chiller.

The cook couldn't get it into the chiller and called for help, so we went to give him a hand. We were only used to handling frozen carcasses, which were easy to shift, but this thing had a mind of its own and was incredibly hard to get a grip of and lift.

Following a lengthy struggle, we finally managed to get it into the chiller where the cook, John Taylor, could start cutting it up.

The captain of the *Agapenor*, Fred Squires, had had some sort of falling out with his officers, and didn't eat in the saloon with them, but ate his meals in his cabin.

The four of us in the catering department ate our meals in the duty-engineer's mess, at the completion of service, and occasionally the captain would sit and have a drink with us. He bought us a beer each from time to time and on one occasion he was with us when the ship's agent came aboard just after lunch.

The agent was invited into the mess and joined the four of us and the captain, who by this time had consumed a fair amount of alcohol. During the course of the conversation, sex reared its ugly head, and we complained about the lack of female company, which was about the only thing in life we were lacking.

Captain Squires asked the agent if he could procure us some women and the agent confirmed that he could, if a requisition order was made out. The captain duly made out the order for three women, signed it, and gave it to the agent. To my horror and frustration, Ron Clarke, the chief steward, leaned across the table, took the piece of paper off the agent and ripped it up. I could have put my head in my hands and cried.

In hindsight, I realise that it was the correct thing to do to keep the captain out of trouble, but at the time I was highly pissed off, and had to go back to reading the steamy Harold Robbins blockbusters for sexual titillation.

Occasionally, the ships would up-anchor and steam around the lakes to test the engines, before returning to the anchorage, and these little jaunts were much anticipated and resulted in a slightly altered aspect each time we re-anchored, which was quite refreshing.

By this time, we had run out of paint and the deck gear was not being used and therefore did not require greasing, so the deck crowds' hours were being reduced until they were only working a couple of hours a day, and not working weekends. They had a lot of time on their hands.

With the ship not moving, a fringe of weeds about three feet long had grown around the ship on the waterline, and this weed was trapping bits of rubbish, including the sewage being discharged overboard, and this was beginning to stink.

The deckies worked from one of the lifeboats to try to get rid of the weed by using long-handled scrapers to remove it. It turned out to be such a long, laborious job that by the time they had completed a section the weed had already grown again where they started, so they gave up.

The rubbish, rotting in the weed, attracted shoals of fish, mainly garfish, which were no good for catching or eating, but also a type of carp of a fair size. About six of these were caught and put into the crew swimming pool, which consisted of a hatch tarpaulin inside a frame which was filled with seawater.

After a day or so, these fish were caught and killed by the cook and appeared on the menu as Bitter Lakes Trout. Having seen what these fish had been nibbling on while in the lakes, I wasn't game to try them, but everyone else did and declared them very tasty. Ugh!

Those of us in the catering department rarely got the chance to visit other ships as the boat usually departed right after lunch or dinner, and the rest of the crowd were too impatient to wait for us to clean up and get ready for a visit, so left without us. If we wanted to visit, we had to take it in turns to have a half-day off so we could catch the boat.

On the occasion I was given a half-day, we visited *Melampus*, and I couldn't believe the state she was in since I had left her. They had taken the water shortage literally, and the alleyways and saloon deck were filthy. The saloon deck was beautiful hardwood parquet decking, which had always been kept clean and buffed. Now it was in such a state it was hard to remember what it had looked like previously. It was sad.

When the boat on which I would be going back to *Agapenor* arrived at *Melampus*, I was surprised to see John Morrow and John Taylor aboard and assumed that the boat must have waited for them to clean up. We had a few more beers in the *Melampus* and later that night returned to *Agapenor*.

As I was heading to the shower, I glanced through the saloon door and the moon happened to be shining through the ports and onto one of the tables. The tables had not been reset for breakfast, which is how they had been able to make the boat.

I was pissed off, as there was so much to do before breakfast that I would never have had time to reset them in the morning. I went up to the office and grabbed the key to the saloon and started resetting the tables. I was in such a foul mood, and throwing silver around, that the chief steward heard the noise and came down to see what was happening.

As I'd had a few beers, I let rip and told him his fortune, and what I thought of the two Johnnies.

Next morning, I had to go up and apologise to him, but after that incident, I refused any more half-days and just stayed on board.

The days were beginning to drag, and we were reduced to having fly-swatting competitions to kill time. The 2nd steward, the chief cook and I used to sit outside the galley with a fly-swatter and see who could kill the most flies, consecutively. Johnny Morrow held the record at 25. Pretty sad!

I celebrated my nineteenth birthday on 9 August, and shortly after that some of the ships began receiving relief crews and heading home. We couldn't wait for the British ships to be relieved and at last, at the end of August, we were notified that it was about to happen, and to get packed.

We were working late the night prior to our reliefs arriving, getting the ship ready for the handover, and I scrubbed the alleyway and saloon deck, and polished the silver, while the others concentrated on the galley, chillers and food-storage lockers.

The big day finally arrived and the launches with the relief crews for the four British ships came alongside early that morning. I showed the guy around, who was taking over from me, and explained the job to him. He didn't seem that interested in the job and kept asking questions about the social aspects, which I didn't think boded well, but what the fuck, I was getting out of there.

Three-and-a-half months later I was on the shore-gang and drinking in the Wheatsheaf at lunchtime, when someone on the table behind me asked the guy sitting with him where he had been, and he replied that he had just returned from *Agapenor* in the canal.

I didn't make myself known but carried on drinking and listening to the conversation. This guy was then asked what state the ships were in when he joined, and he told everyone they were in a shit state when he took over.

I then turned around and said, 'You fuckin lying bastard,' while he went bright red and started stuttering. The guys thought it was a great joke, but I got him to admit that when he took over,

Agapenor was spotless, given the circumstances. I could just imagine what she looked like now, but as I wasn't going back, it wasn't my problem.

We boarded the launch with our baggage, just after lunch, and headed for the western shore of the Bitter Lakes to the tune of Roger Millers' 'England Swings' being played over the speaker system by the relief mate on *Melampus*.

When passing through the anchorage, all the other ships sounded their horns in farewell, which was amazing to hear.

In a way, we were a little sorry to be leaving the ships which had been our homes for so long, and which were to remain anchored in the Bitter Lakes for a period of eight years, earning themselves the nickname of the Yellow Fleet due to the discolouration of the upper-works by the accumulation of blown sand. The ships were eventually rafted together in groups of two or three, to save costs, and the crews gradually reduced, until eventually a Norwegian company was contracted to maintain them.

The cargos were written off by the insurance companies and only the two German ships, *Nordwind* and *Munsterland*, were to make their home port under their own power, arriving in Hamburg in 1975, to a huge reception, from over 30,000 people, having completed the longest voyages on record.

The Blue Funnel ships, *Agapenor* and *Melampus*, were towed out of the canal, sold to Greek companies and continued in service until the end of the decade.

Once ashore, we boarded two buses, with both Blue Funnel crews on one bus, and the Port and Star boat crews on the other, and headed across the desert towards Cairo. I was at the rear of the bus with the chief steward, 2nd steward and chief cook from *Agapenor*, and seated just in front of us was the Scottish radio officer from *Melampus*.

The radio officer produced a silver hip flask of scotch and passed it to the chief steward, who took a swig, and handed it to the cook, who took a swig and handed it to John Morrow, the 2nd steward. John took a swig and went to pass the flask to me, but the radio officer grabbed it back with the words 'Not him, he's only crew.'

I was embarrassed and hurt, as for the past couple of months aboard *Agapenor* there had been no 'them' and 'us' and everyone had been treated like equals, and now we were back to the old bullshit.

The others were embarrassed for me and the atmosphere at the rear of the bus was a bit tense, but I laughed it off and let it go. (Well, I didn't actually let it go, 'cos I still remember it like it was yesterday.)

After a few hours' drive, we eventually arrived at the Omar Khayyam Hotel, Cairo early that evening and checked into our rooms before going to dinner.

When I checked my bag, I found that my 'docking bottle' of scotch had been nicked by the bell boys, so I hope they enjoyed it.

The hotel was surrounded by palm trees and other luxuriant greenery, which made a refreshing change from the arid outlook we had been surveying for the past three months, and this just added to the excitement and sense of freedom at last.

The following morning, we checked out of the hotel and were bussed to the airport, and given a couple of pounds' sub. John Morrow, John Taylor and I immediately went to the airport bar, where we spent the time drinking beer and chatting up the barmaids.

The upshot was that by the time we came to board our plane for the flight home, we were skint and had to rely on the chief steward to buy us a drink on the flight, which he very generously did.

The plane was an Air India flight, landing at Zurich, Frankfurt and then Heathrow, and although we were all in an exuberant mood, we didn't hassle the hostesses, and were all remarkably well behaved, under the circumstances.

On arrival at Heathrow, we were met by officials from Holts, and the TV cameras, and appeared on that evening's news. We had to catch a bus to transfer us to a domestic flight to Speke, in Liverpool, but going through Customs, I was singled out for a bag search, where all my gear was taken out of my suitcase and then I had to repack it. The Customs officer had a good laugh about my panic in repacking my case, but when I got to the bus, one of the Holts officials gave me a big bollocking for holding everyone up. Things really were getting back to normal.

Upon arrival at Speke, we were met by our families in an emotional welcome and then headed off home.

The following morning, we had to travel to a meeting with senior management of Holts in India Buildings, Liverpool, and then paid off. During the meeting, we were admonished not to give interviews to the local papers, as anything which got into the papers disparaging Egypt could cause major problems for those crews still in the Great Bitter Lakes.

My pay-off was a fairly substantial sum of money with which I opened a bank account for the first time in my life, and now I could enjoy a spot of well-earned leave.

A couple of days later, a reporter and photographer from the local paper appeared on the doorstep and Mum invited them in. How they had found out about me was a mystery, as all my immediate family denied having contacted them.

What took place next must have been the weirdest interviews they had ever undertaken, as I was totally tight lipped and tried not to give anything away that could be construed as detrimental to those still in the canal. The reporter kept raising her eyebrows to the photographer in response to my answers to her questions, and I was feeling a little embarrassed about the whole thing.

Eventually, they took my photograph and departed.

It could have been a good story, with the bombing, the retreating army, the aerial dogfights and so on if I had given them the true story, but a rather bland piece appeared in the paper a few days later, along with my photo and the heading 'Chester man views war from the deck of his ship', and to my relief, there was nothing in it that could be construed as controversial.

CHAPTER 11

MOST OF MY LEAVE WAS SPENT IN HOLYHEAD AGAIN, AS KEN had been home and his girlfriend had introduced me to another of her mates, and when Ken went back deep sea, I ended up staying weekends at her place.

I was again on the shore-gang, this time for quite a lengthy period, and when the time came to organise a relief crew to take over from the crew which had relieved us, I was called into the office by Mr Dewhurst, one of the catering supervisors, and asked whether I would be prepared to go back out.

He was expecting me to jump at the chance but was quite surprised when I said no, that I was not.

His first reaction was that I was scared to return, but I explained that I had joined Blue Funnel to see the world and not sit around in the Suez Canal, even though the pay, plus the war bonus, was very tempting.

The main reason for me not wanting to go back out was actually the lack of female company, and the thought of having to go another three-month period without a woman was just too much to think about.

In the event, the crews were given one rostered weekend each in Cairo, to do as they pleased, but I don't think even that knowledge would have made me change my mind, as I could still remember how mind-numbingly boring it had been towards the end.

The atmosphere, when I left the office, was in stark contrast to a meeting I had had with Mr Dewhurst a couple of weeks previously, when he had told me that he considered that I was 2nd steward material and could look forward to promotion sometime in the future.

The only problem with that was that in Blue Funnel promotion to 2nd steward very, very rarely occurred until your late twenties or early thirties, and promotion to chief steward was in the forties, so I still had 10 and 20 years respectively before I could realistically look forward to making petty-officer, so it was hardly a carrot.

MV Machaon

Skinning Out
135

Now that I had refused to return to the canal, a ship was soon found for me, and I was allocated an assistant steward's berth in *Machaon*, a sister ship of the *Melampus*. The only drawback with *Machaon* was that I had to share a double-berth cabin with the assistant cook and he had the top bunk, while I had the bottom. This wasn't a problem, well, not until we reached Bangkok anyway.

We departed Birkenhead and had to sail down the west coast of Africa and around the Cape of Good Hope to Durban, where we bunkered, and then onto Singapore, so it was a long haul before we experienced a run ashore. The people of Aden were probably wishing that the British hadn't left at this point, now that ships were no longer bunkering there due to the canal closure.

We overtook the stream of tankers trekking down the Atlantic and around the Cape to the Gulf of Arabia, and it was strange to pass these tankers in ballast, on a flat calm sea off West Africa, and see them still rolling their guts out, from the effects of the rough seas through the Bay of Biscay. They were all the small three-island jobs back then and not the huge VLCCs that we see today.

We had been a long time at sea, without a break, so a run ashore in Singapore was a welcome relief. One night a group of us was in Bugis Street and I was sitting alone at a table while the group of guys I was ashore with were up dancing with the lady/men and being a little over-exuberant on the dance floor, when I overheard a well-dressed Aussie or Kiwi bloke, on the next table, say to his wife or girlfriend, 'What a bunch of animals.'

I turned to the bloke and said, 'I heard that, mate,' and his partner said, 'You were supposed to,' so I explained that they were just letting off steam, having been a long time at sea, and not doing any harm. In fact, the locals were loving it.

I then said to this bloke, 'What type of person would bring his wife to a place like this anyway, and what type of self-respecting woman would want to come?'

They buggered off shortly after that, but Bugis Street was a popular tourist spot and it was precisely the antics that the *Machaon* guys were getting up to that made it so popular.

It was the usual Far East trip to Singapore, Hong Kong and Japan, with one deviation from the usual run, being a visit to Otaru, in the north of Japan, on the island of Hokkaido, where winter was extremely cold. A walk down the main street of Otaru was a walk down a tunnel of snow with smaller tunnels branching off to each shop or bar, the snow was that deep.

The catering crowd managed to find a good bar, with a big stove, which made it nice and cosy, and drank there every night. The mama-san was fairly young and attractive, and took a shine to me, and as she had a small room at the back of the bar, I slept there nearly every night without paying. The hard part was making it back to the ship in the morning in the freezing weather and fresh snow.

For that reason, Otaru became one of my favourite ports, but, unfortunately, I never returned there after that trip.

MV Machaon in Kaohsiung, Taiwan

After departing Japan, we called into Kaohsiung, Taiwan, which at that time was one of the main destinations for ships about to be broken up for scrap, prior to the ports in India taking over the bulk of this work. It wouldn't normally be a pleasant destination under those circumstances, but we were only calling in to work cargo and expected to be alongside for about a week so that was fine with us.

Author at the stern of Machaon entering Kaohsiung

Due to the ongoing animosity between the Chinese mainland and Taiwan, formerly Formosa, there was a curfew ashore from midnight to 06:00 which effectively prevented the catering crowd from accepting the hospitality on offer by the local bar-girls, as turn-to was at 06:00 and you could not be on the streets before then. The deck-crowd were fine as turn-to for those guys was at 08:00.

Each night at around 23:00 the US Navy shore patrol did the rounds of all the local bars and turfed us out onto the street. 'Hey buddy! You sleeping with that girl?!! If not, get your ass back to your ship!'

Needless to say, we were totally compliant as they were all huge guys with their billy-clubs hanging from their wrists and they didn't take shit from anyone.

What money we saved from the local women was spent on 'knock-off' versions of all the latest LPs which sold for a few cents and came in every colour imaginable, except black. We all bought dozens of these things, but it was the luck of the draw, as some of them only lasted for a couple of turns on the record player.

The weather was good for the duration of our stay, being fine and warm in comparison to our experience of northern Japan and the Arctic conditions we experienced up there.

The other unusual aspect of this trip for me was a visit to Bangkok, where we swung on the hook for almost a week, while waiting for a berth alongside, and the temperature reached 126 degrees Fahrenheit, day after day. I drank that much iced water that I was sick, and we were all having a dozen cold showers a day as the only way to cool down.

The Vietnam War was ratcheting up, and we had to watch as the big, grey American transports steamed into the bay and straight up the river, while we were left swinging at anchor. Eventually, a berth became available, and we picked up the pilot and steamed into the river.

In the evening it was a trip ashore to the Mosquito Bar, but during the day, girls boarded the ship via a rope ladder hung over the stern, and infested the accommodation, so we had to ensure our doors and ports were secure.

The girls were as keen on earning a bar of Lux soap as they were on earning baht, the local currency, as there was good profit to be made on toilet soap ashore, and as we had unlimited access to Lux toilet soap, we were very popular.

I had my share of women over the course of the couple of days we were in port, but the assistant cook was insatiable, and had a different woman in the cabin every couple of hours. The only problem was that he was too lazy to climb into his top bunk and kept having sex in my bunk when I was out of the room.

Whenever I returned to the cabin, I could tell from the way the bunk was messed up that he had been at it, and there were maps of Australia all over my sheet. I would change the sheet, only for him to be at it again, and it was beginning to piss me off. If we had been alongside much longer, we would have come to blows but, fortunately, we departed for Singapore.

We celebrated Xmas in Singapore, and following dinner for the mates and engineers in the saloon, the crew were then served Xmas dinner by some of the mates and engineers. It was a nice gesture, but they were all well pissed, we were tired and still had to clean up afterwards, so it wasn't appreciated as much as it should have been.

New Year's Eve was celebrated at anchor in Port Swettenham and then it was the long slog back around South Africa, only calling into Cape Town for mail, which was delivered by launch.

While we were in Yokohama, I had purchased a motorised plastic scale model of the Imperial Japanese Navy Second World War battleship *Yamato*, which I was intending to take home for my young brother, Stuart, and had written home advising my family of this. The model was 3 ft long and quite impressive. One morning, during inspection, the chief engineer came across it in my locker and asked me to sell it to him, even offering me more money than I had paid for it. I refused the offer and told him that I had already told my brother that I had bought it for him, but the chief became so obsessed with buying the model from me that he went on about it every time he saw me and he was really beginning to get to me.

Crossing the Indian Ocean en route to the Cape, I decided to start assembling the model to get the chief off my back, which it did but then I had the problem, once we were docked in Liverpool, of transporting the partially assembled model home without damaging it, which was a lot easier said than done. No-one was particularly impressed with my effort to build it either!

It was about this time that the radio officer brought me a telegram informing me that I had a new baby sister, and the lads gave me a bit of a hard time about it.

I had to shout everyone a beer and it was embarrassing at almost 20 years of age to think that your mum and dad were still at it.

We were in St George's Channel, off South Wales, and due to catch the tide at the Mersey Bar the following morning when we were informed that an Aer Lingus flight from Cork to London had disappeared, presumed to have crashed, and we were requested to assist in the search for survivors or wreckage. *Machaon* slowed right down, extra lookouts were posted and we began to zigzag through the area.

As we exited the search area without sighting anything, we began to increase speed and returned to our original course. Just then an RAF Gannet flew low across our bow, waggled its wings, and then flew down our wake where it dropped a smoke-float a couple of miles back.

As we knew that whatever had been sighted was unlikely to be a survivor, our first reaction, I'm ashamed to relate, was 'Oh, no, we're going to miss the tide', but then reality set in and we crowded the deck to try and be first to spot whatever it was that had attracted the Gannet.

Unfortunately, it turned out to be a bag of rubbish that the galley-boy had tossed over the side earlier, and was still floating on the surface, so *Machaon* turned around and resumed her course to Liverpool.

We heard later that the aircraft wreckage was located well outside the area we were searching, and all 61 people aboard had been killed.

A few days prior to arrival in Liverpool, the chief steward had, as was customary, asked the catering staff whether, or not, we would be returning for the following voyage. The response, almost to a man, was no, as the chief cook had been a complete arsehole, and we had all had run-ins with him, but the chief steward was too weak to stand up to him when we complained. So, if the cook was coming back for the following trip, then we weren't.

The start of my leave was spent getting used to the novelty of having a baby sister, Nicola, and trying to wake her up when Mum wasn't looking, but most of my leave was again spent in Holyhead, staying at my girlfriend's, as Ken was now away in *Ixion*, on the Aussie run, and I wouldn't be seeing him again for a while.

When leave was up, it was back to the shore-gang to await another ship, and while waiting, I became good mates with an assistant cook named Mick. He was also on the shore-gang and used to catch the same bus as me every morning, boarding the bus at Great Sutton on the Wirral, and after a few mornings we recognised one another through working together on the gang.

At the time I met Mick, he was going with an extremely attractive girl from Chester, who was a nurse, and I occasionally made up a foursome with one of her mates for a night out, but nothing serious, as I was still keen on my girlfriend in Holyhead.

Mick told me that he was thinking of getting engaged, and I encouraged him to pop the question, but he never did. I know his girlfriend's mother would have been over the moon, as she thought the world of him and they had a great relationship.

After a few weeks on the shore-gang, Mick and I were both assigned to *Pyrrhus* when she returned to Vittoria Dock, from coasting.

Pyrrhus was one of the P-boats and sister to *Peleus*, and had gone on fire in Huskisson Dock in 1964, the trip after I had coasted her as trainee boy rating. So much water was poured into her while fighting the fire that she had sunk to the bottom of the dock but was raised, salvaged and fitted out again as good as new. The only signs of the fire were a buckled and uneven galley deck and stove, as a result of the galley being directly above the seat of the fire in No. 3 hold.

The other strange aspect about her as a result of the fire was that there were no cockroaches in either the pantry or the galley, and during the three trips I did in her, I never came across one single 'cockie'.

It was during this period that we were stowing *Pyrrhus* for deep sea, and a large gang were working aboard her. Mick was absent for some reason, and during 'smoko' about 20 guys were in the mess. One of them was a 2nd cook, who asked me whether I was knocking around with Mick and when I said, 'Yes, Mick's a mate of mine,' he said, 'You want to watch out for him; he's a queer.'

I was stunned and said, 'How the fuck do you know?' He replied, 'He was my galley-boy in the *Ajax* and gave me a blowjob.'

I said to him, 'Well, what does that make you then?'

He said, 'Whaddya mean? I'm not queer.'

I said, 'Well, mate, there's no way I'd ever let a bloke suck my cock,' and the whole mess-room just cracked up with laughter.

I didn't, for one minute, believe what this 2nd cook told me, as I knew Mick was sleeping with his girl, but eventually I came to realise that Mick was in fact gay. I never let this affect our relationship, and we remained best mates until we eventually lost contact, a few years later.

My sister Sandra's comment when she found out Mick was gay was 'What a bloody waste'.

Mum and Dad had a bit of an issue with regard to homosexuality, which was a sign of their generation, but as there had been at least one in every ship in which I had sailed, I had come to accept it as a fact of life at sea.

I always wondered what Mum's attitude would have been had I, or my brothers, turned out to be gay, but there was no issue there, as I found out that both my younger brothers had been knocking off the girl next door, at the same time, when they were aged 14 and 12 respectively, and a long time before I lost my cherry.

Mick was a great guy to go ashore with and we always had a good laugh. His natural flamboyance and good looks meant that we always attracted the girls, even though he wasn't interested, which I put down to him being faithful to his girl back in Chester.

Eventually, though, he broke up with her, and for a long time, I assumed that when he 'camped it up' he was just joking.

With the closure of the Suez Canal, the P-boats were now going west-about to the Far East, via the Panama Canal, and home around South Africa, in order to maintain their express service.

There had been some alteration to the P-boat scheduling, and now *Pyrrhus* had taken over from *Peleus* as the 'Xmas ship' and would in future be the ship to arrive back in Liverpool in time for Xmas.

The first port of call was now Curaçao, for bunkers. We did not berth at Willemstad, the capital, but tied up at a bunkering jetty down the coast, away from the town. The bunkering berths were overlooked by an old fort dating from the sixteenth century, and rumoured to be Morgan's fort, but that was extremely unlikely.

We could swim in the clear blue, warm water of the bay, which was protected by big shark-nets. However, when a few trips later we swam out to the nets and dived down, it was discovered that there were holes big enough to drive a double-decker bus through, and it was obvious that they had not been maintained for years, so swimming lost some of its attraction.

It was one-and-a-half days to Colon, the entrance to the canal, from Curaçao and we anchored in the roads with other shipping awaiting transit. Eventually, we moved into the entrance to the canal and entered the Gatun locks, where we secured to the mules, four locomotives, to be towed through the lock.

There was a big viewing platform adjacent to the locks for sightseers to watch the ships locking into and out of the canal, and this being a Sunday afternoon, the bleachers were packed with families.

A group of the catering crowd were relaxing on the foredeck during our afternoon break, and enjoying a couple of beers, when suddenly Mick leapt up onto the bitts, turned his back to the viewing platform and dropping his trousers, gave the crowd a 'brown-eye'. The rest of us were too stunned to do anything at first, until a yell came down from the bridge, when we scattered and left Mick to it, not even bothering to register what the reaction was from the viewing platform.

Mick received a big bollocking but escaped a logging, fortunately for him.

Entering the Gatun Lake, *Pyrrhus* wended her way among the islands dotting the lake, following the channel and passing ships headed in the opposite direction. The transit was so much more interesting than the Suez Canal, and very picturesque, with all the tropical greenery covering the islands and lakeshore, and plenty of birdlife.

We exited the canal through the Miraflores Locks, passing under the huge Bridge of the Americas, passing Panama City to port, and out into Panama Bay, where *Pyrrhus* steered a course north-west for Japan.

The voyage across the Pacific was uneventful, and we finally arrived in Yokohama, and began discharging cargo.

This time there would only be one visit to the ports on the Japanese coast, to discharge, instead of the usual two visits, to discharge and then load.

From Japan, we sailed down to Hong Kong and tied up at Holts Wharf, in Kowloon. Hong Kong was now a huge R&R base for American servicemen on leave from Vietnam and Guam, and there were Americans everywhere, in contrast to British servicemen, who were nowhere to be seen.

More and more nightclub type bars were opening, to cater to the Americans and the regular seamen's bars were losing their popularity. We started to hang out at a new bar called Faces which was situated on the mezzanine floor of a building on Nathan Road and accessed by two long escalators.

Faces got its name from a row of white polystyrene squares stuck to the wall along the length of the long, narrow entrance, with black, stylised faces painted on them. The bar was popular with the Americans but played great music and there were lots of good-looking women.

A group of us were drinking in a packed-out Faces one night when there was a break in the music and the dancefloor was empty. The first song following the break was a Motown song, and Mick and four of the guys formed a line across the dancefloor and did a dance in unison to the song, and kept in perfect step.

I was blown away by this, as I lived with these guys 24/7 and had never, ever come across them practising these moves. They were so good that they got a standing ovation from everyone there, and special attention from the girls.

I was shopping in an apartment store in Kowloon one afternoon and was served by an attractive young woman who spoke good English and was quite keen to have a conversation. After a few minutes I managed to pluck up the courage to ask her to the movies, and to my amazement, she accepted the invitation.

I arranged to meet her in Nathan Road when I finished work and we went to see *Barbarella*, starring Jane Fonda and David Hemmings. It was quite a raunchy movie for its time, with a couple of embarrassing scenes, and I can recall sitting in the dark, glad that she couldn't see me blushing.

She didn't drink, so bars were out of the question, but after the movie she took me to a local restaurant for a shrimp congee, a thick rice soup full of shrimps, which was delicious, and became a regular favourite.

I found out that her anglicised name was Judy and that she had to work late in the department store some nights, but we arranged to go to another movie before *Pyrrhus* left Hong Kong, and we agreed to write to one another.

At one of the ports prior to sailing for the Cape of Good Hope, one of the stewards had visited a Baron boat and been given a small monkey, which he kept in his cabin. How the skipper let him get away with it, I'll never know, but he did.

While he was on duty, he used to tie it up on the after deck, in a bit of shelter, but the Chinese greasers who lived down aft used to tease it mercilessly as they passed on their way to the engine room, and the thing became quite wild. In the end, the only person who could approach the monkey without getting bitten was the steward who owned it.

Everyone else became terrified of it, and if you went on the after deck, you had to check where it was, and how long the rope was which secured it, and make sure you stayed out of range.

Off Madagascar, the monkey had a go at one of the stewards' boys, who then seized the rope and untied it and slung the poor monkey overboard, where it bobbed in the wake.

There was no point in rushing up to the bridge, because they weren't going to turn the ship around for a monkey, so we just watched it disappear into the distance.

The boy rating got a smack in the mouth, threats of violence and the monkey's owner wrote a letter of complaint to the RSPCA, but in the end, I blame the steward for bringing it back to the ship and the hierarchy, skipper, mate and chief steward for letting him keep it on board.

The seas off Madagascar are shark-infested, so I hoped that

one of these sharks had given it a quick end, and it had not lingered on in the water for too long. It was a sad end for the poor wee monkey through no fault of its own, but it would have had to be put down at some stage, as it had become too vicious to be kept as a pet.

The episode put a damper on the crew for a few days, but the mail call at Cape Town soon cheered us up, and a couple of letters from Judy in Hong Kong had me looking forward to the next trip.

The leg of the trip around the Cape was a bit of a drag, as it was a long time without a run ashore, and the haul down the Indian Ocean and up the west coast of Africa to Las Palmas, in the Canary Islands, for bunkers, seemed to go on and on, although we did call in to Freetown, in Sierra Leone, briefly.

We arrived in Freetown after midnight and left before 05:00, so we never got to see anything of it, and Las Palmas was just swinging on the hook, taking on fuel, so no shore leave, even though it looked so inviting, with the town spreading up the slopes of the mountain which is the main feature of the island of Gran Canaria.

CHAPTER 12

WE ARRIVED BACK IN LIVERPOOL IN PLENTY OF TIME FOR MY twentieth birthday, but my relationship with my girlfriend in Holyhead had slowly dwindled away to nothing and she had moved on to a much more worthwhile relationship with someone local, so there was no incentive to travel to Holyhead on this leave.

A new licensee had taken over my local watering hole, the Dee Miller, and I became good friends with Dennis and his wife, Hillary.

Dennis was an ex-Bank Line 2nd mate, so we had something in common, and swapped nautical tales, and eventually I started working behind the bar on busy nights or when Dennis and Hillary needed time off, and over the years was lucky enough to score plenty of one-night stands with the barmaids and the women on the other side of the bar.

I tried to not get too involved, as it was my local community and everyone knew everyone else, and my two brothers also drank in the same pub, so I didn't want any of my private life getting back to my mother, who would have had me married off if she could.

On one night after closing time, I walked a local woman home to her block of flats and we said good night on the ground floor, which was very dark and deserted. One thing led to another and before too long we were at it like a couple of rabbits, up against the wall.

Suddenly, a double-decker bus pulled up at the bus stop right outside the flats, and we became the main floor show for a couple of dozen passengers, who began yelling and offering unsolicited advice regarding my technique.

I kept my head down until the bus moved off and was hoping like hell that no-one had recognised either of us, but it was a very mortifying experience, and not unexpectedly that relationship went nowhere.

On my second trip in *Pyrrhus*, we were calling at Dublin for a short time to top off the cargo, and leaving Vittoria Dock in the evening, I got into a fight with one of the other stewards in the rec room. It was over nothing, and although a few punches were thrown, it was soon broken up and we ended the night amicably.

It was only a few hours to Dublin from Birkenhead, and by turn-to at 06:00, we had been alongside and tied up for a couple of hours.

When the 2nd steward put everyone on the shake, the steward I had the fight with was nowhere to be found and had gone missing. The skipper, Albert Lane, sent for me, and having heard about the fight, interrogated me, intimating that I might have killed this guy and put his body over the wall, during the crossing from Birkenhead.

I had a very nervous few hours until it was established that he had decided, during the night, that he didn't want to go on the voyage, and as soon as we had tied up, he had slipped ashore and caught the ferry back to Liverpool.

The company tracked down a crew member who lived in Dublin and he joined *Pyrrhus* that afternoon, prior to sailing, much to my relief.

This second voyage out to Japan, via the Panama Canal, was uneventful, and as Judy was writing regularly, I was looking forward to reconnecting with her when we finally sailed into Hong Kong.

We arrived in Hong Kong early Sunday morning, and found the harbour, as usual, full of shipping, among which were quite a number of American fleet units on R&R.

Holts Wharf was taken up with other Blue Funnel ships so we were assigned to one of the buoys in the harbour. Approaching the buoy, our stern swung round to within a few metres of an American destroyer, where the crew were assembled at the stern of the ship for church service, and all was solemn and very quiet, but that didn't stop Mick from yelling out and taking the piss out of these guys. I'm sure that had the crew of this destroyer been able to recognise any of us and bumped into us ashore it would not have gone well for us.

When I caught up with Judy, we went to the movies again, but after the movie, we ate in her usual restaurant and then she invited me back to her apartment. I found it hard to believe my good fortune, as she was very attractive, maybe a year or so older than me, and had long, shiny black hair which went down to her lower back.

One of the mates who had seen me ashore with her the previous trip told me he thought she was beautiful, and I was very lucky to have met her, although at first they all assumed she was a bar-girl.

Her apartment was situated just off Nathan Road and was a tiny room with a single bed but was clean and tidy.

I made the most of my night ashore with her but had to be up early to catch the launch back out to *Pyrrhus* in time for turn-to, and kept pinching myself to make sure I hadn't dreamt it all.

Every night after that, if we had a date, Judy always let me stay at her place, and I caught the launch back next morning.

A couple of nights later, when Judy was working late and I wasn't seeing her, I arranged to meet Mick in Faces. I was working late and had a few things to do so Mick went ashore about 30 minutes ahead of me and said he would wait at Faces for me.

I showered and caught the launch ashore and was partway up the escalator to Faces when a commotion on the mezzanine floor caught my attention, and I saw Mick clutching one of the polystyrene drawings from Faces, being chased by a crowd of Chinese staff. He flew down the escalator, and when a member of the public, at the bottom of the escalator, attempted to stop him, Mick smashed him over the head with the polystyrene drawing, which shattered into pieces.

Mick fled out the door, across four lanes of traffic on Nathan Road (no mean feat if you have ever seen the traffic on it), leaping the steel barrier in the middle and made his escape.

I was stunned and watched all this with an open mouth, wondering what the hell had just happened. I carried on into Faces, as I was desperately in need of a beer, and after successfully convincing the staff that I wasn't a mate of Micks and had never seen him before, they served me a beer.

Fortunately, I had only been to Faces a couple of times this trip, so the staff weren't too sure I was an associate of his.

I sat there for about 20 minutes drinking my beer and feeling more and more pissed off with every minute. I finished my beer and headed back to the ship in a foul mood, where I found Mick in his cabin, with his leg in the sink and blood all over the place. He had caught his leg on the steel barrier in Nathan Road when he jumped over it and ripped a huge gash in his leg.

I suggested that he call the mate and get it stitched, but he was scared of the consequences if Faces laid a complaint so we managed to stem the bleeding and bound it up with plasters.

I asked him what the hell he had been thinking, to have ripped the painting off the wall, and he just said he wanted it as a souvenir for his cabin so I told him that he had stuffed up our chances of ever going to Faces again, but it didn't seem to faze him.

On my final night in Hong Kong that trip, and my last date with Judy, she produced a gold ring in the shape of an abacus, which she gave me as a going-away present. I was highly embarrassed, as I hadn't thought of getting her anything, and felt like a big fool. I apologised, but she didn't seem to mind, which only made me feel worse, and we agreed to keep in touch by letter.

Departing Hong Kong, we made Singapore, then Port Swettenham, Penang and then across to Colombo.

Steaming up the Malacca Strait, we had been overtaken by one of the brand-new Hamburg-Amerika boats, and this was quite an event, as the Blue Funnel P-boats were rarely overtaken. We watched her creep up from astern and gradually go past us, with most of her crowd on deck, observing what would have been a rare occurrence for them as well.

I was mortified, as I was very proud of the turn of speed of the P-boats, for their age, but this was a sign of the times, as the new generation of fast, single-screw, aft-accommodation ships came on line.

Departing Colombo, we again faced the long haul around South Africa, and up the Atlantic to Las Palmas for bunkers, and then on to Liverpool where we arrived at the beginning of December.

It was a hell of a long haul without a run ashore, and was beginning to get to everyone, so arrival in the Mersey was a big relief.

I was back on the shore-gang about a week before Xmas and found that Mick had been made up to 2nd cook and baker and assigned to another ship and wouldn't be rejoining *Pyrrhus*.

Pyrrhus arrived back in Vittoria Dock, from the coast, just prior to Xmas and I began to work-by her until we sailed deep sea.

I was home for Xmas Day and Boxing Day but opted to sleep aboard *Pyrrhus* between Boxing Day and New Year's Eve, when we were scheduled to sail, due to the difficulties involving public transport, which at that time of the year were a bit hit and miss, and made getting home each evening, and back again in the morning, too hard.

I was quite happy to go across to the pub each evening, for a couple of pints, and then turn in early with a good book, as the ship was deserted at night, with only the nightwatchman, a mate and a couple of engineers aboard.

One night during that period, Ralph, one of the assistant stewards, invited me to an engagement party at his cousin's house in Birkenhead, which I foolishly accepted. It was good of him to invite me, but as soon as I arrived, I knew it had been a big mistake.

The only person I knew at the party was Ralph, and it was obviously a family thing, and I was well out of place and wishing I was back on the ship tucked up in my warm bunk with a book. I had brought some beers along, so I stood there all night, sucking on cans of beer, and hardly spoke a word to anyone, apart from Ralph. I wanted to leave as soon as I got there, but it was a couple of miles back to the dock, there were no buses or taxis, it was fucking freezing and there was about three inches of frozen snow on the ground.

At about midnight, when I had only had four cans of beer and was stone-cold sober, I told Ralph that I was leaving, but he wouldn't hear of it. He said that if I waited a bit longer, when the party died down, he would get me a blanket and I could doss down on the floor in the front room and walk back to the ship in the morning.

The thought of facing that freezing walk back was not inviting, so I agreed to stay.

A while later, the guy who got engaged, who worked on the docks and was due to work a shift early in the morning, said goodnight and left the party. By this time there were just the hard core of aunts and uncles left at the party, and they must have been wondering who the fuck was the wanker standing on his own all evening and not speaking to anyone. I just wanted to go to sleep.

Ralph found a blanket for me, and I found a space under the table in the front room and dossed down. There were two other people sleeping in the front room, one on the couch and one in a corner, but they were dead to the world and both snoring like crazy.

I was lying on the floor, cold and unable to sleep due to the snoring, wishing like hell that I had given the party a miss and just wanting to be back in my bunk aboard *Pyrrhus*. Around 06:30 I heard footsteps approaching down the street and then the morning papers were thrust through the front door directly into the room and I decided that it was time to head back to the ship. I stepped out of the house onto the ice-covered pavement on a bitterly cold morning and made my way back to the docks.

I joined *Pyrrhus* with my kit on the morning of New Year's Eve and we were scheduled to sail at 17:00.

We worked through the sailing-day inspection, but the wharf was relatively quiet for the remainder of the day, and we were all a little depressed at the thought of departing on NYE. The afternoon session in the Wheatsheaf was rather subdued, and we were all a little downcast as we traipsed back to the ship.

The tugs pulled us off the wharf on schedule and we moved across the dock and into the lock. As we were moving into the lock, we slammed into the wall and one of the railway lines pierced one of the plates on the side of the hull, so the passage out into the Mersey was cancelled, and we tied up in the lock to await the next tide, while welders were sought, to weld the ruptured plate.

The ETD (estimated time of departure) board at the top of the gangway was changed to 24:00 and shore leave was shown to finish at 23:00.

Wow! We couldn't believe our luck and rushed through dinner so that we could get showered, changed and ashore as soon as possible.

The ship's husband, the office 'wallah' who stands by the ship until it departs, was beside himself, and running around telling us if we went ashore, to make sure we were back aboard by the allotted time shore leave expired, or else.

The poor stand-by assistant steward, who had brought an empty suitcase, in anticipation that the ship would be gone by 18:00, was begging us all to make sure we came back on time, and when he asked me if I was going to come back, and not light out for home, I told him I would let him know at midnight.

We piled into a cab and headed to the pubs in Hamilton Square, where all the action was, and gave it a real lashing. When the pubs closed, we drifted back to the ship in ones and twos, and in the event, were all present and correct, come the end of shore-leave.

As I approached the gangway, I bumped into one of the junior engineers, who against all the rules, invited me up to his cabin for a drink. As pissed as I was, I accepted, and soon there were a group of five of us in his cabin, off-duty engineers, the junior electrician and me.

We soon ran out of beer and had to resort to drinking either neat gin, or gin and water, and were well under way when in walked the 2nd mate's wife and made herself at home. The 2nd mate was on duty, as we were locking into the Mersey and would not be permitted to drink anyway. She was totally up herself, and when it came to midnight, she kissed everyone in the cabin Happy New Year, with the exception of me, 'cos I was crew.

I was past fucking caring at that point, as I had had a skin-full ashore and had now given the gin a good lashing, and do not remember making it back to my cabin.

When I was put on the shake next morning, I was as sick as a dog, and was stuck in the heads with stuff coming out both ends and the chief steward banging on the door ordering me to get to work. When I finally convinced him that I was totally unable to turn to, he buggered off and left me to my misery, stuck on the loo.

I spent the rest of the day in my bunk until finally turning to for dinner, but even then, I was far from well and everyone was taking the piss. I was fully expecting to get logged, for self-inflicted harm, and fully deserved to be, but for some reason they never did, and I spent the next few days apologising to everyone who had had to cover for me, which I felt really bad about.

In hindsight, had *Pyrrhus* managed to lock out without hitting the wall, the outcome would have been far different. I would still have been depressed at the thought of sailing on New Year's Eve, but at least I would have been sober come morning, and it only took a couple of days for your mind to swivel away from home, to anticipating the delights of the voyage to come.

The cook who had taken over from Mick was an abrasive Glaswegian, who wasn't too popular with most of the catering crowd.

We also had a Scottish 2nd mate who was a real dour bloke who would barely give you the time of day and was a real misery, who never smiled. One lunchtime he ordered a medium to well-done steak, and when I served it to him, he complained that it wasn't cooked enough.

I took the steak back to the cook, who begrudgingly took the steak off the plate and threw it back on the grill, while I went to get a clean, hot plate. When the steak had been on the grill for a couple of minutes, the cook put it on the plate, then he lifted up his apron, unzipped his fly and rubbed his 'coozer' all over the steak, despite the steak being hot off the grill.

He thought that this was a great joke and waited for me to take the plate back into the saloon, which I totally refused to do. He started to get a bit bolshie, but I told him that if he thought it was such a huge joke, he could go and serve the steak himself, because I wasn't going to.

Eventually, he realised I wasn't bluffing and cooked a fresh steak, but the delay had been so lengthy that the Scots mate was pissed off and had a go at me.

I apologised for the delay, but was thinking, 'Mate! If you only knew.'

I knew that if I had backed down and served that first steak, word would have inevitably gotten out about the incident, which would reflect on my integrity, and one thing that I never, ever did was tamper with anyone's food, regardless of how much I disliked that person.

Midway across the Pacific, we practised boat-drill and lowered the lifeboat and then carried out the usual trick of steaming away and then returning to pick up the boat. While in the water, the crew had spotted a large, coloured glass float, of the type attached to fishing nets, and had salvaged it and brought it back on board.

The next morning, we overtook a surfaced American

submarine, to the west of the Hawaiian Islands, headed to Japan. The mate painted a message on the glass float, 'This way to Yokohama', with an arrow, and tossed it overboard into the path of the submarine, and I imagine that he let the crew of the sub know about it by radio, but whether they bothered to stop and retrieve it, or not, we never found out.

We called at the usual ports on the Japanese coast, but Hong Kong was now my port of choice, and I couldn't wait to catch up with Judy again after receiving regular correspondence from her.

We berthed at Holts Wharf, which overcame the requirement to be dependent on launch schedules for a run ashore, and we caught up again. I had bought her a necklace this time, which she appeared to like, and I had been considering the idea of asking her to become engaged, but then decided against the idea.

I knew that I was still far too immature for marriage, and I also had no intention of giving up the sea, and as we would have had to live in the UK, because I couldn't imagine me making a living in Hong Kong, that would not be fair on her.

A number of the guys on the ship who had met her were telling me I was crazy not to get engaged, but a voice was telling me it just wouldn't work.

One morning I came across a couple of the midshipmen, up in the officers' accommodation, with a couple of young women. As I had never come across females, other than officers' wives, aboard the ship before, I asked them how they had managed to get these young women aboard.

They informed me that they had just asked the mate for a visitors' chit, which enabled them to get the women onto the wharf.

This started me thinking, and that afternoon, when I met Judy ashore, I asked her whether she would like to visit *Pyrrhus*, as I would love to show her over the ship.

She told me that she was keen to visit the ship, so I left her sitting on a bench in a small park adjacent to Holts Wharf, while I nipped back to the ship. I went to the mate's cabin and asked him for a visitors' chit so that I could show my girlfriend around the ship. The mate, who knew that my friend was local, looked embarrassed and told me to go and seek permission from the captain.

I went up to the captain's cabin, told him about my friend and asked for a chit. He asked me whether she was local or expat, and when I told him she was a local, which he already knew, as the whole ship knew about my relationship by then, he told me that he didn't think it was a good idea, as she wouldn't feel very comfortable in the shipboard environment, and gently ushered me out of his cabin.

I left the ship with my mind spinning, thinking about how I could break the news to her, and feeling very embarrassed and humiliated about the whole situation. Judy took the rejection in her stride and didn't seem too upset, and I tried to make up all sorts of excuses to cover my shame.

It was only when I had recovered from the shock later that I really began to resent the ongoing hypocrisy, the 'them and us' class status, the racism, and the total bullshit that was the Blue Funnel Line.

At that point I knew I wasn't going to be joining *Pyrrhus* for another voyage, as I was determined never to sail with this mate, or the skipper, again, and even an alternative to Blue Flu was beginning to look attractive at that stage.

I came across this hypocritical attitude later in my career, but never as bad as in Blue Funnel.

When it came time to say goodbye this time on departing Hong Kong, I knew that it was unlikely I would ever see Judy again. She was far too beautiful, and sweet, to be hanging around waiting for me forever, and there were better catches than me out there. I just wondered how I had managed to hang on to her for so long.

At the end of the trip, the chief steward asked me back for the next trip, but I told him I needed a change of ship and declined to return.

CHAPTER 13

Ken happened to be home in the *Ixion* and while on leave, I caught up with him in Holyhead.

We were drinking in the Edinburgh Castle one night when we got talking to one of Ken's mates, who worked on the Holyhead–Dun Laoghaire British Rail ferries. He told us British Rail were beginning to take on extra crew for the forthcoming summer season and advised us to call into the office the following morning and make some enquiries.

We fronted up the next morning, with our discharge books, to the office, just across the road from the Edinburgh Castle, and had a quick interview.

We were both offered positions in the MV *Hibernia*, commencing at the end of our current leave, which we both accepted and signed six-month contracts with British Rail.

The following morning, we caught the train to Chester, and then to James Street, Liverpool, and fronted up at India Buildings, Holts main office, where we advised the personnel officer that we were leaving Holts.

His reaction to the news caught us both by surprise, as instead of wishing us well, he launched into a bitter diatribe about us never being welcome back if we finished with Blue Funnel, and we would never work for a better company, and that we were making a huge mistake that we would come to regret.

Up to that point, I had been harbouring some doubts about whether or not I had made the right decision in leaving Holts, as I had now been with them for over five years, but his arrogance and dismissive attitude convinced me that I was on the right track, and I walked out of India Buildings with a sense of relief and no regrets.

Dad wasn't so impressed and was pissed off when I told him that I had quit Blue Funnel and was joining British Rail, a company he had worked for, for eight years, when he came out of the army, and a company he did not have much time for. He saw it as a major backward step in my seagoing career and was very upset about the whole thing.

The *Hibernia* was a 5000-ton, twin-screw vessel, with a service speed of 18 knots, built in 1949, and, along with her sister, *Cambria*, operated on the Holyhead to Dun Laoghaire, Ireland, ferry service, with the one-way voyage taking four-and-a-quarter hours.

The normal winter schedule was departing Holyhead every other day, at 03:15 and arriving Dun Laoghaire at 07:30, where the ship lay over for the day, departing Dun Laoghaire at 19:45 and arriving back in Holyhead at 24:00.

Most passengers disembarked to catch the 01:30 mail train to London, but some passengers who had booked a cabin could choose to sleep aboard and catch the morning train to London.

During the height of the summer season, the ships completed two round trips per day, returning light ship (no passengers) from the early-morning voyage, and departing Holyhead again just after lunch.

Hibernia and *Cambria* each carried up to 1500 passengers under normal conditions, but at the height of the season, some 2500 were crammed aboard, and this made any sort of movement between different areas of the ship extremely difficult, with so many people sitting on their luggage in the alleyways. Things were bad enough on a smooth crossing, but in any type of seaway, things got very messy, very quickly.

There were three watches, A, B and C, and Ken and I were assigned to watch C. Two watches were on duty at any one time while the third watch was ashore, so we were always working with different members of the crew. With the different sailing schedules and varied watches, it took me some time to get my head around how things worked, and I was always asking other members of the crew whether we were on or off watch, and what time we were due to sail.

Women made up a large percentage of the crew, which made things very interesting, as I wasn't used to working with women, and they were a bit of a distraction, albeit a very nice one, to say the least.

There was a great atmosphere aboard these boats, with lots of laughter and practical jokes, and life was never boring for one moment, as there was always something going on or someone doing something stupid, which gave us a laugh.

Ken and I were staying at his place in Valley to start with, but eventually we moved into a caravan on a small farm in Trearddur Bay, which caused a few issues for us over time.

The crews were mainly from Holyhead, but as they expanded during the peak season, lots of Scousers were taken on, and then, when the universities broke up for summer holidays, a number of students were taken on for a couple of months.

My first job upon joining *Hibernia* was in the second-class cafeteria as waiter, and as it was only early April, the season had not yet kicked off and I was told it would be pretty quiet, and easy.

We did a few meals while still tied up in Holyhead, but once we were under way, the cashier, Jean, told me she was going to bed during the passage, and would see me again when we were on the Kish lightship, 15 minutes away from docking in Ireland. She told me to put any money that I took during the night in the till, and she would sort it out in the morning.

As soon as she had gone to bed, the two chefs in the galley approached me, and told me to put any money from meals I sold in my pocket and not to ring it on the till, and they would square things in the morning.

Well, I wasn't too sure about this, as I had never stolen anything in my life before, apart from maybe scrumping a few apples when I was a kid, and I felt uncomfortable about the arrangement, but as they were so casual about it, it was obviously what went on, so I went along with it so as not to rock the boat, me being the newbie.

Well, not long after the cashier had left, things really started to kick off and it got really busy. I was like a one-armed paper-hanger, taking orders, running them into the galley, giving change and serving the meals. Time passed so quickly I hardly noticed it, and the chefs were rubbing their hands in glee at the number of diners ordering meals.

I had one-pound, and ten-shilling, notes stuffed into every pocket of my uniform, and things got so bad that every time I went to make change from my pockets, showers of notes cascaded onto the deck. I must have had at least £70 to £80 on me, so to make things easier, I stuffed them all in the till for safe keeping, intending to retrieve them before Jean returned to duty.

Unfortunately, the pressure didn't let up, time flew by without me noticing and next minute Jean was back on duty. She opened the till, saw all the notes inside and said, 'My goodness. You have been busy.'

I told her that I had been so busy that I had not had time to ring up the transactions on the till.

She took four £1 notes out of the till, kept one for herself, gave me one, and one each to the two chefs, and rang the rest of the money onto the till.

The two chefs were choked, as they had been working like crazy all night, cooking meals, and were expecting payback in a big way, so I was not the flavour of the month, and if looks could kill, I would have been as stiff as a board.

What I wasn't aware of was that no matter where you worked, café, snack-bar, bar, cabins, etc., there were fiddles and perks going on everywhere, and everybody was at it. If you worked in the snack-bar, you went ashore in Ireland and bought bread and stuff to make sandwiches, which you then sold and pocketed the money. If you worked in the bar, you bought booze to sell in the bar, and so it went on.

I don't know if British Rail knew it went on and just turned a blind eye, or whether they were being ripped off without realising it, but it was too endemic for it not to have been known about and could have been sorted out if proper checks and balances had been in place.

The thing was that there was no need to steal money and risk getting caught, as the pay was phenomenal during the height of the season, and well above average even in the off-season, even though you did put the hours in to earn it.

As an example, as an assistant steward of 20 years of age and single, I earned between £37 and £45 per week at the height of the season, and between £33 and £37 per week during the quieter period.

Certainly, this was with double runs, and extra shifts, but the money was there if you wanted to earn it.

Compare that with the headline that ran in one of the national newspapers during that period, when assembly workers at Fords in Dagenham were being blasted for sleeping on the job, while earning £26 per week, which everyone considered to be over the top.

But, hey, I was an out-of-towner, the new guy, and I wasn't going to upset things if that was the way they were done. I wasn't a goody-two-shoes, and if money came my way, I accepted it, but I was too fucking lazy to put any effort into making it.

I got moved out of the cafeteria shortly after that, and I think the chefs had something to do with my relocation, but I didn't mind, as every job in the ship was interesting, and different, and I couldn't think of any job that I minded doing, possibly with the exception of anything in first-class, as there was a bit more micro-management up there.

I had managed to get into a relationship with one of the cashiers (not Jean) before I left the cafeteria, and this was now in full swing, and pretty full on.

We had only been in the *Hibernia* for a few weeks, when Ken blotted his copybook for a reason I cannot remember, and was transferred to the *Slieve Donard*, one of the small British Rail coasters, that plied between Holyhead, Birkenhead and Ireland. He wasn't too happy about it, as it was an all-male crew and he was missing out on the 'totty' in the *Hibernia*.

While Ken was sailing in the 'rock-dodger' we occasionally caught up if we were in Holyhead together and went on a pub crawl around the many watering holes, such as the Edinburgh Castle, The Prince of Wales, the Dublin Packet, the Skerries, Britannia, Cambria, South Stack and the Queens Head, to name a few.

Holyhead was similar to Chester, in the number of pubs available, and drinking was the favourite pastime of most of the crew. We drank in the local pubs until closing time, when we joined the ship for the 03:15 sailing. This of course was prior to *The Herald of Free Enterprise* tragedy, and there was no restriction on drinking, as long as you could turn to and carry out your work.

At this early stage on the ferries, I was being moved from job to job, fairly frequently, and one night returning from Ireland I was serving in the second-class bar. There were three of us on the bar, and it was really busy so we were flat out serving pints of Guinness and Irish whiskey, when one bloke who was drinking at the bar took a couple of steps back from the bar, dropped his trousers and crapped on the deck.

He then pulled his trousers up, resumed his position at the bar and carried on drinking. A space opened up around the turd on the deck, but everyone carried on drinking and buying drinks.

The 2nd steward who was on the bar with us said to me, 'You'd better go and clean that up.'

I replied, 'You go and fuckin clean it up, because I'm not touching it.'

It had been cleaned up by the next morning, but I don't know who had been brave enough to tackle it.

Quite a few of the female crew were married, and most of them very attractive, but they nearly all had boyfriends in the crew, and I was fascinated at some of the combinations, as I gradually realised who was doing what to who.

One morning, I was paged over the PA system to go forward and pick up some mail from the first-class bureau. When I got there, I walked into the office and was met by a woman I had not seen before. She was in her early forties, tall, with a good figure and attractive, and when I took the mail from her and looked her in the eye, I just felt that we had a connection.

When I made enquiries about her, I found out that she had been engaged to some bloke ashore, for years, but was going out with the 3rd engineer, who was married.

I was a bit disappointed with what I had found out about her, but filed the information away, and left it at that.

A few weeks later, Ken was forgiven his misdemeanours, and reinstated to the *Hibernia*. One weekend, we went to Chester and hired a car for a week and brought it back to Holyhead, where we used it to drive around Anglesey and visit some of the hard to get to, out of the way pubs.

On the last night before we were to return it to Chester, we were drinking in the Valley Hotel, and had both had a skin-full, so I told him to leave the car in the pub car-park and we could pick it up in the morning. Ken wouldn't have it and insisted on driving the car home, and he managed to prang it.

It was still driveable, but the damage was very noticeable. When we returned the car, he lost the deposit and moaned like hell, but I was just pissed off that it had happened on the last night, and if he'd left it when I told him to, we wouldn't have had a problem.

He then went on to purchase an old green, two-tone Austin, which gave good service and took us all over the place.

I didn't obtain my driver's licence until years later, thankfully, as at that period I was pissed every night, and feel sure that had I been driving, I would not be here now. I chucked in money for petrol, and Ken, very kindly, chauffeured me everywhere.

That poor car endured a lot of neglect and bad use. We had both been invited to my sister's wedding later in the summer, and a couple of weeks before the event, we took a couple of girls out for a trip around the pubs in the middle of Anglesey. At the end of the night, we parked up, but the girl I was with in the back seat had so much to drink that she vomited all down the outside of the rear passenger-side door.

Well, that was the end of that night, which was a little disappointing, as it had appeared so promising, but when we surveyed the car next morning, with the huge splatter of dried vomit down the door, we both agreed to clean it in time for the wedding.

The days slipped by, and the rain had some effect on the slick, but not much, and eventually the day arrived, so we headed to Chester.

When someone enquired about the unusual paint job, we told them that a flock of seagulls had shit all over the car on the way down.

The season was now beginning to pick up, and I was getting more of what were classed as the senior jobs, and less of the work in the cafeteria and suchlike. Eventually, I was given my own cabin section in second class, and remained in that position until I left *Hibernia*.

There were three identical accommodation blocks in second class, consisting of 20 two-berth and four-berth cabins with a total of 54 bunks in each block.

The cabin steward's job was to wait in the second-class bureau, and as the passengers checked in at the bureau, show them to their cabin and assist with their baggage.

I received tips for carrying the bags and assumed that this was the perk associated with this particular job. As I was on such good money, and probably much more than most of the people who were tipping me, I felt rather guilty about accepting their money under the circumstances, so I drew up my own code of conduct.

I refused to accept tips from elderly people, women on their own, or families with children. If any fit young dude expected me to carry his bags, I was quite happy to relieve him of his cash.

On one occasion, I had shown an elderly lady to her cabin, and then left her. She hadn't tried to tip me, but a little later, she returned to the bureau, and tried to give me money, which I politely refused. The other two bedroom stewards saw this and gave me shit for refusing tips, but I stuck to my formula and only accepted tips from people I deemed able to afford it.

I found tipping to be demeaning, especially when I was earning good money, but would probably have accepted it had I not been so well paid.

The good thing about being in charge of an accommodation block was that once the ship sailed, and the passengers settled for the night, you were left to your own devices until the ship docked and the passengers disembarked. You then had to strip the bunks and clean the cabins ready for the next trip.

At one stage, Ken was in charge of one of the other accommodation blocks for a few weeks before he went to first class, and as soon as we had finished making the bunks and cleaning cabins, we shot up the road to the pub in Dun Laoghaire for a few pints.

Ken and the other guy on the third block were always finished well ahead of me every morning and left for the pub 20 to 30 minutes before I was finished, saying they would see me up there.

No matter how fast I worked, and sometimes I was waiting outside the cabin and got stuck in as soon as it was vacated, I just couldn't finish at the same time. This started to get to me, and I knew they weren't cutting corners as they still had to pass the daily cabin inspections, so I figured that I must be a slow worker.

I stewed on it for quite a while, until one afternoon in the pub I asked Ken how he and the other bloke were so much quicker at the job than me. Ken laughed his head off, and then told me that they didn't bother changing the bottom sheet on the bunks, unless they were obviously soiled, which saved them a huge amount of time.

Well, I was a bit dubious and thought it sounded a little grubby, but if everyone else was getting away with it, then I'd give it a go.

The next day, I tried it and finished well ahead of my usual time, so we all went to the pub together.

That night we were embarking passengers, and I was feeling pretty pleased with myself, when the very first passenger I showed to a cabin, an old Irish lady, came to find me in the bureau, and in front of everyone, said, 'Young man, the sheet on my bunk is dirty and you need to replace it.'

I was mortified, and had to strip the bunk, change the sheets and make it up again, and mumbled something along the lines of having missed that one. I couldn't believe that everyone had been getting away with it for ages, but the very first time I tried it, I got caught out.

I decided there and then that in future I would do the job by the book, regardless of how much time it took me.

Another issue was the piss-pots, which were kept in a small locker under each bunk, even though there was a perfectly good toilet in each alleyway. These were a holdover from the old days and not something that I agreed with. If anyone ever used one, and they did from time to time, I just took it out on deck and tossed the whole thing over the side, pot and all.

There must be dozens of these things sitting on the bottom of the Irish Sea, and they are probably worth a great deal as collectors' items, with the BR crest on them.

I kept a few in my locker for daily inspections and when the 2nd steward asked me which cabins I wanted him to unlock for inspection, I always made sure that the piss-pot was in the locker under the bunk just in case anyone checked.

CHAPTER 14

IT WAS ABOUT THIS TIME THAT WE RENTED AN OLD CARAVAN on a small farm in Trearddur Bay, just outside Holyhead, from an old lady who lived in the farmhouse which was about 40 metres away from the caravan.

She was a right pisshead and had a boyfriend who kept bashing her up every time they went on a bender. She was forever banging on the caravan door in the middle of the night for us to come over to the house and sort him out, and we would try to sneak into the caravan without her seeing us and pretend we weren't home when she came knocking.

It was a bit hard with the car parked outside so we started parking the car up the lane away from the caravan.

At first, we shared the caravan with a lad off one of the other watches, Ken Tatlock, but after a few weeks he got a better offer of accommodation and moved on.

As we only had a set of Ken's mother's old bedsheets between us, for the two beds, we borrowed some from the ship, and changed them on a fairly infrequent basis.

As we both had a steady stream of females visiting us, this was probably not as frequent as it should have been, but as the condition of the caravan didn't really entice you to stay and chill out, we only used it for sleeping or sex.

Now that I was living in the caravan, with no shower or washing facilities, I began using the showers on the ship. They were big, open concrete showers with no doors or any other type of partition, buried in the bowels of the ship and hardly ever used, as the regular local crew all chose to bath or shower at home.

I had to give them a good clean-out at first, as they were pretty gross, but the pressure was good and the water was always hot, so I used them as often as I could.

One night, I was showering and had put shampoo on my hair, so had my eyes tightly closed while I soaped myself all over. When I rinsed the shampoo out of my hair and opened my eyes, I found that the lads had brought some of the female crew into the shower-room to watch me.

I got a helluva fright, but as the showers were such huge affairs and my towel was on the other side of the room, there was not much I could do to cover my embarrassment and had to endure the cat-calls and humiliation.

It was an occasion that I could only wish that I had been endowed with a much bigger set of tackle, but, unfortunately, it was what it was.

For the next few days, I had to endure the dirty jokes and innuendo, whenever I met any of them, especially from some of the older women, but had to take it in good spirit, or they would never have let it go.

One afternoon in Dun Laoghaire, I was in the pub with the boys when I bumped into the attractive bureau assistant I had met in the first-class bureau. We had a couple of drinks together, and then left to walk back to the ship, leaving the rest of the lads in the pub.

When we got back aboard the ship, we arranged to meet in one of the cabins of my section, while the rest of the crew were ashore or asleep. Once we were in the cabin, things were just starting to get interesting, when we heard someone in the alleyway outside the cabin. She panicked, thinking someone had followed her down to the section, and quickly got dressed.

When I checked the alleyway, there was no-one around, but the moment had passed, and I was cursing whoever had interrupted us, but I now knew that she was definitely up for it, and only had to wait for a more suitable occasion.

The problem aboard ship was that you always thought you were too smart for everyone, and that you had done a good job of covering your tracks, but this was rarely, if ever, the case, and any relationships soon became common knowledge.

A few days after our meeting in the cabin, one of her friends, a fellow bureau assistant and older lady, came to see me and expressed her concern about what was going on, and in particular the big age gap between us, which she didn't think was right. I told her that we hadn't actually done anything yet, and that the difference in age was up to the lady in question, as I was quite relaxed about it but would understand if she decided not to carry on with the relationship.

I found it pretty difficult, talking to someone who was a lot older than me, about my supposed relationship with her friend, and felt like telling her to fuck off and mind her own business, as she was making me feel uncomfortable.

I had to acknowledge that there was a big age difference between us, as I was 20 and she had to be in her early forties, but she was a good-looking woman with a great figure, and her age didn't bother me.

Her mate must have mentioned the conversation she had had with me, as things cooled off for a while, and I was beginning to think that it was not to be.

However, a week or so later, *Hibernia* was berthed overnight in Holyhead, and C watch was watch aboard, while the other two watches were ashore. This meant that C watch did the clean-up the next morning, but even quite a few of C watch had gone home for the night and would return to the ship next morning, for work.

At about 01:00 the IRA, or someone claiming to be from the IRA, phoned in a bomb threat, claiming that a bomb had been placed somewhere in the ship. No-one, for one moment, believed it was a viable threat, and we all knew it was a hoax, but we had to go through the motions, and the ship was searched by the bomb-squad.

All the crew aboard were instructed to meet in the first-class bar, which was situated on the top deck and at the furthest point forrard of the accommodation, and well away from the hold where the bomb was supposed to be.

About a dozen of us congregated in the bar, and most of us bought a drink, and then settled into one of the booths to discuss the situation and pass the night away.

Among the crowd in the bar was the bureau assistant from first class, who came and sat in the seat next to me and reached out and held my hand. Sitting opposite us was the chief steward, who, upon seeing us holding hands, raised his eyebrow, but didn't make any comment.

After a couple of hours, the all-clear was given and we were permitted to go to our berths for the night. She held me back as everyone dispersed, and when everyone had gone, she unlocked the bar door, pulled me inside, then relocked it and we had sex on the bar floor.

It had been unexpected, but a very welcome surprise, and she certainly knew what she wanted.

This meant that I was now being intimate with two women on the same watch, which was slightly awkward, but this was the sixties, and casual sex was all the rage. I knew that my cashier girlfriend was also seeing someone else at the same time she was seeing me, and I just accepted that.

Once word got out that we were seeing one another, no-one seemed to care, or bother about it. She finished with her engineer, and I bumped into him in the Railway Club one night when he was with his wife. He gave me a filthy look, but I just thought, 'Mate, at least I'm not cheating on my wife,' and didn't let him get to me.

She swapped positions with the second-class bureau assistant, who went to first class, and she came to the second-class bureau.

One immediate result of this was that she suddenly started slipping me money on each watch, and when I queried this, she told me that it was part of the fiddle the bureau assistants ran, whereby on the weigh-sheet, they showed a cabin in each section, vacant for the passage, when it had in fact been sold, and the money was split with the three cabin stewards.

They had not been cutting me in on this, as I was a newbie who was only there for the season, and I was an out-of-towner to boot.

I found it hard to believe that they were getting away with it, as it was obvious to anyone checking the weigh-sheet what was going on. At the height of the season, the ship would be full, with all cabins taken, and yet, on every trip, the weigh-sheet showed three vacant cabins, one in each section.

I began to realise just how extensive these perks were, but it wasn't my problem and I wasn't going to rock the boat. If British Rail couldn't be bothered to put in place the checks and balances to prevent this type of behaviour, then they deserved to be ripped off.

I just wished, a little later in life, that I had done something constructive with all this money I was earning, instead of just pissing it up against the wall, as just about every penny went on beer, and having a good time.

The other good thing about her transferring to second class was that we were at it at every opportunity, as working so closely together gave us ample scope to meet up and find a secluded spot.

The only problem with having an assignation in a cabin in the section was that if you turned off the light in the cabin you were in, the bulkhead on both sides of the cabin looked like the 'sky at night', with pinpoints of light shining through, where generations of stewards had made holes in the bulkhead to spy on attractive passengers.

If I did arrange to meet a female in a cabin in my section, I always ensured that the light was off, to avoid featuring in a peepshow.

Apart from the females in the crew, there were also the passengers, as during the height of the season, a great many young females travelled on their own or in pairs and on the afternoon trips across to Ireland very few, if any, passengers booked a cabin, so you could approach these women and offer them the use of a cabin for free.

Quite a few accepted the offer and then it was just a case of obtaining a few cans of beer and you had a party going on, which usually led to the inevitable over the course of the four-and-a-quarter-hour crossing.

We also managed to take girls that we had met in the pubs in Holyhead across to Ireland for the day, as when we took them aboard with us when joining the ship at midnight, no-one ever checked up as to whether they were crew or not, and the same applied on the Irish side.

They could just come and go as they pleased, and security was non-existent.

On one occasion, I met a girl in the Edinburgh Castle, and when I went to her house to take her on a date, while I was waiting for her to get ready, her mother started talking about engagement rings, which made me feel uncomfortable.

The next time I called to take her out, her mother told me that she was aware that I had left the *Hibernia* in the company of a woman and wanted to know who the woman was. I managed to take her over for a trip to Ireland in the *Hibernia* but thought the talk of engagement rings, and then the close scrutiny, was a little freaky and over the top, so I ended the relationship and bailed out.

The girl was nice enough, but the mother was just a bit too weird for me.

It turned out that the girl's brother was the ticket collector on Holyhead station, and I had to pass him every time I joined or left *Hibernia*, so the mother would be aware of every move I made.

The investiture for Charles, Prince of Wales, was held on 1 July 1969, at Caernarvon Castle and the Royal Yacht *Britannia* was anchored in Holyhead harbour for a few days, which attracted hordes of sightseers to Holyhead.

The Welsh Nationalists were foaming at the mouth about being under the English yoke and the subjugation of Wales by the English. Why the hell anyone gave them the time of day was beyond me, but they were all over the news with the focus being on Holyhead due to the Royal Yacht.

Every time we departed Holyhead, the passengers flocked to the port side of *Hibernia* to catch a glimpse of the yacht and watch the ensign being dipped in salute.

Towards the end of July, we began to get the university

students joining the crew for the peak of the season. They were mainly from Cardiff and Bangor universities and a mix of male and female students.

I'd noticed one particular young girl of 19 who had joined C watch but had not had much to do with her or even spoken to her often.

One night, C watch was watch on duty departing Holyhead and I was sitting in the darkened second-class bureau talking to one of the other seasonal stewards when the door opened and this young stewardess slipped into the bureau. I excused myself and left the office, thinking that they wanted to be alone. As I stepped into the alleyway, the bloke I had been speaking to dashed after me and asked where I was going, to which I replied that I was giving them some privacy.

He then blew me away when he told me, 'Mate, she's here to see you, not me,' as I had not spoken more than a dozen words to her since she had joined *Hibernia*. I rejoined her in the office and sure enough, she was keen to have a relationship, but before it went any further, I found out a few things about her.

She was at Cardiff University, along with her boyfriend, who was in the *Cambria*, so they were, literally, like ships that passed in the night, as *Hibernia* and *Cambria* were always on opposite sides of the Irish Sea, apart from the couple of hours at midnight, when one ship was just arriving at Holyhead as the other was getting ready to depart.

I suggested that she request a transfer to *Cambria*, which she could have done with no difficulty, but she told me that she preferred things as they were.

I thought it must either be a fairly open relationship, or a relationship that was doomed, but as she was only 19 years of age, it didn't much matter, and was no concern of mine.

To complicate things even further, her boyfriend's brother was also in C watch in *Hibernia*, but she didn't attempt to keep our relationship any great secret and he never said anything to either of us, or ignore us, when he used to see us together up the pub in Dun Laoghaire.

It was a rather surreal experience to be sleeping with three women, each of whom knew about the other two, and having none of them tackle me about it, and initially I was walking on eggshells, expecting the shit to hit the fan, but nothing ever happened and we just carried on regardless.

My twenty-first birthday was coming up on 9 August, and we would be over in Dun Laoghaire for the day, so I arranged with the landlady of the local pub to put on food and drinks for the crew of the *Hibernia* and invited everyone, catering, deck and engine room.

The day cost me a fortune, but I had nothing else to spend my money on, and unknown to me, the crew had had a whip-round for me and presented me with an envelope of cash, which went a long way to defraying the cost.

The chief steward and one of the deckies got into a fight over a woman (what else?) but apart from that, the afternoon went well, and we were all pretty merry when we went back to work.

It was about mid-August that we got kicked out of the caravan at Trearddur Bay, for having too many parties and too many women visiting, according to the old lady who owned the farm.

This was totally untrue, as we were too knackered to have more than the occasional party, and the place was such a dump that we rarely invited women, and not too many self-respecting women would have slept there anyway.

We didn't argue with her, as we had both had enough of her and her boyfriend continually arguing and fighting, so we were happy to call it quits.

On one occasion, the boyfriend had bashed her so badly that

one of us went up to the telephone box on the main road and called the cops, but when the police turned up, she refused to press charges, which pissed us off.

I think that she actually relished all the drama and the attention she got when he was having a go at her, and it wasn't going to end anytime soon, so we were out of there.

We ended up back at Ken's mum's in Valley but didn't spend too much time there. On one day off we drove to Chester for the day and forgot to fill up with gas before leaving Chester on the way back to Holyhead to join the ship at midnight.

We'd had a few beers and figured we would find an all-night gas-station in North Wales, but we ran out of gas at Colwyn Bay, and as we had by this time missed the ship, we went to sleep in the car. A policeman woke us up first thing next morning by banging on the window and we found out that there was a 24-hour gas station just around the next corner, about 200 metres up the road.

The cop had a good laugh at our expense and gave us a lift to get the gas.

It was the first time either of us had missed the ship, so we got off with just a telling off and a warning, with no loss of pay.

With all the fornicating and the heavy drinking, we were walking around like zombies some nights, particularly if we ran into some heavy weather, where the overcrowded alleyways and public spaces made moving about the ship a nightmare.

It only took one person to start vomiting, to trigger everyone else and soon the decks were awash, and the smell horrendous.

In heavy weather we collected Kleensaks full of sawdust and wandered around the public spaces throwing the stuff over pools of vomit to soak it up.

As soon as the passengers had disembarked, all the sawdust was swept up and the decks mopped, and the acid from the vomit kept the decks gleaming white and in pristine condition.

The lack of sleep began to take its toll after a while, and one night when I had been without sleep for 48 hours, through one thing and another, we were watch below, so I got my head down as soon as we departed Holyhead, expecting to get four hours' sleep before berthing in Dun Laoghaire.

I had just dropped off, when Ken shook me awake to tell me that he had two girls in one of his cabins in his first-class section and he needed me to come forrard and take one of them off his hands.

I wasn't interested, but he wouldn't let up, so I very reluctantly climbed out of my bunk and put on my uniform.

I trudged along the deck to first class and located the cabin number Ken had given me. When I entered the cabin, I found Ken in the top bunk with his girl, and another girl alone in the bottom bunk.

I took off my uniform and climbed into the bottom bunk, where I commenced kissing this girl. After a while I put my hand on her breast, but she gently removed it, and we carried on kissing. I put my hand on her breast again, and again she gently removed it, so I put my hand between her legs and again she removed my hand.

After a few more minutes of kissing, I put my hand between her legs again, only for her to remove it, so I jumped out of the bunk, got dressed, and without saying a word, left the cabin and headed back down aft to my bunk, where I promptly fell asleep.

Ken had a go at me next morning, but I'd done enough to help him out, and told him so.

September saw us approaching the end of our six-month contract, and despite both Ken and I being offered permanent positions in the *Hibernia*, we had decided that we still had plenty of the world to see and intended to go back deep sea, if we could find a company to take us on.

We had both overstayed our welcome in Holyhead and were barred from a couple of pubs, so figured it was time to move on and let people's memories blur a little, plus Ken had just split with his long-time girlfriend and things were not going too well between him and the new boyfriend.

One of my last jobs in the *Hibernia* was to act as nightwatchman while she was berthed in Holyhead and carry out the fire watch. The usual shoreside nightwatchman was unavailable and the 2nd steward had asked me to fill in, as no-one else was interested.

The fact that it was a Saturday night may have had something to do with that.

The job entailed punching a time-clock at all the fire-points located around the ship, on the hour, every hour, from 24:00 to 08:00, and I would be the only person in the ship during that time, and I would be paid an extra eight hours' pay.

I had been shown the location of all the fire-points and the route I had to cover, which would take me about half an hour to complete, but one of the stewardesses offered to stay with me and keep me company, which I had accepted, and she was waiting in my bunk.

The route took me from stem to stern and through every deck, but I was running down the alleyways and leaping up and down companionways to get it over with as soon as possible so that I could jump into my bunk and have sex with my companion.

The first round took me about 20 minutes, but as I got to know the route, I got faster and faster and at the end was getting around in under 15 minutes. If anyone had bothered to check the time-clock next morning, they would have found all the time stamps crammed into the first 10 or 15 minutes of the clock, and nothing in the remaining space.

We ended up having sex eight times during the shift, but I have to admit that the last two were only steam.

She headed home at 08:30 and we arranged to meet in the Railway Club at 11:00, but when I got there, I was struggling to keep my eyes open and had to call it quits before the Sunday lunchtime session was over.

CHAPTER 15

A FEW DAYS LATER KEN AND I WERE SAYING OUR FAREWELLS to the crew of *Hibernia*, and it turned out to be a lot more emotional than I had thought it was going to be. I was beginning to think that we had made a big mistake in not accepting the offer of permanent employment with British Rail, but it was too late now, and we were bound for the Shipping Federation Office at Mann Island, Liverpool.

Before I left *Hibernia*, one of the girls told me she was pregnant, but she said it in such a casual, flippant manner, that I just thought she was joking and thought no more of it.

The crowd gave us a great send-off from Holyhead and then we were on our way.

The jobs at the Shipping Pool in Liverpool were the usual load of rubbish, tramps and Trident Tankers, with the usual supercilious, sarcastic bastards behind the counter that I experienced at every other shipping office I had the misfortune to deal with.

Always made me wonder why they stuck with the job, when

they all seemed to hate it so much, but I don't suppose there was much call for their unique people skills!

We were after a ship that went to Australia, as Ken had told me about all those Aussie women, and the great times he had had down there, so I was really keen to get down to the Antipodes and experience things for myself, and Liverpool was not the port to find a ship bound for Aussie.

As there was nothing to take our fancy at Liverpool, we asked the bloke behind the counter would it be okay if we went and tried our luck in London. He told us that he really couldn't give a fuck where we went, so we thanked him politely and headed off to make plans to get to London.

We caught the train to Euston Station on a Thursday afternoon and booked into a cheap hotel near the station, and the following morning did the rounds of the shipping offices in the city, such as Port Line, Blue Star Line and Shaw Savill.

Port Line and Blue Star line could offer us nothing, and didn't seem the least interested, so we figured out that head office was not the place to be seeking seagoing employment.

We tried Shaw Savill, but they could only offer us jobs in the *Northern Star*, or her sister, *Southern Cross*, and we had both heard enough horror stories about both these 'ten-pound-Pom' ships not to want to go there.

They were infamous for the fights between the crew and the immigrants headed for Australia, so we rejected job offers on both those ships.

Someone suggested that we give the New Zealand Shipping Co. out at the Royal Docks a go, so we caught the underground train out to the East End and got off the train at Plaistow, where we caught a cab to the Royal Albert Dock, and the offices of NZSC.

We handed our discharge books to a young lady behind the

desk and she disappeared into a back office but did not close the door, and we overheard a male voice in there making complimentary comments about Blue Funnel and their standard of training, which sounded pretty positive to us.

The gentleman in question, Mr Larsen, the catering superintendent, came out of his office, asked us a few questions, then told us that there was a ship up in Liverpool requiring a couple of A/Ss, and could we join her on Monday morning.

We asked if she went to Australia, to which he replied in the affirmative (what he meant was that they all went to Australia, but not necessarily on that particular trip) so we agreed to join her.

He sent us around to the Shipping Federation Office at King George V Dock, to sign on.

It was a hell of a long walk around to KGV and we were tempted to call into the Connaught on the way back for a couple of pints, but decided against it, in case Mr Larsen smelled the beer on us, which wouldn't have been a good look.

With our paperwork in order, we returned to NZSC offices and Mr Larsen gave us instructions for joining the MV *Otaio* at Gladstone Dock, Liverpool, first thing Monday morning.

We caught the train at Plaistow and returned to the city, where Ken made arrangements to catch up with the Irish girl that he had slept with the night that I walked out on her mate, in the first-class cabin in *Hibernia*.

I was too embarrassed to catch up with them and figured if she hadn't been prepared to turn it up in the privacy of a cabin, she was hardly likely to turn it up on a night out in London, so I stayed drinking at the bars and pubs around Euston Station, in the hope of picking someone up, but that was wishful thinking, and I was in bed by the time Ken returned from his date.

We checked out of the hotel next morning and caught the train back to Chester, for me, and Holyhead for Ken, arranging to meet up on Chester Station first thing Monday morning, to catch the train to Liverpool.

The *Otaio* was a 13,000-ton refrigerated cargo ship, with a service speed of 17 knots, and was the cadet ship for the NZSC, but we weren't aware of that when we joined her in Gladstone Dock, as she only had a skeleton crew aboard for coasting, and no cadets had yet joined her.

MV Otaio (Credit: Chris Howell)

We introduced ourselves to the 2nd steward, a New Zealander, with the nickname of Kiwi Kate, for obvious reasons and were allocated our jobs. I ended up engineers' steward, again, Ken was saloon-bobby and tiger and some old bloke was officers' steward.

The 2nd steward introduced us to the chief steward, who turned out to be a very heavy drinker, and when he was on a bender, the 2nd wouldn't let anyone near him and acted more like his mother. He was like a Rottweiler guarding its puppy.

When I first saw the size of the saloon, I was blown away: it was so big, although only two tables were in use when we joined her. We were beginning to get an understanding of what was ahead for us, as we came across all the accommodation which was currently not in use.

We eventually locked out of Gladstone Dock into the Mersey and sailed around the coast, up the Thames, and into London, where we berthed in the Albert Dock.

The work rate gradually began to pick up, as more and more crew joined the ship in London. These were mainly the teaching and training staff, but one morning we were woken to the strains of a bugle sounding reveille, which was the turn-to call for the cadets.

The cadets were both deck and engine room, and the deck cadets worked under the supervision of the bosun and lampy, so there weren't many actual crew aboard her, apart from the catering crowd.

The *Otaio* also had more than her share of special lunches, for shippers and others, which were a real pain in the arse when you were trying to get up the road to the pub for a lunchtime session.

We drank in The Steps, which was the nickname for the Custom House pub, mainly, and the first time we went in there, we thought we were talking to an attractive barmaid behind the bar, but gradually we realised we were actually talking to a barman.

Despite wearing long sleeves, I noticed, when she was pulling a pint, that she had huge scars on both wrists, as a result of attempting to commit suicide.

We gradually, over time, found out that she had been at sea, and was obviously trapped in the wrong body, which was pretty tragic, as she would have been a stunning woman, and she was no longer permitted to go to sea, having seriously tried to top herself.

She always came over and talked to us, if the pub was quiet, and I think Ken must have been jealous that she spent so much time talking to me, as when we got back home and we were having a drink with Dad in Chester, he told him that I had been trying to chat up a 'queen' down the docks in London, and Dad, being a homophobe, wasn't very impressed.

At the beginning of November, we departed London and sailed around the south coast for Falmouth, where we were due to go into dry-dock, and the rest of the crew, including more of the cadets, joined the ship.

Ken and I were beginning to have second thoughts, as the bullshit connected to the *Otaio*, being a cadet ship, was beginning to ramp up, culminating in our returning from ashore one night in Falmouth to find three cadets at the head of the gangway checking the ID of everyone coming aboard, and discovered that this was to be the norm for the remainder of the voyage.

How the hell could you get women back on board with that level of scrutiny, was our first concern, but when we also found out that *Otaio* was not, as we had first thought, going to Australia, but to New Zealand instead, the alarm bells really started ringing.

Quite frankly, New Zealand was not on my radar, as I hardly knew anything about the place, apart from what I had learned at primary school, and that was so far off the mark, it wasn't funny. About the only facts I could recall were that the people lived in grass-huts with huge wood carvings around the entrance, and that males and females all wore grass skirts.

I had never come across anyone who had been to New Zealand, so my ignorance remained unchallenged, and I was in for one hell of a shock when I eventually did get there.

To really top things off, we turned to one morning to find that the other A/S had done a runner and skinned out during the night, without telling anyone, and to really put the lid on things, a directive arrived from head office that the chief and 2nd stewards were to ensure that boy-ratings were no longer bullied.

Where the fuck that came from, we would never know, but can only surmise that it was an early version of Health and Safety, but at first, we just took it to be some sort of joke.

We may have thought it was a joke, but the bosses were taking it seriously, and instructed the boys, that they were no longer to take instruction from the ratings, and they were only to carry out duties given by the bosses. This meant that we could no longer just dump our trays by the sink and expect the boys to clear up but had to do everything ourselves.

The little bastards were just loving this and on top of being short-handed, things were headed to a blow-out.

Well, that happened that afternoon when I was attempting to get afternoon tea out to the engineers, the mates, and the training staff and teachers, all at the same time.

The 2nd engineer had a go at me for being a little later than usual with the engineers' tea and coffee, and I blew big time and we very nearly ended up having a fight. The chief steward got involved and I told him his fortune and told him that if he didn't have a relief steward to replace the bloke who had skinned out, by the following day, then he would be looking for someone to replace me as well.

The next morning, a local guy from Falmouth, Cliff, turned up for duty and things returned to some semblance of normality. He was a nice guy and a good worker, but by then Ken and I had decided that we weren't going deep sea in the *Otaio*.

We were only on Home Trade articles for coasting and had told the boss that we wouldn't be signing on to go deep sea, and he would need to find replacements.

A day or so later, being Saturday, Cliff asked us whether we were going ashore that night, and when we said that we were, he arranged to meet us in the lounge bar of the local pub at 20:00.

Ken and I turned up at the pub on time but there was no sign of Cliff, so we settled down at a table on the edge of the dancefloor with a couple of pints. Next minute, the lights dimmed down, the curtains on the stage parted, and out stepped Dusty Springfield, singing one of her big hits.

We were sitting there with our mouths open when we realised it was Cliff in drag.

He finished the song to huge applause from the crowd in the lounge and then came over to the table and sat with us while having a drink.

After a time, he excused himself, and disappeared, and sometime later the lights dimmed again, the curtains opened and out stepped Shirley Bassey. He again received a huge ovation and then came over and joined us.

He could have made a serious living at this, as he had the lip-synching of the songs down pat and all the mannerisms of both singers, but he was quite happy to be at sea, although he told us that he wasn't planning on going deep sea in *Otaio* but would pay off when we did.

A couple of days later, we paid off and caught an early train to Truro, where we changed for London.

I didn't regret leaving the ship due to the fact that there were no actual crew, other than the catering staff, which would have put a bit of a block on the social side of things, plus there was no crew bar, which would have made it rather hard to meet women in port.

The bugle calls were a bit over the top as well, so she was a ship I was quite happy not to have sailed in.

We were home for a couple of weeks and had heard nothing

from the office, so one morning we decided to phone Mr Larsen from a public telephone booth in Chester.

He seemed surprised to hear from us, and when we told him that we had been told when we paid off *Otaio* that the office would be in touch with us to allocate another ship, he asked us if we were in a position to join a ship in Liverpool the following morning, which was due to sail that night.

We told him we could join her first thing next morning, so he gave the name of the ship and the berth in Liverpool she was on.

Ken caught the train to Holyhead to pick up his gear, while I shot around Chester, buying stuff that I needed and then home to pack.

We met on Chester Station early next morning, and caught the train for Liverpool, getting off at James Street and taking a cab to Gladstone Dock, again, to join the MV *Westmorland*, a Federal Steam Navigation Co. refrigerated cargo ship of 8000 tons. She was one of four sisters, the other three being *Taupo, Tekoa* and *Tongariro*, which all belonged to the New Zealand Shipping Co.

Federal and NZ Shipping were a combined company under the P&O Shipping group, but ships with English county names were classed as FSNC ships, while ships with Māori names were classed as NZSC ships. It was all pretty confusing at first, but we got the hang of it after a while.

Westmorland wore the light green hull livery with white upper-works and the beautiful red Federal funnel. I wasn't too sure of the colour scheme at first sight, as I was so used to black-hulled ships, but it very soon grew on me and I now consider it to have been one of the most distinctive colour combinations of any class of ship.

The four sisters were fitted with D-frames on the masts, which gave them a unique silhouette and enabled them to work cargo either side of the ship, with just the one derrick.

She had a service speed of 21 knots, giving her an average daily run of over 500 nautical miles, and her only vice was a disconcerting habit of her engines suddenly stopping for no apparent reason, due to an ongoing problem with her turbos.

This gave a very eerie feeling when she was pounding along, mid-ocean, at 21 knots, when suddenly the engines cut out and she drifted to a halt in dead silence, while everyone rushed to the bridge and engine room, and the 'not under control' signal was flown.

This occurred on about eight occasions when I was in her but, fortunately, never in any kind of seaway, and the problem was usually fixed in about 30 minutes.

We climbed aboard with our bags and found the chief steward, Billy Battson, who introduced us to Eddy the 2nd steward, who showed us to two single-berth cabins in the cross-alleyway on the main deck.

With the ship being only four years old, the cabins were modern and spacious and located just across from the heads and showers, which was very handy. The only drawback with my cabin was that a cargo winch was situated directly above my bunk on the next deck just a few feet above my head, and this became problematic when we were working cargo at night, unless I had taken enough lubrication to knock me out.

The 2nd steward then took us up to the saloon to introduce us to the saloon-steward, another Ken.

At first, we were wondering 'what the hell!' as we had assumed that the chief steward was gay, but this turned out to be not the case, but the 2nd, Eddy, and the saloon-bobby, Ken, definitely were.

I'd heard that the London and Southampton ships were a lot more gay-friendly than the ships from northern ports, and now we were seeing the evidence of this. Not that it was a problem, as apart from Charlie in *Peleus*, no-one had ever hit on me.

We turned to and were soon flat out finding our routine and getting to find our way around the ship.

I was officers'/engineers' steward, Ken was crew messman and gay Ken was saloon-bobby and captains tiger.

Fortunately, there was none of the sailing day rigmarole associated with Blue Funnel sailings, and the ship was just left to itself, with no inspections or extra shore-side people in for lunch, so the whole day just proceeded as normal.

As soon as lunch was over, we shot ashore to the Caradoc for a lunchtime session and on the way back picked up a couple of transistor radios to install in our cabins and were back aboard for afternoon tea and then dinner.

The ETD board at the head of the gangway was showing 21:30 with shore leave finishing at 20:30, so as soon as dinner service was completed, we took off to the Caradoc for our last shore-side drinks for a while. I'd had no breakfast, lunch or dinner so I grabbed a pie at the pub and made do with that.

Just as we were finishing our pints to return to the ship, a group of deckies from *Westmorland* turned up and told us that the ETD had been put back so shore leave was extended. They weren't sure of the time, but we thought that if we kept an eye on them, we would be pretty safe, as the ship was going nowhere without the deck crowd.

After about another hour of drinking we all traipsed back to the ship, where the mate, Mike Hill, was waiting at the head of the gangway and ripped into the deck-crowd for holding the ship up.

CHAPTER 16

THE ETD HAD BEEN PUT BACK, BUT NOT AS MUCH AS THE deck crowd thought, and the mate was not pleased. While he was bollocking them, the stewards and motor-men snuck into the accommodation and down to our cabins, where we commenced to party with cans of beer and spirits.

The deck crowd were all on stand-by, with the exception of the watch-keepers on the four-to-eight watch, and there were five of us in my cabin with others coming and going.

As I had only had the meat pie at the pub to eat all day, and consumed a fair amount of alcohol, my stomach was beginning to play up and I had a bad case of flatulence going on.

I was sat on my bunk with the two Kens sat either side of me, one of the ABs from the four-to-eight was sat on my day-bed and one of the motor-men in a chair at the table. We were all fairly pissed and having a good yarn and a laugh, when I felt I had to fart so I raised a buttock and let rip. Ken, the saloon-bobby, was sat on the side I let rip and he suddenly leapt to his feet, smashed a beer bottle, held it to my face and accused me of taking the piss out of him.

Next minute, the AB stood up and pulled his deck-knife from his pouch and told Ken to drop the beer bottle. I thought, 'Holy shit! What the fuck's going on here?' From a pleasant night on the piss, I was suddenly in the middle of a 'Mexican stand-off'.

Ken threw the bottle onto the deck and stormed out of the cabin, while the rest of us went back to drinking and I tried to stop myself shaking. The AB and the motor-man decided to call it a night shortly after and left, which left me and Ken having a nightcap before turning in.

Next minute, the cabin door opened and Ken the saloon-bobby, staggered in, slumped into the chair at the table, mumbled something which we couldn't understand, put his head down and promptly fell asleep. Ken and I finished our drinks and then tried to wake him, but he was dead to the world and wouldn't wake up.

We each grabbed an arm and half carried, half dragged him back to his cabin where we threw him, fully clothed, onto his bunk.

Before we left the cabin, Ken suggested we open his porthole to let the cold air wake him up, as by now, we had locked out into the Mersey and there was a freezing wind blowing, so we raised the deadlight and the port and hooked both to the overhead hook.

This being the end of November, we figured that the cold would soon wake him up and he would get into his bunk, so we left him to it.

At 05:30 the following morning we were put on the shake by Eddy, the 2nd steward, who told us that he was having a heck of a job waking the saloon steward and he also told us that he had had a 'dream' during the night, when Ken, the saloon steward, had come to his cabin and told him that he had taken an overdose of sleeping pills. Ken had obviously taken the pills then gone to Eddy's cabin before returning to my cabin, where he passed out.

This started the alarm-bells ringing, so we all shot round to his cabin where we found him still fully clothed on the top of his bunk, still in exactly the same position we had left him the night before, and the cabin like an ice box.

Eddy, the 2nd, palmed an empty pillbox from the table and dashed up to the chief steward while Ken and I slapped the shit out of the comatose Ken in an attempt to wake him.

Next minute Billy, the chief steward, appeared, took one look at the scene, and dashed up to the bridge to sound the alarm.

By this time, we had dropped the pilot off Point Lynas and were well down the Irish Sea, so a distress call was put out and we altered course toward Cork in southern Ireland, where the Cork lifeboat set out to meet us.

Fortunately, there wasn't much of a sea running when the lifeboat came alongside, so Ken was strapped into the Neil Robertson stretcher and lowered over the side and into the boat below.

I was hoping he wouldn't wake up at that stage, as he would have gotten the fright of his life.

The lifeboat got him ashore and transferred to hospital, where he gradually made a recovery, though they credited his survival to the fact that we had opened the port and the extreme cold had slowed down his metabolism, which meant that the pills he had taken were not absorbed as fast as they would have been, had the room been at a normal temperature.

Of course, we only found all this out much later, and at first, I was feeling fairly guilty about the whole incident, having precipitated it with my upset stomach.

The lads told me not to worry about it, as to try and bottle someone for farting was a bit extreme, and there must have been more to his over-reaction, but I figured that they obviously hadn't smelt my farts!

The Old Man, John North, interviewed us a day or so later, in an attempt to find out what was behind the attempted suicide, but of course, none of us mentioned the bottle and knife stand-off, so they just put it down to personal problems.

Of course, this meant that we were now short-handed, so the job was divvied up between Ken, Eddy, me and the pantry-boy, and the work load ramped up accordingly.

Ken became tiger/saloon steward, with some of the accommodation thrown in, while I took over all of the mates' and engineer's accommodation, while the pantry-boy took over the crew messman's position and Eddy did most of the pantry work.

We were carrying a couple of supernumeraries from head office, who were carrying out a time and motion study, but the fact that we were now a man light in the catering department had buggered their calculations, so they left us alone. We were now working a lot more overtime, which would have skewed their findings, so they concentrated on deck and engine room.

By now, we realised that we were bound for New Zealand and not Australia, but from what we were picking up from the rest of the crew, this appeared to be no bad thing, as they regaled us with stories of women ringing up the ship and inviting the crew to parties ashore, and the crew bar heaving at all hours of the night and all weekend.

New Zealand sounded too good to be true, so we took all this talk with a pinch of salt, but if even a fraction of what they told us was true, it sounded as though we were in for a good time.

As we got to know the crew better, we realised we had fallen in with a great crowd, as everyone got on well together, and even the mates and engineers were a friendly bunch, for the most part, and the atmosphere in the *Westmorland* was so much more laid back than in Blue Funnel.

Inspection was held only a couple of times a week, but one

major difference was that inspections took place in port as well as at sea, which was to catch me out from time to time.

We had a good run down to Curaçao for bunkers and then Panama and once out into the Pacific, work commenced on decorating the crew bar ready for the Kiwi coast. The first attempt looked fantastic but had to come down as the deck-head had been covered in decorated paper, which was deemed a major fire-hazard.

The second attempt didn't look quite so good but was given the tick of approval by the mate, and it was interesting to see some of the lads excel at design and come up with some innovative ideas, which gave the bar plenty of character and atmosphere.

MV Westmorland

Two weeks out from Panama, just before lunch, a dark smudge appeared on the horizon dead ahead. It was a beautiful day, with hardly a cloud in the sky and we were out on deck on the 'bronzie' after lunch as we approached Cape Palliser on the south-eastern tip of the North Island, New Zealand.

We rounded the Cape in the middle of the afternoon, crossed

Palliser Bay and rounded Pencarrow Head into the entrance to Wellington Harbour.

It was dinnertime as we slowly passed the wreck-site of the MV *Wahine*, with one of the Holm boats acting as tender to the wreck.

The *Wahine* was a 9000-ton inter-island ferry, running between Lyttelton in the South Island and Wellington in the North Island, when she was caught in the tail of a cyclone at the entrance to Wellington Harbour on 10 April 1968.

She lost steerage at the entrance to the harbour and drifted onto Barretts Reef, where she was holed, and then drifted up the harbour before foundering.

Fifty-three passengers and crew lost their lives through drowning or exposure.

The *Wahine* was only two years old when she foundered and when we passed the site, it had been just over a year and a half since she went down. They had salvaged everything above the waterline but were still carrying out salvage work below the surface. It was a rather sombre moment as we passed close by and most of the crew were at the rail to pay their respects.

Dinner was a fairly easy affair that night, as everyone was busting a gut to get ashore and weren't wasting any time over dining, so Ken and I spent most of our time out on the saloon-deck, taking in the sights of Wellington.

Wellington came as a major surprise to me as I honestly thought we would be tying up at some rickety wooden jetty in the middle of the jungle, so the modern high-rise buildings and colourful roofs of the houses were a welcome surprise, with not a grass-hut or grass skirt in sight. So much for British primary school education!

It was 23 December 1969, the day before Xmas Eve, and after dinner we were showered and changed in no time and headed ashore. It was a beautiful evening, so we went ashore in just jeans and T-shirts and proceeded to head to the city centre via the pubs and bars along the way.

To say it was a little disappointing would be an understatement, as we had been led to believe that the bars would be pumping and the places heaving with women, but the city was deserted and all the bars empty.

We had not realised that with Wellington being the seat of government, and Parliament being closed for the holiday period, the city had emptied out, as everyone headed home for the Xmas and New Year holidays.

After a month at sea and all that anticipation, it was a huge anticlimax, and by the time we had found our way to the Bistro Bar at the Royal Oak in Cuba Street we were well over it.

The much-vaunted Bistro Bar was almost deserted and I wasn't impressed by the way you had to queue in line at the bar inside a rail to stop people jumping the queue, and had your jug filled by the bar-staff holding a gun on a flexible hose which dispensed beer. It looked pretty industrial to me, with all the stainless steel, and I was beginning to have my doubts about New Zealand.

Come closing time at 22:00, we went outside in search of a cab and, boy, it was fucking cold. The jeans and T-shirt had been a major mistake as the temperature had plummeted and a freezing wind was blowing down the street, and I had never been so cold in my life and this was the height of summer. I couldn't believe it, I just wanted to be wrapped up in my warm bunk.

We finally found a taxi rank and eventually made it to the head of the queue and were just about to climb into the cab when two young women came dashing up to us and asked us if they could share our cab. I couldn't give a fuck, as I just wanted to get into the cab, out of the cold and stop my teeth from chattering.

We agreed to let them share the cab and when they found out we were going back to a ship with a bar, they were keen to join us, so when the cab dropped us at the wharf, we invited them to come aboard.

As we were climbing the accommodation ladder to the main deck, Ken and I were wondering where all the noise was coming from, and as we entered the cross-alleyway leading to the crew bar, it hit us in a tidal wave of sound.

When we stepped into the bar, it was crammed bulkhead to bulkhead with women and the noise was horrendous.

We partied into the night, and then slept with the two girls we had brought aboard, and next morning there were women everywhere, in the mess, the showers and elsewhere, and no-one seemed to care.

There was no sneaking around and they moved about the ship openly, in various states of undress, visiting their mates in different cabins, and just about every member of the crew had a woman in his cabin.

It just seemed to be too good to be true, but I gradually came to realise that everything the lads had been telling us about the Kiwi coast was proving to be right on the money, which was amazing.

My girlfriend invited me to the beach with her two-year-old son, so we spent the afternoon at Oriental Bay, the closest beach to the city, and had a good time, as the weather was fine and hot, and we arranged to meet in the Royal Oak that night before I returned to the ship to finish work.

She slept aboard again that night but told me that she was going to New Plymouth for the rest of the holidays to be with family, and although *Westmorland* was going to New Plymouth next, she would be returning to Wellington about the time were leaving, so we never got together again.

It was Xmas Day but things were pretty low-key, as we didn't make too big a deal over Xmas dinner, but the bar was heaving that night as the pubs ashore were closed for the day, so we were very popular.

I met another girl, Margaret, who took me home on the train to Porirua to pick up a couple of changes of clothes, where she introduced me to her father, who didn't seem too impressed with me, so he must have been a pretty good judge of character.

He didn't say goodbye when we left to head back into town.

The majority of women on board were 'ship-girls' who would hook up with a member of the crew for the duration of the time the ship was in port, and would often follow the ship around the coast, and then join another 'home-boat' when the ship left the coast, but they were totally loyal to whoever they were with, while the ship was on the coast.

There were some real characters among them and one girl, nicknamed Monkey, got her name when the captain of one ship, returning from ashore one night, came across her swinging from the cargo-hook hanging from a derrick and told the guy she was with to 'get that monkey off my ship'.

They knew all the British ships and companies, and often had their favourite companies and ships.

The main companies at that time were Port Line, Blue Star, Federal, NZSC and Shaw Savill and they had nicknames for a number of the ships. The Federal boat, *Essex*, was known as the 'easy-sex' and the Shaw Savill boat, *Majestic*, as the 'magic-stick'.

They were a friendly crowd, but you certainly wouldn't want to cross them.

We also saw quite a bit of Carmen, the well-known Wellington transvestite, who spent a fair amount of time in the bar, and as the crew bar was pumping at that holiday period, the mates and engineers also spent a fair amount of time drinking in there.

The atmosphere was amazing and I couldn't believe how readily the women were accepted on board, the only stipulation being that they had to be ashore during inspections and if they were caught in your cabin during an inspection, you were in trouble.

Just after Xmas, a replacement for Ken, the guy we had put over the side in Cork, finally came aboard to take some of the pressure off. Unfortunately, he turned out to be a Dutch engine-room crewman, who had paid off a Dutch ship for medical reasons and he didn't have a clue about catering and what's more, had no intention of learning.

He was a lazy bastard, which was most unusual for a Dutchman in my experience, who wanted to spend all his time in the bar and if you had to go looking for him, you always knew where to find him.

After a couple of days of this we got fed up with the situation and petitioned the boss to get the agent to replace him, which they did.

The replacement wasn't much better to start with, as he was another ex-engine-room crewman, but a Kiwi this time, and he had been in the *Kaitawa*, a Union Steamship Co. collier, which was lost with all hands in May 1966 off Cape Reinga, in bad weather.

He was meant to be aboard her that trip but for some reason had paid off and had a lucky escape, which I think was still playing on his mind. He was a bit of a strange dude, but harmless enough, and at least he made an effort to pick the job up and give it a go.

He had a disconcerting habit, every breakfast time, of eating the crusts of toasted bread straight from the 'gash-bucket', into which they had been thrown. When we asked him if he couldn't at least eat the crusts before they were tossed into the 'gash', he just laughed and carried on doing it.

We figured that some of the ships he had been in must have

been crap feeders. Either that or he had a few issues, but we were just grateful to have someone to ease the workload, so we put up with his weird ways.

We celebrated New Year's Eve in Wellington and a few days later sailed up the west coast of the North Island around to New Plymouth, berthing around 09:00.

While we were tying up, the deck-boy was badly injured when the cable for the accommodation ladder, on which he was standing, snapped and the ladder crashed to the wharf.

Fortunately for the deck-boy, he was harnessed to the ship, but the chain yoke of the ladder caught him on the way down and caused his injuries.

He was admitted to New Plymouth Base Hospital and paid off the *Westmorland*. Over the ensuing days he had numerous visits from the rest of us, but I think most of us were more interested in the nurses than the deck-boy, as they used to hang out of the nurses-home windows and give us a very warm welcome whenever we visited the hospital.

One of the more memorable sights at New Plymouth was the sight of Mt Egmont, as it was known then, now Mt Taranaki, towering over the city. The mountain was a perfect cone shape, similar to Mt Fuji in Japan and with snow on the peak in winter, looked like a picture postcard.

New Plymouth was the major service port for the oil and gas industry, which operated off the Taranaki coast, and had a bit of a Wild West frontier atmosphere about it, with oil and gas guys from all over the world adding to the mix in the pubs and bars.

A recent killing involving a couple of rig workers was all the news at the time and was a big event for a town the size of New Plymouth.

As soon as the ship was alongside and the shore-side telephone installed, it started ringing off the hook, with invitations to parties, and we were kept busy scribbling addresses down.

As soon as dinner was over, a group of us went ashore, jumped into a cab and headed for one of the addresses which had seemed most promising.

When we got there, we were disappointed to find that the youngest woman in the room was in her mid-fifties, so we rang the ship and got hold of old Hughie McLean, the bosun, and told him to get a couple of the old guys to come to this party, which he seemed keen to do, and then we caught another cab up town and went to the hotel in the main street.

The lounge-bar was pretty lively, with plenty of women, and Ken and I copped on to a couple of sisters. I chatted up the older sister, who was a few years older than me, and Ken got talking to her sister.

The only problem with my girl was that she was recently separated from her husband and he was there that night along with a few mates. He obviously hadn't accepted the fact that they were separated, because he kept making himself a real pain in the arse and despite her telling him to piss off on more than one occasion, he just wouldn't let go and I figured that I was going to be in a fight before the night was over.

She eventually suggested that we go back to the ship for a drink and despite it not being quite closing time at the pub, I was happy to oblige, as I didn't quite fancy taking on this guy and all of his mates so decided that discretion was the better part of valour.

She slept aboard that night but had to go to work next morning so I called her a cab first thing in the morning, escorted her off the wharf and arranged to meet in the hotel that night.

Her ex was there again that night but not quite as pissed as he had been the night before, but he still kept hassling her so we headed back to the ship, as there were few other options of going to other hotels.

It was fairly obvious that she and her ex had a few issues and I had the feeling that she was actually getting a kick out of the situation and in no hurry to resolve it.

After a few nights of this, I made the cardinal error of chatting up another woman before finishing with the girl I was going with and I was in my cabin talking to this other woman when the door flew open and my girlfriend walked in, told me my fortune and stormed off the ship.

When the girl I had been talking to in my cabin became aware of the situation, she insisted on being taken ashore and put into a cab, which I very reluctantly did.

I was returning to the *Westmorland* along the wharf and feeling sorry for myself, when the ship berthed ahead of us, an Avenue Shipping Co. vessel, whose ships are all named after Irish counties, began pulling away from the wharf to depart New Plymouth.

As I got closer, I could see a girl standing on the wharf, waving goodbye to someone on the Avenue boat, and when I got talking to her, found out that she was farewelling her long-time boyfriend, an AB on the ship. I invited her aboard *Westmorland* for a drink, which she readily accepted and soon one thing led to another.

Ken's girlfriend, the younger sister of my ex-girlfriend, refused to speak to me again, and I couldn't really blame her, so I stopped going ashore with Ken for the remainder of the time we were in New Plymouth.

The problem for me, and many others, was that there were so many attractive (and some not so attractive) available women on the Kiwi coast that I was like a kid with a box of chocolates and didn't know which one to pick, or I wanted to try them all.

CHAPTER 17

It was a bit of a relief to finally depart New Plymouth, round Cape Reinga and head down to Auckland with a clean slate.

Sailing into Auckland, up the Waitemata Harbour, passing bush-clad Rangitoto Island to port, on a beautiful summer's afternoon, with all the boats on the harbour and the multi-coloured roofs of the houses, which were even more impressive than those in Wellington, was a sight to remember and I fell in love with Auckland from that first impression.

We berthed at Queens Wharf at the foot of Queen Street, the main street in Auckland city, and just along the wharf from the main ferry terminal for the harbour, with ferry boats coming and going all day long.

It was just a short walk from the wharf gate to the Snake-pit, a well-renowned seamen's bar, situated in the basement of the South Pacific hotel on Queen Street, and as soon as work was finished for the day we made a beeline for the place, having heard so much about it.

Coming down the stairs from the entrance on Queen Street

we were met by the sight of a woman standing on one of the tables
with her skirt up and her knickers down, giving everyone a 'brown-
eye' and thought that the place was certainly living up to its
reputation.

The place was packed and we settled down with a few jugs of
beer until closing time at 22:00 when a loud alarm bell started
ringing and did not stop until everyone had vacated the bar. We
thought this was a pretty uncivilised way of saying 'Time please,
gentlemen,' but it had the desired effect, as no-one could sit
through it for long and you were happy to get out of the place.

We all headed back to the *Westmorland* in various stages of
inebriation and found the bar packed with women and the crews
of other 'home-boats' which were in port. The crew bar stayed
open as long as someone was prepared to man it, and we set up a
roster, but whenever any of the guys on the roster had had
enough and wanted to pack it in, someone was always prepared
to jump in and take over, so it kept ticking along into the wee
hours.

We had no problem finding a partner and most of the crew
were soon paired off with Auckland women for the duration of our
stay in port.

We didn't stray far from down-town Auckland, as that was
where all the action was, with visits to all the seamen's hangouts,
such as the Akarana, De Bretts, Ma Gleason's, the Occidental and
the Queens Ferry in Vulcan Lane and of course the Snake-pit,
which was everyone's favourite watering-hole. It was the venue of
choice for the lunchtime sessions, as it was so close to the ship.

We were also regular visitors to the White Lady pie-cart in
Fort Street for our late-night burgers as we staggered back to the
ship at all hours.

The commodore chief engineer, Frank Kent, had his wife with
him for the trip and she was a lovely lady who always engaged me

in conversation when I was cleaning their accommodation and we had some lengthy chats.

I was staggering along the wharf back to the ship, after one lunch session, in the company of three ship-girls, who were singing and performing and being a bit boisterous, when I looked up at the ship and saw the chief engineer's wife staring down at me from the boat-deck.

She didn't look too impressed, and I was wishing there was somewhere I could crawl into and hide.

She didn't speak to me again for a while and it took a few days for the atmosphere to get anywhere back to normal.

I was serving breakfast one morning after a particularly heavy night on the grog, when I suddenly felt ill and had to dash out to the saloon-deck, where I threw up over the side into the harbour.

The Devonport ferry just happened to be gliding past at that moment, packed with all the office-girls and boys, headed to work in the city, and they really gave me some shit as I hung over the side puking my guts up.

On the final night in Auckland, Ken and I only had $5 between us, just enough for a couple of beers, and as my girlfriend was ashore visiting some mates and not coming back until later that night, and Ken had arranged to see his bird in Ma Gleason's, we headed off up there. The intention was to just have a beer each there and then return to the bar in the ship.

When we reached Ma Gleason's, which was a bit of a dive with all sorts of shady characters hanging out there, we told Ken's girl that we were skint and couldn't afford to buy her a drink, as we only had enough money for a quick drink.

She told us to hang on for a bit, then went to speak to some old guy and disappeared out the door with him. About 20 minutes later she returned, came over to our table and gave Ken $10.

We were blown away but weren't going to look a gift-horse in the mouth, so Ken accepted the money.

We now had enough money to go to the Snake-pit, but she wanted to stay at Gleason's, obviously to earn some more money, so she told us to go to the Pit and she would meet us up there later on.

She couldn't earn money in the Snake-pit, as if you had to pay for it in the Pit there was something wrong with you.

We didn't need to be told twice and were off like a shot, but as soon as we walked in the door of the Pit, two women hit on us and made it very clear that they were really interested in us.

We were in a bit of a bind, as we knew our girls would catch up with us at some stage, but at the same time we didn't want to miss out on the new girls, so we decided to take them back to the ship.

How we ever believed that this was not going to end in disaster is beyond me, but the alcohol must have kicked in to give us a rosy view of proceedings.

When we got back to the ship, I grabbed a key to one of the spare empty cabins in the crew accommodation, and took the new girl in there, as I knew that my girl, who would be returning from ashore, had a key to my cabin, but Ken decided to use his own cabin.

All went well until about midnight, when all hell broke loose down the alleyway as Ken's bird from Gleason's came aboard and was beating on his door. When he finally opened the door, she gave him a hell of a kicking and a right verballing before storming ashore.

We certainly had a lot to learn about the way the Kiwi coast worked.

I managed to sneak the girl I was with ashore and into a taxi in the early hours and next morning made out that I had fallen asleep somewhere when I returned to my cabin before turn-to, but it was obvious that the girl in my cabin knew precisely what had been happening.

She got her own back, as when we departed Auckland that evening, she was waving goodbye from the wharf wearing a brand-new Wrangler jacket and it was only after a couple of days at sea I realised it was my brand-new Wrangler jacket, but I deserved that and more, for the way I had behaved.

The tugs towed *Westmorland* off Queens Wharf and into the stream, where we sat quietly, before we gave three blasts on the ship's horn, the engines kicked in and next stop was Panama.

I really didn't want to leave, as I had such a fantastic time on the Kiwi coast that I could have quite happily turned around and done it all over again, and I was hooked on New Zealand.

The return trip across the Pacific and transit of Panama Canal was uneventful and we called into Curaçao for bunkers, berthing in the capital, Willemstad, but were advised against going ashore due to riots which had been occurring spasmodically throughout the latter part of 1969 to the present.

The city was very picturesque with a mix of old Spanish and Dutch buildings, and we were disappointed not to be able to check out the local bars.

We departed Curaçao early February on course for Liverpool and were about five days out and four days from the UK, when we ran into a massive storm with huge seas which reduced our speed to below five knots and just making steering-way.

The seas were tremendous and threw us all over the place, making it impossible to sleep, as when she rolled, you were either standing on your feet in your bunk, or on your head and when she pitched you were having to hang on to avoid being pitched out of the bunk. When she buried her head in a sea, the vibration as the bow tried to throw off the water and return to the surface made it seem as though you were standing on a springboard.

Subsequently, we were all exhausted and worn out by the constant movement, which overcame any fear of foundering, and although distress messages were being received from ships in trouble, there was not much we could do, as we could barely help ourselves, and anyway, they were too far away for us to offer assistance.

The force of the seas breaking aboard had split the welding where the accommodation joined the main-deck, forrard and the crew mess-room was flooded with water, which spilled down the alleyway, and when the seas abated slightly, it was discovered that there was a big split in the fo'c'sle deck and the forepeak was flooded with tons of water.

Gradually, the storm subsided and we managed to pick up speed but the seas were still quite rough, although compared to what we had just been through, it seemed quite calm. The water in the mess-room gradually escaped through the broken weld, but there was still a couple of inches sloshing across the deck with the roll.

We had crept into the lee of southern Ireland and were receiving television reception on the mess-room TV, although only very grainy and distorted, when I went into the mess-room that night to find some of the lads sitting in a row of chairs, one behind the other down the centre of the mess, watching TV as the water sloshed across the deck with the roll and splashed back from the bulkhead, the middle of the mess-room being the only area they could sit to avoid the splash.

I wish I could have taken a photo, as it looked really comical as they raised their feet in unison to avoid the surge of water, while concentrating on the TV.

We were anchored off the Mersey Bar with four or five other ships, waiting for the tide, and the storm swell was still so strong that when you looked along the line of ships at anchor facing out to the Irish Sea, it looked like the Grand National with the horses taking Becher's Brook, as the ships in unison climbed the waves and fell down the other side.

When we were tied up alongside in Gladstone Dock, huge pumps were put aboard to begin pumping out the fore-peak, and when we left the ship following pay-off, water was cascading over the bow and into the dock, so a serious amount of water had been taken on in the storm.

Leave passed relatively quickly with a few nights out in Chester and Holyhead, but I was without a girlfriend at the time so was looking forward to getting back out to New Zealand.

I received instructions from head office to rejoin the *Westmorland* in Cardiff, and early one morning, met Ken and Pat Carroll, the donkey-man, on Chester Station to catch the train for Cardiff, South Wales.

When we joined *Westmorland*, we found that she was scheduled to do a double-header, on the MANZ run, and would be away about nine or 10 months. We discovered that MANZ stood for Montreal, Australia and New Zealand, and we would do the run twice before returning to the UK.

We also found out that the ship was operating under IDF or Inter-Departmental Flexibility, and the crew would be signing on as general-purpose seamen, which meant that we could be switched from department to department as required, as overall crew numbers had been reduced and IDF meant that the ship could operate with a smaller crew, resulting in reduced running costs.

The reality turned out to be that although the catering crowd worked on deck and in the engine room, the deck crowd and the engine-room crowd never worked in the catering department. This arrangement pissed the deckies off no end, as the catering crowd were taking all their overtime and during the voyage, we worked on deck for two hours every day we were at sea, washing down, chipping, red-leading, painting and greasing, and making good money.

The new format caused quite a bit of friction during the course of the voyage, particularly with the dyed-in-the-wool union guys, who were really not happy with the way things were panning out, but it wasn't down to us, so we just got on with the job.

The *Westmorland* had been berthed adjacent to the coal-berth in Cardiff for a number of weeks and when we climbed aboard, we found she was in a filthy condition, with a thick layer of coal dust everywhere, and cleaning the accommodation was a bit of a challenge.

The captain, mate and chief engineer were all bringing their wives along for at least part of the voyage and they would all leave at various stages of the trip, with the chief engineer's wife being aboard the longest. Frank Kent, the commodore chief engineer, was on his final trip before retiring.

A couple of days after joining, I began to itch down below and upon closer inspection found three itchy lumps on the side of my penis and immediately jumped to the conclusion that I had picked up an STD. I went along to the mate and told him, and he referred me to the doctor at the local Shipping Federation offices.

The doctor took one look at my condition and referred me to the STD clinic at the local hospital and told me to return and see him with the diagnosis when I came back from the hospital. He didn't give me any specific directions to the clinic, so I just turned up at the hospital to find the reception desk manned, totally, by women and not a male in sight. When the lady behind the desk called me forward and asked what was wrong with me, I stammered something about having cut myself on my inner thigh and need to see a doctor. When she tried to get me to be more specific, I just kept stuttering and wishing the ground would open and swallow me. She looked at me in a strange way and must have thought she had a right one here, but eventually gave me a slip of paper and told me to take a seat.

While I was waiting, I spotted a male orderly and immediately approached him and told him I needed to see the pox-doctor. He took me outside and pointed me in the direction of the STD clinic and then returned inside, no doubt to have a good laugh and joke at my expense.

When I got to see the doctor at the clinic, he asked me when the last time I had had sex was, and when I told him that it had been two months previously, in Auckland, New Zealand, he looked puzzled and asked if I was sure.

I told him that I was certain, so he wrote a few things down in his notes, examined me and then told me to get dressed.

I was expecting to be given an injection and a course of tablets but received neither and was just told to soak my penis in a glass of hot, salt water every night. He gave me a letter for the mate and sent me on my way.

I thought that I had better return to the Shipping Federation and let the doctor know what had transpired, so called in there on my way back to the ship, where I approached an attractive young woman behind the counter and asked to see the doctor.

She informed me that the doctor wasn't in, and I was about to leave when some short-arsed little prick came dashing out of a back office and gave me a right verballing, telling me, 'Who the hell do you think you are?' and 'The doctor's a busy man and not at your beck and call.'

He must have thought I was chatting up his office girl or something and she had the grace to look embarrassed at his reaction, but I had had a very stressful morning and was not in the mood to take shit from him.

I asked him whether he knew which ship I was in and when he replied, 'Of course not,' I said, 'Good, go and get fucked then,' and walked out of the shipping office.

As I was returning to the ship, I bumped into the Old Man, John North, and his wife, at the dock gates and I was hoping they had no idea what I was doing ashore in the middle of the day.

I was expecting to be paid off and was dreading the idea of having to return home and make up some excuse for not having sailed in the *Westmorland*, but the mate read the letter from the doctor and told me to get back to work, so I left it at that.

We eventually departed Cardiff for the short trip to Newport, just a few miles up the coast and Newport was such a memorable place to visit that I can't recall a single thing about the place, or even which pubs we drank in.

Fortunately, we were only there for a couple of days before departing for Swansea.

On approach to Swansea, we were forced to make an emergency stop when some dickhead in a sailing dinghy tried to cross ahead of us, only to capsize directly in front of us.

I was in the saloon at the time laying up my table, when the deck began vibrating and all the silverware began bouncing off the table onto the deck, as the ship went full astern to try to avoid the bloke in the water, which we managed to do, although I didn't think he'd be cutting across too many bows in future.

The majority of the crew were the same as the previous trip, with just a couple of changes, while the catering department had only one change and that was the crew mess-man.

He was a little Aussie bloke of about 60 years of age and gay, but he could drink like a fish and was a good laugh to go ashore with. He'd been in all the big ships and knew a lot of famous people, so he had some hilarious stories to tell.

I was officers' steward again, a job that I loved, as it kept me out of the limelight, and Ken was captain's tiger/saloon steward, a job that he didn't relish, particularly as the Old Man's wife was aboard.

She was an attractive woman for her age, being late forties/early fifties, and rumour had it that she had been a top model, which I could believe, as she had the figure and bearing of a model. She always reminded me of the film star Lauren Bacall, as she had the high cheekbones and light hair.

She was always polite and said good morning when she came into the saloon, but as the trip wore on, she and Ken had a few disagreements.

Prior to departing Swansea to go deep sea, we had a bit of a session in the boss's cabin one night which got a bit argumentative but managed to clear the air a bit, as there were still quite a few issues arising from the new IDF regime, which we were trying to come to terms with, and which were causing a few problems.

Bill Battson, the boss, was one of the best, if not the best chief stewards I had sailed with and despite his boyish looks, he didn't let anyone fuck him about and I had seen him stand up to the Old Man, the mate and the chief engineer on many occasions and although he could be one of the boys at times, he ran a well-regulated catering department and would soon pull you into line if you pissed him off.

The deckies were nearly all returnees from last trip who we got on well with and the mates and engineers were a bunch of good blokes that we were to have many a session in the bar with, over the course of the voyage. So *Westmorland* was a very happy ship, apart from me, as she prepared to depart Swansea for the trans-Atlantic voyage to the St Lawrence River and our first port of call, Quebec.

We departed Swansea mid-March and headed out into the North Atlantic, where we were met by a series of spring gales.

Westmorland was fairly light and high out of the water, as she would be loading cargo in Canada and USA, bound for Aussie, and she moved about a fair bit in the weather. The catering department were out on deck every afternoon for two hours, soogeeing (washing down) the accommodation from top to bottom, to get rid of the accumulation of weeks of coal-dust. Seeing the pristine white paintwork emerge from the covering of grime, which gave a great contrast, was a big morale-booster.

The freezing cold water which flowed up the sleeves of our oilskins, from the long Turks-head brushes used to apply the soogee, was uncomfortable but soon forgotten in the comfort of a long, hot shower afterwards.

The bosun told us that he was impressed with our efforts, as he was expecting the job to be a shambles and that he would have to get the deck-crowd to go over the job again, but there was no need for that, as the paintwork gleamed.

I quite enjoyed the work on deck and did not miss my afternoon nap, which is usually how I spent my two-hour afternoon break, as the work was such a contrast to our normal work that it was something of a novelty.

The only unhappy person aboard was a short-arsed Scots guy, Keith from Leith, who was a real union guy and a bit of a 'bush-lawyer', but he wasn't the most popular bloke on board and we tended to ignore his whinging and complaining.

Off the Grand Banks, we were hit by a huge wave from the port-side which pushed us over on the biggest roll to starboard I had ever experienced. We were in the pantry, just completing clean-up for the day and someone shouted 'Hang on' as she went over.

A 20-litre container of Teepol, a type of detergent, had been left on one of the benches and began to slide and like a complete idiot, I let go of whatever I was hanging onto and tried to grab the container. The next minute I found myself slamming into the steel railings around the companionway down to the galley on the deck below and just managed to grab the rail as I went over. I found myself staring at the tiles on the galley deck with the muscles in my arms straining to hang on.

After what seemed to be an eternity, *Westmorland* slowly began to roll back to port and I was able to push myself off the railings, but I was in agony and thought that I had broken both my legs, as I could not walk and collapsed on the deck.

The lads carried me down to my cabin and put me on my bunk and sent for the mate. When he rolled my trouser legs up, there were two huge indents into each of my shin-bones where I had crashed into the railings, but fortunately, they weren't broken. The mate gave me some painkillers and I tried to get some sleep.

Next morning, I found that I could just about hobble around, and as the day wore on, the pain got a little easier.

That night, I had my legs propped up on a chair with cushions, and ice-packs on my shins, while I soaked my dick in a glass of hot, salty water, as per the pox doctor's instructions, when Ken popped in to see how I was doing and I'd forgotten to lock my cabin door.

Ken fell about laughing when he saw me and reckoned it was the funniest thing he'd ever seen. I made him swear that he wouldn't tell anyone, which he promised, but I was on edge whenever we got on the piss and were swapping stories in the bar for the rest of the trip.

I just thought that this trip, which I had such high hopes about, was turning into a nightmare and I was wondering what else could go wrong.

CHAPTER 18

We entered the St Lawrence River, which had only been open for a couple of days to shipping, due to the winter ice, of which there were still huge sheets many miles in length covering the river, and the houses ashore still had deep deposits of snow covering the roofs.

It was very picturesque, with the snow and ice, and the many islands dotting the river, and it was fascinating to watch the *Westmorland* ploughing through these pristine sheets of ice, on her way up river.

We passed one of the Empress boats, of Canadian Pacific Line, ploughing through the ice on her way downriver en route to Liverpool, which was quite a sight, and overtook an Indian ship with a badly twisted bow, which had tried to get through the ice a few days earlier but sustained the severe damage in the process.

We arrived in Quebec, quite late at night and too late to go ashore, and were on our way upriver again early the following morning on our way to Montreal.

The first night in Montreal, a group of us decided to visit the old Expo '67 site where the 1967 Montreal World's Fair was held, as everyone had heard so much about it. The site still operated, with numerous bars and entertainment venues and was a major tourist attraction, with The Dubliners, a well-known Irish band, performing at one of the venues that night.

Following the show, Ken and I decided to head into the city for a few drinks, so we caught a cab up town, to Your Father's Moustache, one of those franchised entertainment venues.

Some of the Abs, including John Garrioch, were caught at the Expo by the cops, lowering all the international flags which flew outside the venue. The Montreal police gave them a ride back to the ship in their police cruisers and even put the lights and sirens on for them, which you can't imagine too many police forces doing.

There wasn't much doing in Your Father's Moustache, so we moved on to a nearby German Beer Hall where the beer was served in big steins and we got talking to a couple of women who were both quite a bit older than us and in their late twenties, early thirties.

They were both friendly and easy to talk to, but in my current condition I wasn't that interested, and just played along to help Ken out.

They turned out to be two nurses from the local hospital, who shared an apartment in town and they both arranged to meet us again in the same venue, the next night.

I wasn't too keen, but again went along to help Ken out, as there was not much else I could do.

We had a good laugh at the beer hall and they invited us back to dinner at their apartment the following evening. I definitely didn't want to go this time, but Ken talked me into it and I reluctantly agreed to accompany him.

They cooked us a huge steak dinner, and following a few drinks, Ken ended up in bed with his partner, while I sat up talking and eventually made my excuses and caught a cab back to the ship.

She must have been thinking I was gay, as although she had not shown any inclination to get me into bed, I was pissed off that I couldn't try.

After a few more nights out and me keeping the relationship purely platonic, the time finally arrived for *Westmorland* to depart Montreal for Halifax, Nova Scotia and New York and I was quite relieved.

Heading down the St Lawrence River, there was nowhere near as much ice present as there had been on the way up, but there was still the odd large sheet about.

Halifax was a bit of a non-event and not much of a run ashore, so we were quite happy to depart for New York.

A day or so later we passed under the Verrazano Bridge at the entrance to New York Harbour and then turned to port, into Kill Van Kull Channel, between Staten Island and New Jersey, into Newark Bay and tied up alongside in Newark Harbour.

We had all been expecting to berth in Manhattan, so it was a bit of a shock to be way out at Newark, which was in New Jersey and a long Port Authority bus ride into Manhattan.

Newark was a huge wasteland of docks, with no facilities, apart from a Seamen's Mission and we were heavily advised against drinking in the town of Newark, due to racial problems.

The first morning in Newark, I was picked up in a huge American car from the agents and taken to the local pox doctors, where he examined me, but didn't prescribe an injection or pills. I told him about the hot salt-water treatment, which he told me to continue with, but didn't seem too convinced of the efficacy of the treatment.

I was getting extremely concerned, as the itch wasn't getting any better, but no-one I had seen seemed to know what was causing it, or appeared to be too worried about it.

The trip into Newark and back was a bit of an eye-opener, as the place was very run-down and depressed and I could see why we had been advised against drinking there, as even without the racial problems, it seemed to be a very dangerous place with a lot of dodgy characters about.

One afternoon, the assistant-cook and I went into Manhattan by bus to buy some stuff to decorate the crew bar and came back with a load of psychedelic posters, which didn't impress some of the older members of the crew, but which turned out to be quite effective when we put them up and the lights were dimmed.

Manhattan was full of shops with gear like that and we could have shopped all day, but it was a good job we didn't bring back some of the more outlandish stuff we came across.

We had a couple of nights out in Manhattan and visited Times Square, but got lost on the way to Greenwich Village, so we very nervously approached a cop to ask for directions and he very kindly escorted us all the way and took us to the door of the NY Your Father's Moustache.

Once inside, a few of us were invited onto the stage to take part in a beer-drinking contest, which the Aussie mess-man off the *Westmorland* won, by downing a glass of beer in just a couple of gulps.

Another night we went for dinner at Jack Dempsey's restaurant and had a great night out.

A dance was held at the Seamen's Mission one night and although some of us went along, more out of curiosity than anything else, you knew you weren't going to get anywhere with these women as they had all been invited along by the padre just for the dancing and to give us some wholesome company.

Departing Newark, we sailed down the coast to Chesapeake

Bay and berthed in Newport News, just across the bay from Norfolk, the big US naval station.

Heading into the Bay we had passed a steady stream of US Navy vessels and transports, all fully loaded and bound for Vietnam, so the deckies were kept busy lowering and raising the ensign at the stern and we came across a Blue Funnel ship outward bound and down on her marks. She was one of the ships built for Silver Line and bought on the stocks, so didn't have the usual Blue Flue silhouette; it was possibly the *Telamon*.

There wasn't too much nightlife in Newport News, and what there was, was packed out with US Navy ratings, as a big carrier was fitting out a couple of docks over from us, so they owned the town.

The junior electrician met one of these navy guys ashore and invited him back to *Westmorland* for drinks and dinner. The poor guy spent all night sat at attention, surrounded by mates and engineers in uniform with gold braid and when the skipper, mate and chief engineer walked into the saloon, he nearly had heart failure.

To top it off, the chef, Dan O'Mahoney, had been on the piss all day and the food was absolute crap. The entrée for that meal was Welsh rarebit and I was embarrassed to serve it as it was so bad.

This bloke must have had a great time regaling his mates back on the carrier with horror stories of the lousy food served in Limey ships.

One great thing about being in the States was the number and the variety of radio stations playing the latest pop music and country & western, and we all looked forward to Thursdays, when the latest records were released on the air.

There were a number of acts that we wouldn't have heard of in the UK and the Top 40 was a who's who of the best bands around at that time, with a fair percentage of British acts included.

From Newport News, we made our way down to Curaçao for bunkers, and berthed at the bunkering berth down the coast from Willemstad, so no run ashore this time either, and then headed to Panama for the canal transit.

Westmorland catering crowd

Crossing the Pacific, the catering crowd were on deck for two hours overtime every afternoon and the bosun gave us the job of chipping the MacGregor hatch-lid section covers. Each folding section of the covers had a small, raised lip on the joint, which was too small to get the head of a windy-hammer into, so we had to use chipping hammers. The head of the hammer only just fitted the space, which made it difficult to get a good blow at it to dislodge the rust and paint, so there were numerous barked knuckles and bruised fingers. It was slow, laborious work in the hot sun of the Equator and by the time we had finally managed to complete every hatch-cover, it was time to start all over again. The very welcome shower at the end of the deck session came as a huge relief.

A couple of weeks run across the Pacific brought us to Brisbane, Australia and we arrived at a time of massive flooding in Queensland. As we headed upriver into Brisbane we were passing the carcasses of drowned sheep and cattle, which were floating out to sea, so it wasn't a great welcoming sight.

The following morning the agent sent a taxi to pick me up and take me to the pox-doctors in the city.

The driver wasn't the most friendly of souls and when I asked him what the name of the river that flowed through Brisbane was called, his reply, 'The fuckin Brisbane River, of course,' killed any further conversation stone dead.

I put his surly demeanour down to the fact that we were headed to the VD clinic, and he probably assumed that I was just another 'Pommie' seaman coming down-under to infect the local sheilas with the clap, so I gave him the benefit of the doubt and tried not to take it personally.

At the hospital, they inspected my member and ummed and ahhed a bit but again no injection or medication was forthcoming, and as I had given up the hot salt-water treatment as useless, I was becoming concerned again, as it had now been a long, long time since I last had sex and although the itch was nowhere near as bad as it had been and the blisters were slowly disappearing, I really needed someone to tell me what I was suffering from and whether it was ever going to clear up.

They referred me to the STD clinic in Sydney which was the next port of call, and the taxi ride back to the ship was long and silent.

I wasn't that impressed with Brisbane, as the city didn't appear to have much soul, but that may have had something to do with the recent flooding and the fact that they were in recovery mode, so I reserved judgement. The fact that I was not actively chasing women, due to my medical condition, may have coloured my view of Brisbane, as I tended to rate ports solely on my success, or lack of, with the opposite sex, so it may not have been a fair assessment.

We arrived in Sydney in pouring rain, which did not let up for the entire time we were there, and as I had always considered Aussie to be the land of eternal sunshine, to say I was underwhelmed would be a bit of an understatement.

The following day, Dave, an AB who was also suffering with some sort of condition, and I were picked up and taken to the clinic by taxi and dropped off, but the driver told us we would have to make our own way back to the ship.

At the clinic I was seen by a specialist and they took some blood, at last. I was terrified of needles but was relieved to find that they were at least taking my problem seriously enough to do some tests to try and confirm what was wrong with me. The specialist told me that he would have the results when we returned to Sydney after we had visited Melbourne, Adelaide and Melbourne again, which would still be a few weeks away, but I had gone this long so a few more weeks should be manageable.

I caught up with Dave in the hospital reception area and we tried to get a cab back to the ship, but it was still pouring down and one thing that we both had to learn about Sydney was the absolute impossibility of finding a taxi when it was raining.

We finally gave up on the taxi and asked someone to point us in the right direction for a bus to Glebe Island. We managed to catch a bus but found that we had to change buses partway through the trip and the instructions we were given were so confusing that we became totally lost, so we did what any self-respecting seaman would have done and found a local pub.

Having given up any chance of returning to work, we settled down for a few beers and after a couple of hours, rang the lads on the ship and asked them to swing by the pub and pick us up when they finished work.

By the time the lads arrived I was well pissed and fell asleep at one of the tables, so they left me there and headed off into town to a night-club.

When one of the barmaids shook me to wake me up, I ended up vomiting all over the table, floor and my trousers, so I was in a bit of a state by the time I finally found my way back to the ship.

When I apologised to the boss, Billy, next morning, for not making it back to work, he told me that he had not expected me back so not to worry about it, which after all the effort we had made to get back didn't sit that well with me, but at least I didn't get logged and lose pay.

The problem was that it had counted as a half day off and I owed the rest of the crowd to cover when they took a half day, so I had that hanging over me.

We swung on the hook for a couple of days off Melbourne, before entering the Yarra River and berthing in the port, and during that couple of days experienced four seasons in one day, as the weather was so changeable and went from one extreme to the other.

When we arrived in Adelaide, we found that Port Adelaide is a long way from Adelaide city so I did not make it into the city and the few who did get there told us we weren't missing too much.

There was a good Seamen's Mission at the port which we made good use of and as I was still not seeking women out, that was fine by me.

Back in Melbourne, on the way back up the coast, I became friends with a heavily pregnant woman I met ashore. There was nothing between us romantically but she was a good laugh and very friendly. She invited me home for meals and to watch television, but definitely wasn't looking for anything else, which, with her in her condition and me in mine, was a good thing and I had a couple of nights off the beer as she couldn't drink, which was a win-win.

I got her shoe size off her and promised to bring her back a pair of boots from the States, which I did and dropped them off to her next time we were in Melbourne.

One of the local seamen's pubs in Melbourne, which was situated just outside the docks, had been taken over by Greeks and they were trying to get rid of the seamen and turn it into a local taverna so we weren't very welcome.

They objected to us singing along to the jukebox and things got a bit tense at times, but we hung in there as there was nowhere else to go that was so handy to the ship and we were spending a fortune, which should have helped, but didn't.

The next time we returned to Melbourne, we weren't allowed in and it had gone totally Greek.

Back in Sydney, I went back to see the specialist at the STD clinic and get the results of my tests. When I went in to see him, the first question he asked me was what brand of washing powder I was using for washing my clothes. When I told him that I used the 'hungry enzyme' powder which was new on the market, he advised me to change back to one of the other washing powders and make sure that I rinsed my underwear thoroughly when I did my laundry.

It appeared that my problem was a skin reaction to the new washing powder, and not a sexually transmitted disease at all.

I didn't know whether to laugh or cry, as on the one hand, I was over the moon to find I hadn't caught it off a woman, but on the other hand, when I thought of all the opportunities I had had to turn down and all the stress it had caused me, it was one of the most traumatic periods of my life.

When I took the results and my clearance back to the mate, he told me that he hadn't been too worried about it, as he had boned up on all his medical books, but couldn't find anything of a similar nature which was a STD.

I just wish he had let me in on that fact and tried to put my mind at rest.

That night I headed up to Monty's Hotel on the Pyrmont Bridge, a famous seaman's hangout with a big circular bar and ships lifebelts all over the walls and also a famous hangout for women of easy virtue.

I had more than a few beers and picked out the easiest woman in the place, but next morning, when I woke up alongside her, I instantly regretted my decision and thought it would be pretty ironic, if after all I had gone through, I picked up a genuine dose of the clap and couldn't believe my stupidity.

Fortunately, nothing of the sort eventuated and when I was sure that I was in the clear, I swore that I was going to be a lot more careful in future and make sure that I used protection on every occasion.

The crew bar was nowhere as busy on the Aussie coast as it was on the Kiwi coast and women were a little harder to get on board. This was probably due to the more extensive nightlife in Sydney and the Aussie ports compared to New Zealand, but overall I preferred the Kiwi coast and the more laid-back atmosphere.

One night, Ken and I came out of Monty's at closing time and were tossing up whether to return to the ship or to go up-town nightclubbing.

We opted to go up-town and spotted a taxi coming along the road so waved for it to pick us up. It was going so fast that when he slammed the brakes on, it was 50 metres past us before it came to a stop. The driver slammed it into reverse and backed up to us, and luckily there was no other traffic about.

We jumped in the cab and told the driver to take us into town, but he took off at such a speed that I was beginning to think we had made a major mistake as his driving was so erratic.

Approaching a set of traffic lights on red, he didn't slow down but drove at speed into the inside lane and we thought he was going to run the lights but just as we got up to the lights they changed to green and he shot through.

Unfortunately, some dude coming from the right tried to beat the red light and slammed into the side of our cab in the middle of the intersection, causing it to roll a couple of times before coming to a halt on its side.

Ken was on the side that was hit and copped most of the impact and he was lying on top of me, knocked out and bleeding all over me.

A group of passers-by pushed the cab over onto its wheels and helped me out and sat me on the kerb while I tried to figure out what had happened.

Technically, it was the fault of the guy who ran the red light but if the taxi-driver hadn't been driving like a maniac, it could have been avoided. When the taxi-driver was talking to the cops, he was sounding like the aggrieved party, which he was, but it still pissed me off.

The driver was unhurt but Ken and I were put in an ambulance and taken to hospital. Despite me protesting that I was not injured and the blood in which I was covered belonged to Ken, the nursing staff insisted on stripping me to examine me.

When the nurses began to take my gear off, they found I was wearing a T-shirt, sweat-shirt, shirt, pullover and jacket and they began to take the piss out of me for wearing so many clothes, but I told them I was used to being in the tropics and despite what everyone had told me, Sydney was fucking cold at night.

After a couple of hours, they discharged me but detained Ken overnight for observation, as he had a big gash on his head, so I returned to the ship in the early hours of the morning and Ken was released from hospital next day but spent a couple of days in his bunk, recovering.

There was some talk of compensation for Ken's injuries but, in the end, nothing came of it.

From Sydney, we sailed up to Brisbane and then departed for the trip across the Pacific back to the States.

On the way, we passed one of our sister ships, *Tongariro*, headed to Australia and both ships altered course slightly to pass a mile or so apart, starboard side to starboard side. She was a magnificent sight as she went flying past and we knew that she was seeing almost a mirror image of *Westmorland* as we passed at a combined speed of around 42 knots. The only difference was that she was ploughing into the sea and throwing up a huge bow-wave, while we had a following sea with relatively little bow-wave, as we watched her gradually disappear astern.

A few days later, we passed Fatu Hiva in the Marquesas to port and sailed quite close in but did not see any signs of life, as there are only a few hundred people living on the island. Still, it was quite a sight to see this island in the middle of nowhere, rising sheer out of the ocean, with steep cliffs dropping down to the sea, where the breakers crashed ashore dramatically.

Hermann Melville was supposed to have jumped ship there in the 1840s before he wrote the novel *Moby Dick*, and I could see the attraction, as it certainly was a beautiful island and a welcome sight on a long sea voyage.

CHAPTER 19

After transiting the Panama Canal, and bunkering in Curaçao, we sailed up the east coast of the States and entered the Delaware River bound for Philadelphia.

We passed Wilmington and approaching Philadelphia, passed under a huge road bridge where dozens of workmen were carrying out maintenance on the underside of the bridge.

As we passed close under the bridge, the workmen all started yelling and wolf-whistling and we wondered what the hell was going on. It turned out that the captain's and mate's wives were sunbathing in bikinis on the monkey-island and the workmen all had a bird's-eye view.

There was a great amount of history in Philadelphia but once again most of us only saw the inside of the local bars adjacent to the docks and I was to, later, much regret missed opportunities to visit some of the famous historical sites and museums.

The first bar we went to, they refused the assistant cook service, as he was still a few weeks shy of his twenty-first birthday and they were pretty strict on it, despite our trying to get them to change their minds, so we moved on to try to find somewhere with a more relaxed attitude.

In one bar, we came across a couple of old guys who had been in the US Army and had fond memories of Liverpool during the Second World War so we had a good session with them. But even here in Philadelphia, there was an undercurrent of racial tension and people warned us to stay out of Black areas, which was a bit sad and an indictment on the United States in 1970.

Shortly after this, when we were again berthed in Newark, Ken and I walked into a bar in Manhattan which was crowded and found that we were the only two white faces in the bar and the atmosphere was a bit tense, but as soon as we ordered a beer and they picked up on our accents, the tension was broken and they began talking to us and we had a good laugh and a few more beers.

From Newark we were calling at Boston so we entered the Cape Cod Canal to take the short cut and avoid having to sail around Martha's Vineyard, Nantucket and Cape Cod.

At 08:00 I was out on the after deck enjoying a cup of coffee and watching us coming up on a small sailboat motoring ahead of us, which we were catching rapidly. The morning was still and peaceful, with not a cloud in the sky and the canal bank to port was lined with a thick forest of pine trees.

Suddenly, the *Westmorland* gave three long blasts on the horn to let the bloke in the sailboat know we were about to pass, and the banks of the canal came alive with people appearing out of the forest to see what was going on and the source of the noise.

A good many of the crowd on the canal bank were young women in shorts and bikini tops so the rest of the crew were soon out on deck to wave and yell as we passed.

It turned out that there was a huge campground in among the trees and as this was the height of the holiday season, it was packed.

Sailing into Boston, I saw my first Boeing 747 airliner approaching Logan International Airport to land and was blown away by the size and the majesty of the aircraft as it touched down.

We ended up berthed in the heart of Boston and once again the history, the sites and the buildings were amazing. Everywhere we went, we saw places of interest and tried to get around some of the beautiful parks in addition to the bars.

I did regret not getting over to the USS *Constitution* and the museum, as we had heard so much about it, but I did make some effort to see the sights.

The next port of call was Montreal, and Ken had been keeping in touch with his Canadian nurse, so we arranged to catch up with them again and met in the bar where we had first seen them, and then they invited us back to their apartment for the night.

My girl must have wondered what the hell had happened to me since I was last in Montreal, as I was all over her and although we slept in the same bed, she resisted my frenzied advances in no uncertain terms, and I was very frustrated on my return to the ship next morning.

We were in Montreal for quite a lengthy period and hosted a reception and dinner for the shippers one evening. The catering crowd weren't too pleased about this as it meant no shore leave that night, but the reception was fairly memorable for the variety of cheeses and wines on offer, a fair amount of which we consumed at the end of the evening.

The next scheduled stop was to be Three Rivers, which was just a few hours downriver from Montreal and when our nurses found out, they offered to come with us and then hitchhike back to Montreal.

I wasn't too sure about this, as there didn't appear to be much in it for me, apart from getting in the shit if caught, as she was still not putting out for me, although Ken was doing alright and getting more than his fair share from his girl.

Looking back, I feel that the main issue getting in the way of our relationship was the big difference in our ages and although it didn't bother me, I think she had some concerns.

Anyway, sailing day arrived and I let Ken and the girls overcome my concerns so we brought both of them aboard and settled them in my cabin.

Just prior to departing Montreal, I stepped out of the galley on my way to check up on the girls, just as the 3rd mate was about to put his pass-key in my cabin door on crew inspection. I just about had heart failure but managed to say, 'It's okay third, I'm aboard,' and he withdrew the key and moved on to the next cabin.

When we finished work for the day, we brought the girls dinner to the cabin, and had a few drinks, then Ken took his girl to his cabin and I turned in with my girl, where she finally took pity on me and gave in.

I'd like to say it was well worth waiting for, but I don't recall much about it so it couldn't have been that memorable.

There was the possibility that I had other things on my mind, as I lay awake, worrying about a possible change of orders during the night, which would have had dire consequences, as if we didn't stop at Three Rivers, the next port of call was Newark and I didn't think the girls would be too pleased about that.

Not only would it be a much longer hike, but the girls would have to cross the US/Canadian border and I wouldn't have thought that they had their passports with them.

When I awoke next morning, I was relieved to find the engines silent and *Westmorland* tied up alongside in Three Rivers.

That afternoon, we escorted them ashore, telling anyone who saw us that the girls had come down by bus to see us, and said our goodbyes, as they started hitchhiking back to Montreal.

We expressed our concern about them hitching lifts and offered to pay their bus fares, which was cheap enough, but they insisted that that was the way they got around Canada and everything would be fine.

That was the last I saw or heard from my girlfriend, as we didn't write and I didn't make it back to Montreal again.

It was a different matter for Ken, however, as his girlfriend turned up on his doorstep in Holyhead a few years later, having decided on a change of career and becoming a marine engineer on a ship which came into Liverpool, where she tracked Ken down.

I don't think that his then wife was too impressed, but you had to give this girl top marks for perseverance.

We were only in Three Rivers for the day, so only saw the local bar, and then we were off downriver headed to Newark.

I didn't make it into Manhattan on this visit, but we did get invited to a party in a local suburb of Newark, at the home of an ex-British seaman and his American wife.

It was our final night in Newark, as we were sailing in the early hours of the next morning, and as luck would have it, I met an attractive nurse at the party and was making headway.

The lights in the room were fairly dim and everyone was fairly pissed, so this nurse and I were lying on the floor behind the couch making out, when the hosts' three-year-old daughter, who should have been in bed, came around the couch and sat on the floor staring at us.

That put paid to any further amorous advances, but she gave me her telephone number and I told her I would call her from Newport News in a couple of days.

When I got back to the ship, I offered the wharfies a bottle of scotch to go on strike for the day, so that I could see her again, but they thought I was joking. I was, but only half.

When we arrived in Newport News, I went ashore and found

a public phone box and called her. We had a long conversation, but the operator kept butting in every few minutes telling me to insert more coins and the call ended up costing me a small fortune by the time I had finished.

We exchanged a couple of letters, but the fact that I would not be back in the States for the foreseeable future, and that the Aussie and Kiwi coasts were on the horizon, meant that things just drifted to a close.

From Newport News we sailed down the coast to Charleston, South Carolina, where we tied up at the bottom of a main street, which viewed through the trees looked just like a street out of the movies, about old southern towns. We had arrived in the early hours of the morning and were due to sail at lunchtime so we did not get the opportunity to explore, but it looked a very picturesque and interesting place.

Heading downriver out to sea, we passed creeks and bays filled with hundreds of mothballed navy ships and transports from the Second World War.

Leaving the States for the final time, we bunkered at Curaçao again and then through the canal and across the Pacific to arrive in Brisbane for the last time on this trip.

I never had any luck with the women in Brisbane, until the final night, which was a Friday night, and we were scheduled to depart at midnight, with shore leave expiring at 23:00.

We decided that there was no point in going nightclubbing, so a group of us arranged to meet in one of the pubs in the CBD after work, for a few beers.

When Ken and I went ashore, after work, the ABs had already been there for a while and we joined them to make a party of about seven around one of the tables. We were having a laugh with the barmaids, who were taking the piss out of the way we pronounced 'jug' as in jug of beer and just keeping to ourselves as we knew there was no point in chatting up women if we were leaving that night.

It being a Friday night, there were many groups of office girls enjoying Friday-night drinks, but relatively few males in the place, so the women kept sending over invitations to join their groups, which we just ignored, as we didn't see the point.

As the night wore on and we became more inebriated, we finally got around to joining some of these groups of women and pairing off with some of them. By the end of the night, I found myself with one of these women in the ladies' toilet and she was all for having sex in one of the cubicles. The only thing that saved me was that I was not quite so drunk that I could bring myself to have sex, while other women were constantly coming and going in and out of the loo.

Ten o'clock closing finally prevented me making a fool of myself in an embarrassing situation and it was time to leave. As I was leaving the toilet, I had to step over one of the ABs and his woman who were lying on the floor outside the toilet, but fortunately they were both fully clothed.

The taxi dropped us off at the docks and we made our way across some railway lines to the concrete wharf opposite the ship. The wharf was about chest height and there were access steps up to it but they were a fair distance away on either side of where we had been dropped off and we couldn't be bothered walking the distance to use the steps.

We decided to run at it from a few metres away and attempt to jump up at it. Unfortunately, I was so pissed that I just kept bouncing off the wharf back onto my arse and in the end, after a few attempts, the lads decided to haul me up onto the wharf by my arms.

When I woke up next morning, I was wondering where I had

got all these scrape marks across my belly and down my legs, until it slowly came back to me.

Brisbane, which up to that point I had not been very impressed with, had been saving the best for last and shown what a good run ashore it could have been.

Sydney had warmed up a bit since we were last there and the weather was much more like you would expect Aussie weather to be and it was a much more pleasurable experience this time around, without the constant rain.

We were still having women stay the night on board and getting away with it most of the time, but there was the occasional slip-up.

We were storing the ship one morning and I was partway up the accommodation ladder with a case of stores on my shoulder when the mate came dashing out of the crew cross-alleyway, leant over the side and yelled, 'Saul! There are two women in your cabin. Get them off this ship immediately.'

Well, I knew there was one woman in my cabin, but I had forgotten about inspection, and Ken had dumped his girlfriend in my cabin, to keep my girlfriend company, while inspection was taking place. I wasn't too concerned about it but the inconvenience of having to call a taxi and escort them off the ship annoyed me somewhat, especially as the wharfies were all having a laugh at my expense and the sheer hypocrisy of the situation pissed me off.

I was up in the officers' accommodation about 30 minutes later when I overheard the mate dictating a shopping list to the junior electrician's girlfriend, who had obviously slept aboard all night, as she was still wearing the same clothes from the night before, when dining in the saloon.

It pissed me off that even in the seventies, mates' and engineers' women were classed as girlfriends, even if they had been picked up in the crew-bar, but crew women were classed as ship-girls, no matter how respectable they were.

Officers' women could come and go as they pleased and dine in the saloon, but crew women had to be sneaked about the ship, even though everyone knew they were aboard, and if they had a meal, you had to forego your meal.

I practically lived on cheese rolls.

When we berthed in Melbourne, we found that there was some sort of problem with the rubbish disposal service and were obliged to stack the black plastic rubbish sacks on the port-side after deck.

What started out as a couple of sacks gradually grew into a mini-mountain of rubbish during the time we were alongside and the stench was horrendous, along with the swarms of flies which were attracted to it.

I was amazed that the wharfies did not walk off the job in protest at having to work cargo adjacent to a rotting pile of rubbish sacks.

Upon departing Melbourne, as soon as the deckies came off stand-by, the first job they were given was heaving all these sacks of rubbish over the side and many of the sacks were thrown overboard before we had even made our way out of Port Philip Bay.

I imagine that they would have all ended up washed ashore all along the Australian coast as very few of them were heavy enough to sink, but they were no longer our problem and we were happy to see the last of them. It was good to have the rubbish gone, along with the swarms of flies, and have the decks hosed down and back to normal.

I'd caught up with my pregnant friend, who was no longer pregnant and had a beautiful daughter but still no man in her life. I gave her the boots I had bought for her in the States. The relationship was still purely platonic and we were both happy with that.

It was about this time that Ken began to get himself offside with the captain over various little failings which gradually accumulated and grew to a head over time.

One of these incidents involved the captain's wife, who came into the saloon alone one lunchtime, due to the fact that the ship was entering a port and everyone was on stand-by.

Ken and I were standing at our dumb-waiters at the pantry end of the saloon, which had glass-mirrored bulkheads on both sides of the pantry door.

Ken stepped forward to pull out her chair and as she was taking her seat and he was pushing the chair in, he began making faces behind her back, trying to amuse me.

I could see out of the corner of my eye that she was looking directly into the mirror at Ken and could see everything he was doing, so I continued to stare straight ahead and ignored him.

When he went to take her order from the menu, I shot into the pantry ahead of him and when he entered the pantry, I told him that she had been watching everything.

He just said, 'Oh shit!'

She must have told Captain North, because Ken said that the atmosphere in the captain's cabin was decidedly frosty, next time he went up there.

The mate's wife had flown home and the captain's wife was due to fly home from Auckland, leaving the chief engineer's wife as the only woman on board after that.

Again, I didn't bother going into the city of Adelaide, as it was too far from the port, and just hung around the mission and bar at the port.

We left Adelaide, bound for Whangarei in Northland, New

Zealand and after a four-day passage, tied up alongside in Port Whangarei, which was a little distance from the town.

The junior electrician hired a car for a couple of days, and Ken and I and a couple of the ABs agreed to share some of the cost in exchange for being given lifts. However, on the first trip out we did, Ken and the two ABs bailed out at a party that we called at and decided to stay.

I was invited to stay as well but felt sorry for the junior electrician, who was left in the lurch, so I opted to put some money in for gas and stay with him.

Things turned to shit, however, when he expected me to pay half of the cost of the car, now that the other three had bailed out, despite me only doing the odd trip with him and not having use of the car.

We picked up some nurses from the nurses' home, but when the girl that I was with found out I was crew and not on the upper deck, she didn't want to know and insisted on rejoining her sisters up in 'officer country'.

After that, I tended to hang out at The Settlers Hotel, the only handy watering hole in town, but it was rather dangerous, due to the number of under-age girls hanging around so you had to be very careful.

I was quite happy to depart Whangarei and sail down to Auckland, and back to the real action of The Snakepit, The Akarana and Ma Gleason's and the home-boats crew bars, which were all pumping.

From Auckland, it was around the east coast to Napier, where the wharfies threatened to go on strike if we didn't stop encouraging their wives and daughters to come back to the ship and drink in the crew bar.

There wasn't a lot going on in Napier at that time so the crew bar on the *Westmorland* was an extremely popular place for the females and we were making the most of it.

As we had now been away for over eight months, with no time off, other than a half-day on the Aussie coast, the boss, Bill Battson, told the catering crowd that he would allow us all to have a weekend off in turn so we drew straws for the honour.

Mine came out first, so I decided to head off to New Plymouth for the weekend to see my girlfriend from the previous trip. Unfortunately, being such short notice, all flights from Napier to New Plymouth were fully booked, so I had to go by train.

Had I known what the journey by rail entailed, I would not have bothered, but it didn't look too far on the map so I bought the tickets.

I left the ship at 06:30 Saturday morning and went by taxi to the railway station. The cab driver had seemed like a friendly enough bloke and was chatting away quite happily until we pulled up at the station and I handed him a $20 bill for the, admittedly, short trip.

He went ballistic and accused me of taking all his change, so I had to go into the station and purchase something from the kiosk, where I got the same reaction. I hadn't realised that $20 was such a huge amount of money, but apparently it was.

The next shock was when the train pulled in and I climbed aboard to find that it was narrow-gauge and like something out of the Wild West. Being narrow-gauge, it never got above 70–80 kilometres per hour and the trip took ages. We had to change at Palmerston North and finally pulled into New Plymouth late Saturday afternoon.

By the time we had a Saturday night out and a bit of a walk around New Plymouth on Sunday morning, it was time to repeat the whole trip over again and I finally got back to the ship late

Sunday night, wishing that I hadn't bothered and regretting my wasted weekend.

While we were in Napier, a presentation of a silver salver and a set of glasses was made, on behalf of the crew, to the Commodore Chief Engineer Frank Kent, who was retiring at the end of the voyage.

The presentation took place in the officers' bar and a bouquet of flowers was presented to his wife by the youngest member of the crew, Junior Ordinary Seaman John Bradley.

In Napier, we loaded a small deck cargo of wool bales, destined for Lyttelton, which the catering department were given the task of securing on the fore-deck, under the supervision of the bosun, Hugh McLean.

We tommed the bales off and secured them with wire ropes which were tightened with bottle-screws. The bosun checked our work and declared the wool bales secure before fetching the mate, Mike Hill, to inspect our handiwork. He told us that we had done a good job and that the cargo was as secure as it could be.

We departed Napier that evening and although the trip down to Lyttelton was fine, with smooth seas, the deck cargo, mysteriously, managed to come adrift as someone had slackened off the bottle-screws.

Everyone knew it had to have been Keith from Leith, the rabid union guy, but it couldn't be proven and as no damage was done due to the smooth passage, no-one cared too much.

CHAPTER 20

By this stage of the voyage, we had proven that we could do the deck-work we were given to do and do it to a high standard. Despite only being given the mundane jobs of soogeeing, chipping, red-leading, painting, greasing and preparing mooring ropes, we did it to a reasonably high standard and the bosun and mate were more than satisfied with our efforts.

In addition, the galley-boy and the pantry-boy were both going for their steering-tickets and spent hours on the wheel most afternoons at sea and appeared to be making a good fist of it.

It was about this time that Ken finally sealed his fate with the Old Man and transgressed once too often.

He had taken the Old Man his morning tea and then commenced to vacuum the captain's day-room, but following a very heavy session on the piss the night before, made the fatal mistake of sitting down in the captain's easy chair and fell asleep with the vacuum cleaner running.

When Captain North woke Ken up, he finally decided that he had had enough and got the boss to 'demote' Ken to mess-man and 'promote' me to tiger.

To say that I was totally pissed off would be an understatement, as it meant that I was now at the Old Man's beck and call and required to do late lunches whenever the agent or friends of the skipper were aboard, while Ken swanned about in jeans and T-shirt all day and spent most of the day in the crew bar.

The nightwatchmen even cleaned the mess for him every night, so he had it sweet.

On the last night in Lyttelton, before departing for Picton, I ended up on the piss in the British Hotel with the crowd off the Shaw Savill boat *Carnatic* and forgot about the time, with the result that the agent had to come and get me out of the hotel and return me to the *Westmorland*, just prior to sailing.

The mate and the chief steward weren't too happy with me, so I copped a bollocking off each of them but, fortunately, no logging.

Picton was to be our final port of call on the Kiwi coast before heading for home, and back in 1970 it was a fairly quiet place, with not much happening apart from the daily ferry arrivals and not much in the way of exciting watering holes ashore.

Ken's girl came down from New Plymouth and booked into a motel ashore, and a girl I knew from Wellington came across on the ferry to spend a couple of days and there was quite a procession of women arriving on the ferry from Wellington to spend some final time with their men prior to *Westmorland* sailing deep sea.

We were just topping off a full cargo of frozen lamb destined for the UK and the frozen lamb carcasses were level with the hatch coaming, when Ken and I decided that we would like to take one home with us.

We approached one of the wharfies, who was standing on top of the cargo and stacking the lamb neatly, and before we had even finished the request, he tossed one of the frozen carcasses over the hatch coaming to land at our feet.

We both shit ourselves, as we had not checked whether the coast was clear and where the mates were. Ken grabbed the lamb and dashed along the deck, heading for the companionway to the galley freezer and just as he got there the 2nd mate appeared from around the forward accommodation.

Ken flung the lamb down the hatch, without checking to see whether anyone was down there and fortunately there wasn't, otherwise we would have had two bodies to hide in the freezer.

The 2nd mate hadn't spotted us, so we put the lamb in the freezer and agreed with the assistant cook to split the carcass three ways if he would butcher it for us.

He made up three nice-sized parcels and with it being the middle of winter when we paid off in London, we had no problem keeping it frozen until we eventually got home.

Mum was delighted, although I had to tell her I had bought it, otherwise she wouldn't have touched it, but in the end, it seemed like a lot of effort to go to, just for a bit of frozen meat, and I was never tempted to repeat the process.

When we finally departed Picton for the UK, we knew we were cutting it fine to make it home for Xmas, but we were all hoping that we would be able to make up some time to get there before the festivities were over.

Since we had experienced those North Atlantic gales in March en route to Montreal from Swansea, the weather had been fine and the seas smooth and calm, and any sort of sea-way was just a distant memory. So much so, in fact, that rough weather procedures had been largely forgotten, and one night, on the run between Curaçao and London, I took the Old Man's supper tray up to his cabin without damping down the tray napkin, and to make matters worse, I placed the tray on a hard surface.

During the night, we ran into a forecast storm and the result

was a right mess the next morning when I went to clear the supper
tray away.

John North was not happy with me, but since I hadn't wanted
to be tiger in the first place, I wasn't that concerned, but I was
pissed off at my lack of foresight, as I had known the storm was
imminent and should have prepared for it.

The Old Man must have been going through the crew
discharge books in preparation for voyage reports and had noticed
that I had been trapped in the Great Bitter Lakes during the 1967
Six Day War. He asked me to write an article for the company
magazine, *Crossed Flags*, on my experiences in the canal, which I
agreed to do and managed to complete the article prior to docking
in London.

The article appeared in the May 1971 edition of the magazine,
and although I had promised to provide some photographs, when I
got home, I couldn't be bothered to trawl through my vast
collection of photos, so I didn't bother and the article was
illustrated with a couple of hand-drawn pictures by someone from
head office.

Xmas Day morning found us racing up the channel to make
the tide at the Royal Docks that night and we passed numerous
Scandinavian ships steaming down channel, outward bound and
sporting Xmas trees at the fore-mast.

We couldn't help feeling sorry for them, as the mood aboard
those ships would have been fairly bleak and depressed, but we
were so looking forward to the end of the trip that we weren't the
least interested in Xmas Day festivities and hardly celebrated
Xmas lunch.

Dinner time found us sailing up the Thames, approaching the
Royal Docks, so with everyone on stand-by, dinner was a bit of a
hit-and-miss affair and we tried to get it out of the way as swiftly as
possible, as most of us had bigger things than dinner on our minds.

Locking in to the Albert Dock from the river, a line of cars were waiting at the swing bridge over the lock for us to pass through and a group of young women in one car were swigging out of bottles, while dancing on the road to the car-radio. They gave us a great welcome home, and it was at that point that it hit home that we had missed Xmas after all, as by the time we could get ashore that night or home the following day, Xmas celebrations were effectively over, so we would have to settle for New Year.

By the time we had managed to clear customs, we just had time to get to the Connaught for the final couple of pints before they closed for the night. There was talk of us catching the train to the West End, but fortunately we had only had a couple of pints so common sense prevailed. We continued on board with a few cans, but the atmosphere was lacking and we had had a long day, so most of us hit the sack early.

Billy Battson, the boss, had told Ken and I that he would have either of us back for another trip, but would never have the two of us together again. He reckoned that if one of us was in trouble then the other one wasn't far behind.

Neither Ken nor I was intending to come back as it had been a long trip and we were in need of a break, but I was soon regretting that decision after only a few days at home, as I was soon missing the *Westmorland*.

The following morning, we paid off and caught the train at Euston to Chester and Holyhead. Unfortunately, with it being Boxing Day, rail services were severely curtailed and the train we boarded at Euston was absolutely jam-packed and we couldn't get a seat, so we were stuck in the corridor with our baggage.

The toilets were overflowing before we even left Euston and the train stopped at every station on the way, so it was a long and tedious journey.

Getting home was a bit of an anticlimax, as once I had caught up with everyone, it was into the old routine of down the local every night, which soon got old. We had accumulated 52 days' leave, which was a substantial amount and a long time to make our pay-off spin out.

I started doing some nights at the pub, for my mate Dennis, to earn some beer money and spent some time in Holyhead catching up with Ken, but he had a new woman in his life and I began to get the vibes that I was not welcome, as I was encouraging him to get on the piss with me and she didn't like it at all.

Going back too soon off leave meant you were paying additional tax so I wasn't too keen on that, but Ken had soon run out of money and with still a couple of weeks of leave left, he decided to apply to head office for another ship.

I lost touch with Ken for a few weeks after that and didn't think we would be sailing together again.

I was sitting in my local one evening, when the lady who ran the off-licence came through to the bar to tell me that there was a telephone call for me. As I didn't know anyone who had a telephone and no-one, apart from my parents, knew I was at the pub, I was wondering who the hell could be wanting me on the phone at that time of night.

I followed the lady through to the off-licence area and picked up the phone to find Ken on the other end. He was coasting *Dorset* and had rung me to tell me that there was a vacancy for an assistant steward become available and that I should telephone Mr Larsen at the Royal Docks first thing in the morning.

I asked Ken what *Dorset* was like and his reply, that she was 'chatty but happy', meaning that she wasn't much to look at but the crew were a happy bunch, was to haunt me for the next four months.

I put the phone down and went back to my beer and first thing the following morning I went to the public telephone box across the road from Mum's and put a call through to head office in London.

When Mr Larsen came on the line, I told him that I had heard that there was a vacancy aboard the *Dorset*, and that I was willing to take it.

He asked me if I could get to Avonmouth by that evening, as she was sailing the following day and I replied that I was sure that I could, so he told me to join her as soon as possible and that I would be reimbursed the rail fare when I signed on.

I ran home and threw some gear into my suitcase and then caught the bus into Chester to purchase a few things I needed and then called at the railway station to check up on train timetables. I established that a train left Chester at 14:30 for Birmingham New Street, where I changed for Bristol Temple Meads and then changed again for Avonmouth.

I purchased the tickets and then called into the Dee Miller on the way home to say goodbye and let them know that I wouldn't be available to cover the bar any more, for a while.

I made my farewells to the family and caught a cab to the station, where I began the disjointed journey down to Avonmouth, arriving at about 20:30.

I caught a cab to *Dorset* and hauled my bags aboard, to be met by Ken, who took me to the chief steward, where I signed on and had my rail fare reimbursed and up to this point everyone seemed friendly enough and it appeared that I had made a good choice in joining.

Ken and I then dashed ashore to the Royal Hotel, just outside the dock gates, just in time for last orders and met up with the 2nd steward and some of the galley-staff, who all seemed happy and friendly enough so I was beginning to relax and enjoy myself.

Dorset was a 10,000-ton, single-screw vessel with a service speed of 16 knots, built in 1949 and beginning to show her age.

SS *Dorset* (Credit: Chris Howell)

The crowd were mainly a mix of Londoners, South Welshmen and Stornowegians, with Ken being the only North Welshman and me being the token Scouser, and if I thought that I had a bit of an alcohol problem, it was nothing compared to some of this mob, especially the greasers and firemen, who were to prove particularly adept at putting the grog away.

Ken and I shared a huge double-berth cabin, adjacent to the crew-bar, which was to cause a few issues further down the track, and the third assistant steward, Cyril from Swansea, had another double-berth cabin to himself.

There was a distinct mark on the bulkhead outside our cabin, which, apparently, had been caused by a racehorse carried on a previous trip.

The story was that a racehorse was being carried on the

after-deck, when *Dorset* ran into a huge storm and the horse was in danger of being swept away, so it was brought into the alleyway from the deck and stabled there until the storm died away.

The following morning, I turned to and completed my mornings work, but as I had been in such a hurry to join the ship the previous day, I had not had time for a haircut and I needed one badly.

Come morning 'smoko' I approached the boss and asked him if it would be okay if I nipped ashore for a few minutes to get my hair cut, which, in view of the effort I had made in joining the ship, I considered to be a reasonable request.

I was totally unprepared for his response, where he accused me of using the haircut as an excuse to call at the pub and have a few beers and spent the next few minutes ranting and raving about how he was not going to let me put one over on him and he had come across my type before, who were more interested in drinking than working.

Well, he may have been right about that, but in this instance, I genuinely needed a haircut and when I pointed out that if there wasn't someone on board who cut hair, then, by the time we got to New Zealand, I would be a right sight.

He very reluctantly agreed to let me go, but advised that he would be timing me and that I had better not call at the pub, or be late back to the ship, as we were due to sail shortly after lunch.

When I got back from the run ashore, I told Ken about the weird reaction of the chief steward and he told me that he had omitted to tell me about how the vacancy had occurred in the first place.

The assistant steward whose place I had taken had been leaning on the rail when he saw the chief steward coming up the gangway on joining the ship and had turned to Ken and said, 'I ain't sailing with that fucker,' packed his bags and walked off the ship.

The chief steward was 29 years of age, which was a young age to have made boss, and came from the passenger ships, the *Rangitoto, Rangitane* and *Ruahine*, and probably felt that a cargo ship was a bit of a come-down for him.

He was from Essex and so far up himself, he used to walk around wearing sunglasses even when it was pissing down with rain.

He'd only done a couple of trips as boss and was obviously out to make a name for himself, never mixed with the crew, only officers, and during the course of the trip the catering crowd came to detest him.

His 2nd steward was a Glaswegian, John Cuthbertson, who was a good guy but never stood a chance with this prick and by the end of the trip we had grown to dislike him as well, but he was only doing what he had to, so we shouldn't have blamed him for the crap that went down.

The crew had recently been reduced in size and the catering department lost an assistant steward and a boy-rating, and in order to enable us to cope with the reduced numbers, the company no longer required us to carry out scrub-outs of alleyways or any accommodation decks and had put on board a large quantity of squeegee-mops to speed up the operation.

We departed Avonmouth mid-afternoon and were no sooner out into the Bristol Channel than the chief steward collected all the squeegee-mops from the storeroom, tossed them over the side and told us that we would be doing scrub-outs in the traditional manner.

To a degree, I agreed with him, as I thought mops were a waste of time and only spread the dirt around and much preferred to scrub out, as it was the only way I knew, but the problem was that we simply didn't have the time on top of the rest of the work.

Ken, who was saloon-bobby, simply ignored him and continued to wash the saloon deck with a cloth wrapped around a broom-head for the remainder of the voyage, which drove the boss mad, but he couldn't do much, as the company had set the rules.

I compromised, and did a different part of my alleyway, each day, by scrub-out and the rest with a damp cloth, to speed things up, but it still drove this nut-case wild.

The 2nd steward had strict instructions to check that we had turned to and were on the job by 06:00 every morning and so every single morning for the remainder of the trip, the 2nd steward's head would peep over a companionway or peer around a corner of an alleyway to check that we were on the job and we would each give him a little wave, to acknowledge that if we were to be treated as children, we could act like children.

The atmosphere aboard this ship was decidedly weird and did not bode well for the future.

The deck crowd were mainly Stornowegians from the Outer Hebrides and all appeared to be related to one another in some way or other and there were some real strange ones among them. They weren't a particularly friendly bunch and tended to stick to themselves, which was fine by me, as I couldn't understand a fucking word they said. When they spoke to me, I just smiled and nodded my head and hoped for the best.

More than one of them referred to me as 'that Scouse bastard'.

One night in the crew bar prior to arriving Curaçao, the bosun, who turned out to be gay and was rumoured to be having it off with the mate, got into a fight with one of his ABs and lost badly, so that was the end of any discipline on deck and the trip just spiralled down to new depths.

By now I was beginning to curse Ken for telephoning me and

getting me into what was rapidly degenerating into the 'voyage from hell' and the behaviour of the boss was becoming more and more extreme. He never, ever held a normal conversation with any of us, and was forever demanding greater effort or picking us to pieces over minor shit and it was getting harder and harder to resist hauling off and belting him whenever he addressed me.

His three assistant stewards may not have been perfect, but we were all excellent workers who were good at what we did and compared to the rest of the crowd, he just didn't realise how lucky he was.

Our first port of call in New Zealand was Mount Maunganui in the Bay of Plenty and we arrived early evening, just after dinner.

After clearing Customs, we asked the boss for a sub so that we could go ashore for the first time since departing the UK.

Despite having the New Zealand currency on board, delivered by the agent, he refused us a sub and told us we would have to wait until the following day, which really pissed us off, so, as I had a couple of pound sterling left over from the UK, the three of us went ashore to the bar just outside the wharf gate and had a couple of beers anyway, despite losing out heavily on the exchange rate.

Back in the day, Mount Maunganui wasn't the large, modern, busy port that it is today and *Dorset* was the only ship in port, so there were no ship-girls hanging around the pub, and it was pretty quiet and the pub was deserted apart from us.

Mount Maunganui was a popular holiday destination for Kiwis and we were told that at the height of summer, the beaches and bars were packed with young people, sunbathing and partying, and meeting women wasn't a problem.

However, summer was coming to a close and the beaches and town were now mostly empty and deserted, despite the weather still being sunny and warm.

There was another bar in town, apparently, but we never came across it and continued to hang out at the wharfies pub, the Anchor Inn, in the hope that women would turn up eventually, but all we ever saw in there were wharfies, surprisingly.

The boss had talked us stewards into purchasing the last dozen short-sleeved officer-style shirts, with the shoulder epaulettes, from the slop-chest, by assuring us that they were legitimate catering uniforms, that we would be permitted to wear on any ship in the future.

They were much easier to use than the white mess-jackets that we currently wore, as they only required washing and ironing and not starching, so we were happy to purchase them but subsequently found that, other than aboard the *Dorset*, we were not permitted to wear them, as people confused us with junior officers.

On Sundays, the wharf was closed and the public were permitted access, to stroll and view the ships, and as *Dorset* was still the only foreign-going ship alongside, the crew bar was particularly busy, as the shore-side pubs and bars were closed on Sundays.

The only problem was that no-one had taken the trouble to decorate the bar and it wasn't very inviting, being just a bare room with a rudimentary bar tucked in one corner, and the usual assortment of alcoholics scattered about the place, mumbling to themselves and making it pretty difficult for the rest of us to impress and chat up women.

Compared to the *Westmorland*, the atmosphere among the crew was abysmal, as none of the departments mixed with one another and there were a few fights.

The engine-room crowd were a bunch of real pissheads and two of them got into a fight when one guy climbed out of his bunk in the middle of the night and pissed in his cabin-mate's boots.

The chief cook fell asleep while smoking one night and set his mattress on fire and was lucky not to have suffered more serious burns than he did and the accommodation stank for days with the smell of burnt foam rubber.

All in all, *Dorset* was not the happiest ship I'd ever been in, and the chief steward's malignant presence just made matters worse.

CHAPTER 21

From Mount Maunganui we steamed down the east coast around to Wellington and looked forward to catching up with some of our old flames.

The first night ashore was the early part of the week, either a Monday or a Tuesday, and pretty quiet around town, so we ended up at the Royal Oak, in the bistro bar. There were not too many people in the bar and a group of us were drinking around one of the leaners and thinking about heading back to the ship, when I glanced across the room and caught the eye of a very attractive young woman who was drinking with another group of people.

She smiled at me and nodded but I didn't have the balls to go across and talk to her so just kept drinking with the lads.

A couple of the blokes in the group she was drinking with were big Māori boys, who were wearing motorcycle gang regalia and looked like bad-asses, and when one of them left the group and came over to talk to me I thought he was going to have me on for trying to get off with his girl, but all he said to me was, 'Hey bro, that girl fancies you,' and went back to the group.

I decided to go over and introduce myself and got talking to

her and she told me that she had to go to work and would I like to
go with her.

I began wondering what sort of work she would be starting this
late at night and figured that she must be a nurse or work on hotel
reception, or something similar, so I agreed to go with her.

I went back and told the lads, who told me that she was setting
me up and I was going to be robbed when I set foot outside the bar,
but she was so hot that I was quite willing to take the risk.

I gave my wallet and watch to Ken for safekeeping but took $5
and put it in my pocket for taxi fare and took off out of the bar
with her.

She still hadn't told me what she did for a living, but we
headed off down Cuba Street and walked for a few hundred
metres until we came to the Purple Onion, a world-famous strip-
joint.

She took me inside and introduced me to some guy, who I later
found out owned the place, and then took me out back of the stage
to a tiny dressing room, where five women were in various stages of
undress, and introduced me to all of them.

I still hadn't twigged to what was going on and just figured that
she had called in to see someone and that we would be heading off
to work eventually, but the girls were all very friendly and
welcoming and didn't seem to mind me being there while they got
changed and I was trying my best not to stare and appear to be too
creepy.

I'd found out that her name was Maryanne, and she took me
out into the theatre and took me to a seat alongside a booth where
the owner sat in front of a turntable. She told me she wouldn't be
long and then disappeared back-stage, the show began and the
penny finally dropped!

There were about a dozen other people in the audience, all of
them fairly old guys and as strip-joints weren't my normal habitat,

I felt a little uncomfortable to start but soon relaxed as the show began.

The girls were all attractive, with good bodies and stripped completely to their own songs, which the owner played on the turntable in the booth.

Maryanne was the youngest performer, with the best looks and the hottest body, and I couldn't begin to believe that this was actually going to lead anywhere, as I had it at the back of my mind that this was still a set-up and was going to end badly for me.

As soon as the show was over, she came and joined me, we said goodnight to the girls and the boss and headed out into the street. Everywhere was now closed, so I invited her back to the *Dorset* and was pleasantly surprised when she accepted and began to believe that maybe it wasn't a set-up after all.

When we got back to the ship, the bar was closed and all hands were turned in, so I sneaked her into my cabin and into my bunk while trying not to wake Ken, who appeared to have had a few more beers and was out to it.

When I turned to next morning and was telling the lads all about it, none of them would believe me and thought I was having them on, which I could fully understand, as if someone had tried to tell me the same thing, I would have found it to be pretty far-fetched as well.

The next night we all went to the Royal Oak again and met a mate of Maryanne's who she introduced to Ken and then we went to the Purple Onion, where Maryanne tried to get her mate a job as a stripper but she was a bit too young and inexperienced and when she auditioned and ended up with all of her kit off before the song was even halfway through, the boss told her to go away and practise a bit more.

We all ended back aboard *Dorset*, with the girls staying the night.

Dorset was berthed in Wellington for three weeks and I ended up at the Purple Onion almost every night, except when Maryanne had the night off. Word got around the ship and a few of the guys came along to check the place out and on the busier nights of the week the place got quite lively.

One night, partway through our stay, the boss of the joint called me over and said he had a bad cold, was not feeling well and would I cover for him by playing the girl's music.

It simply meant that before each girl came on, I put their particular record on the turntable while they stripped and then took it off at the end and it became my regular job, although I wasn't paid for it.

I quite enjoyed doing it but felt a bit embarrassed at the end when everyone was leaving and they came over to thank me for a great show, which made me feel a little grubby.

It was too good to last, however, and eventually the day arrived when we were due to depart Wellington. ETD was set for 24:00 and Ken and I were in bed with our girls, saying goodbye, about 21:00, when the chief steward came in on a crew check and found us both in our bunks with our women.

He didn't mind about the women, just told us to have them ashore before we sailed, and then ran around the officers' area bragging about all his guys being in bed with women, while the deck crowd and the engine-room crowd had failed to score.

Cyril, the A/S from Swansea, wasn't too pleased about this when he found out, as he was married with a couple of kids and didn't mess around with women.

To be quite frank, the deck and engine crowds were hardly ever seen with women and *Dorset* had a bad name on the coast that trip. If there were ever other 'home-boats' in port at the same time as *Dorset*, you could always guarantee that their bars would be packed out while ours was deserted.

Ken and I took the girls across the road to Wellington railway station and as it was cold and raining, we gave them a couple of blankets to keep warm. We said our goodbyes and put them on the train and returned to the ship without the blankets, which we let them keep, compliments of the chief steward!

The following morning, we berthed in New Plymouth, which was to be our final port on the Kiwi coast.

New Plymouth wasn't doing it for us any better than Wellington or the Mount as there were other 'home-boats' in and the women preferred to be in their bars, rather than ours, and the crew bar aboard *Dorset* continued to resemble a duty-messroom, rather than a bar.

One afternoon, we three assistant stewards went ashore shopping, as it was to be a long haul across the Southern Ocean to Cape Town, before we got the opportunity again.

It was a wet, dismal afternoon and we didn't even make it into the pub after shopping but tried to get a cab back to the ship, which was impossible due to the queue lining up for a taxi, because of the wet weather. We waited in line for ages but there were very few taxis available and the queue was moving very slowly, when we spotted a bus with 'port' on the destination board pull up around the corner.

We abandoned the taxi queue and shot around the corner before the bus could pull away, piled aboard and bought our tickets. The time was 15:30 and as we had to turn to at 16:00 and it was only a short distance to the port, we assumed we had plenty of time.

However, the bus had only gone a short way towards the port when it veered off the main road and up into the hilly suburbs of New Plymouth, where it proceeded to meander from stop to stop before eventually rejoining the main road and continuing on to the port, which we arrived at, bang on 16:00.

As there were two ships ahead of *Dorset* on the wharf, we still had a fair distance to go once we left the bus, so we found ourselves climbing the gangway at about 16:10 with our old mate, the chief steward, waiting for us.

He started to give us a right bollocking for being late back from ashore and just wouldn't let it go. He probably thought he was getting us back for an incident earlier in the voyage, crossing the Pacific, when he tried to get us to turn to on Good Friday to polish brass portholes.

We had refused to do the work, as it was not classed as essential duties, and there was nothing he could do about it, so he was obviously going to make the most of this opportunity we had given him.

I went to my cabin and changed into blues and then returned to the saloon, to prepare my table for dinner service.

The boss followed me around the table, raving about the fact that he was not going to put up with us being late back to work, and he was going to make sure that we all paid the price for our tardy behaviour. This constant haranguing went on for about 20 minutes, non-stop, when I finally snapped and decided that I had had enough.

I had been using a cloth to polish the silver and glassware on the table and I threw this cloth in his face, walked out of the saloon, went down to my cabin, where I changed back into my jeans and shirt, all the time with the boss jumping up and down and foaming at the mouth in rage, walked ashore to the Breakwater Hotel at the end of the wharf and ordered a beer.

By the time Ken and some of the lads came ashore after dinner, I had had a few, so we caught a cab into town and continued drinking in the Egmont, where the boss turned up in the company of one of his officer mates and Ken had to stop me having a go at him.

The following morning, when the 2nd steward put me on the shake, I refused to turn to, and when the boss came down to my cabin to get me to turn to, I told him where to go.

At lunchtime, I left the *Dorset* and crossed the wharf to where another of the company ships was berthed, went aboard and settled down in the crew bar for the afternoon and then returned to the *Dorset* after dinner.

The following morning, I turned to as normal and got on with my normal duties, until mid-morning, when the boss escorted me up to the bridge, where the mate logged me a day and a day, and a day and a day, meaning that I got fined four days' pay for the two days I was absent from duty.

Ken and Cyril hadn't been too impressed with my protest, as the additional work had fallen on them, in my absence, but I had wanted to make a big enough statement that the office would have to ask me about it when we returned to the UK and I could lodge a complaint about the chief steward.

This guy was seriously beginning to get to me with his constant whingeing and complaining and having fined me four days' pay for my transgression, he was a little smug about it but insisted that I had forced him into it.

The fact of the matter was that I didn't give a stuff about the money, as I had never seen it, so didn't miss it, but his sanctimonious attitude really pissed me off.

I'd managed to retrieve a two-foot piece of flat steel bar from the scrap bin at some stage and I had this wrapped in a piece of mutton-cloth and hidden under the mattress on my bunk, and I started to fantasise about sneaking into his room in the middle of the night, belting him over the head with the steel bar and putting him over the side while we were crossing the Southern Ocean.

I was that obsessed with the idea that one night I actually spent time out on the boat-deck, checking who used the alleyway during the change of the 12-to-4 watch and to see if there was a window of opportunity.

Obviously, I didn't have the balls to go through with it, but, looking back, I'm amazed at how much time I spent thinking about it and planning it. I always wonder what the person who found the steel bar under my mattress after I left *Dorset* made of it. They probably thought I had it for protection.

From New Plymouth, we began the long haul across the Southern Ocean to Cape Town.

We were meant to be in Cape Town for about three days, but as it never stopped raining, we ended up being there for over two weeks. No sooner were the hatch-covers taken off than they had to be put back on again, due to torrential rain which never let up, and although we only had a relatively small amount of cargo to pick up the time spent loading was never more than an hour or so at a time.

It was a depressing time, as the trip was bad enough without this delay, but the abysmal weather just made things worse, although it didn't prevent the boss from continuing to wear sunglasses on even the most dismal, dark days.

Going ashore was a bit of a risk due to the racial tension, and a number of Europeans were reported killed on the streets at night, so it didn't pay to go ashore on your own. A group of the boy-ratings were held up and robbed at knifepoint one evening but luckily escaped injury.

Our main watering-hole was Delmonicos and we were in there one night when the chief steward came in with a girlfriend. We got the DJ to play a request from the crew of the *Dorset* to the chief steward, Lynn Anderson's 'I Never Promised You a Rose Garden' which was top of the charts at the time, but the miserable prick couldn't see the funny side.

Eventually, we managed to complete loading cargo and

departed Cape Town on the final leg of the voyage up the west coast of Africa to the UK.

Apart from bunkers at Curaçao and Panama Canal transit, we had only called at four ports to discharge and load cargo, but the trip had taken over four months and the 16-knot speed of the *Dorset* hadn't helped matters.

A day or so out from London the chief steward called me into his office and asked me if I was coming back next trip, to which I replied, 'You've got to be fuckin' kidding me,' and walked out of the office.

He had taken me totally by surprise, as the last thing I expected was to be asked back and I was wishing that I had had some inclination of what was coming and could have come up with a much more memorable response.

None of the catering crowd agreed to return the following trip, with the exception of the boy-ratings, who didn't have much say in the matter, and this would have been a black mark against the boss, hence the reason he had been forced to ask me back.

Had either Cyril or Ken agreed to come back next trip, then he would in all probability not have asked me back, but all three ratings refusing to return was not a good look and he knew it.

Even the 2nd steward, John Cuthbertson, had refused to return and earlier on in the voyage had written home to begin the process of joining the Glaswegian police force as a consequence of the disillusionment he felt due to the abusive nature of the chief steward.

The man was totally despised by the catering crowd and when, some months later, during another trip in the *Westmorland*, someone stepped into the galley and announced that he had passed away due to some type of illness, I felt not the least bit of remorse and I doubt that few who had sailed with him would have, either.

Upon arrival in London, I went looking for the Seamen's Union representative and found him drinking with the chief steward in the boss's cabin, so I very politely explained to him why I resented paying my union fees when this was the service we received and didn't bother registering my complaints.

I was interviewed by a bloke from head office, who didn't even mention my loggings and just wanted to know why I was refusing to return for another voyage in the *Dorset* and as by that stage, I just wanted to be shot of the *Dorset* and get away, I just made some rather bland statement and left it at that.

When Ken and I left to catch the train from Euston, there weren't too many fond farewells, apart from Cyril, the other A/S, as we hoped never to set eyes on most of the crew again and left with no regrets.

Ken was now heavily involved with his girlfriend and the next time I caught up with him on leave, he told me that he was giving up the sea and had successfully applied for a job with Rio Tinto, who had just built a new factory at Holyhead.

At first, I thought he must be joking but it turned out that he was deadly serious and didn't want any repeats of the *Dorset* experience.

His girlfriend introduced me to a friend of hers who was about 10 or 15 years older than me and divorced but wasn't going to 'put out' without some sort of commitment from me, which wasn't forthcoming, but still didn't stop me from trying at every opportunity.

Both girls lived out at Amlwch, which was a small town on the opposite side of Anglesey to Holyhead and miles from anywhere, in the middle of the countryside.

One evening, Ken dropped me off at my girl's place and told me that he would pick me up in a couple of hours on his way back to Holyhead from his girl's place.

After a couple of hours of trying and getting nowhere, my girlfriend had gone to bed and I was waiting on the street corner, for Ken to pick me up.

After waiting for over an hour, I figured that Ken had either decided to stay at his girl's place or had gone home without me, and as I had no idea how to find his girl's place, I decided to start thumbing a lift back to Holyhead. My girlfriend's place was in total darkness, so I didn't want to go waking her and her family up, so started walking.

Fortunately, it was a dry night, as there was no traffic about and I had walked miles before a car finally appeared and the driver, who was headed to Bangor, offered to drop me on the A55, which was the main route across Anglesey, where I had more chance of picking up a lift.

He dropped me off on the A55 near Rostrevor and after thanking him, I continued walking, as I still had almost the entire length of the island to traverse to get to Valley and Ken's place.

The traffic here wasn't much heavier than outside Amlwch and what very few cars there were didn't stop. I'd walked miles and as it was now the early hours of the morning, I was resigned to walking all the way to Valley and if I could have got hold of Ken, I would have happily killed him.

Eventually, along trundled an old horse-float with two men in it and they very kindly stopped and offered me a lift. There was no room in the cab, so one of them hopped out and opened the side door so I could ride in the back and, fortunately, there were no horses.

We continued at a sedate pace, with me hanging onto one of the stalls and eventually they dropped me off outside the Valley Hotel, where I thanked them profusely, before walking over the railway bridge to Ken's place.

When I got into the house, I found Ken in bed, snoring his

head off, and woke him up to find out why he had left me in Amlwch. He thought it was hilarious and told me that he assumed that I was going to 'score' and would be spending the night with my girlfriend and he would have picked me up the next day.

I asked him why the fuck he thought she was going to let me sleep with her, when she quite clearly hadn't shown any intention of doing so to date, but he still thought it was a great joke and as I was so knackered, I just had to turn in and go to sleep.

CHAPTER 22

AT THE CONCLUSION OF MY LEAVE, THE OFFICE TOLD ME TO join the *Manapouri* in Liverpool for a coastal run but upon joining her, I discovered that the mate was Mike Hill who had been mate in the *Westmorland* when we were on the MANZ run and we had both had enough of one another.

After working-by for a couple of days, he called me up to his office and informed me that there was a vacancy for an A/S in the *Westmorland* and if I was interested, he could arrange for a transfer, so I took the hint, packed my bags and moved a few docks over to Canada Dock, where it felt like coming home.

There was a coasting crowd in her, but both the other assistant stewards were planning on going deep sea in her at the conclusion of the coasting voyage, and although I went ashore on my own for the first few nights, I soon got to know these guys and we started knocking about together.

The assistant stewards were Tony, a Lancastrian, and Alan, a Geordie, and we all got on well together.

One Thursday night, Tony and I picked up a couple of women in a bar up town and they were both keen to come back to the

Westmorland with us, so we paid a taxi driver a couple of quid to put both women in the boot of his black cab and drive them through the dock-gates to the ship.

It was the girls' idea and they both knew the cab driver so they had obviously done it before and Tony and I could hardly believe our luck.

The following day being Friday, I was heading off for the weekend at the end of the day for one final visit to Holyhead, prior to heading off on the coastal trip.

I told the girl that I was with that I would drop her off in town when I took a cab to the station, but she didn't want to leave her mate and wanted to remain on board for the weekend.

I wasn't going to leave her in my cabin for the weekend, so arranged for one of the ABs, Dave, to look after her for the weekend, which he was only too keen to do.

I duly caught the train to Holyhead, where Ken was now renting a cottage in Newry with his girlfriend and where I spent a fruitless time trying to seduce her mate, who was determined to hold out and not give in to my lechery.

Early Monday morning, I returned to the *Westmorland* and found Dave, the AB I had left the girl with, waiting for me at the head of the gangway and he was not very happy.

It turned out that on the first night he had slept with her, she had had a very heavy period and flooded his mattress so she had to go home the following day and he had spent the weekend trying to replace his mattress, which was ruined.

I fell about laughing when he related the tale and realised what a lucky escape I had had, and he eventually came to see the funny side of things and we became such great mates that he was best man at my wedding a few years later.

Tony's girl was still on board and not keen to leave any time soon. She was a tall (over 6 ft), attractive girl with long, straight ash-blonde hair and her nickname was Horse, although she certainly didn't look like one.

One evening, I had just had a shower and was getting dressed to go ashore when all hell broke loose in the cabin next door, which was Tony's, and there was a lot of banging and crashing on the bulkhead.

I shot around, thinking that there was a fight going on and when I opened the door, I found Danny, one of the motormen, cowering in the corner, while Horse, who was completely naked, beat up on him.

Tony and I eventually managed to calm her down and I found out what had happened.

It appeared that Tony was keen to add to his collection of 'blue photos' prior to going deep sea and asked Horse to pose for him so he could take some pictures of her naked with his Polaroid camera, to which she had willingly agreed.

Danny, who I had sailed with in the *Dorset*, was a big West Country boy with a strong West Country accent and when sober was a really nice guy, but when pissed was a total pain in the arse, which was why I never went ashore with him.

You never knew what he was going to say, or do, to anyone when he had been drinking and he could start some serious trouble if you didn't watch him carefully and if you did go ashore with him, you spent the whole evening apologising to people and trying to avoid trouble.

Danny had had a few beers and was in Tony's cabin while he took the photos, as Horse didn't mind an audience, apparently. She had been lying on Tony's bunk and adopting various suggestive poses while Tony took the photos and Danny quietly looked on saying nothing.

Next minute, Danny took a final swig out of his beer bottle, leant forward and thrust the empty bottle into her vagina.

That was the point that all hell broke loose and attracted my attention from next door.

We managed to get Danny, who still thought it was a great joke, out of the cabin and calm Horse down, but the moment was gone and she refused to do any more posing, much to Tony's disgust.

From Liverpool, we sailed across to Belfast, which was a bit depressing, being at the height of the Troubles, and a run ashore was not even considered.

I had to go ashore for a haircut one afternoon but was more than happy to return to the ship afterwards as the atmosphere was not pleasant and the place was really run down.

The next port of call was Avonmouth, where we experienced a similar incident to when I was in the *Pyrrhus* and hit the lock wall while locking in and punctured one of the hull plates.

We were to be in Avonmouth for a period of almost six weeks, with a couple of visits to the dry-dock included and in all that time only experienced three or four days of rain.

The Royal Hotel was to become our second home and we were in there every lunchtime and evening without ever missing a day.

I met a girl who drank there regularly and reminded me of Barbara Windsor of *Carry On* fame, except that she had a West Country accent. One night she invited me home with her and after a really long taxi journey to the outskirts of Avonmouth, we pulled up at her local pub where a band was playing on stage. Despite not being able to sing a note, she insisted on getting up on stage with the band and belting out a song, which was a bit embarrassing, and everyone was eyeing me with pity, as they obviously knew her.

When the pub closed, she took me a few doors up the road to where she lived and where her mother was babysitting for her and as soon as her mother left, we had sex on the carpet in the living-room.

I then had to find my way back to the docks and as there were no taxis or buses around, she gave me directions to the docks and I started walking.

There was absolutely no traffic about and Avonmouth was like a ghost town, even though I was on the main road to the port. I had been walking for about half an hour and still had miles to go when a police car pulled up beside me and I thought they were going to offer me a lift. A sergeant and a constable got out of the car and came up to me and told me that someone matching my exact description had been reported trying to break into a house just up the road and wanted to know my movements.

I produced my seaman's card and explained that I had just walked from my girlfriend's home, but I wouldn't have been able to find it again, or the pub, so I was hoping that they would not be asking me to.

After a few more questions, they reluctantly decided to let me go on my way and went back to their car. As they were getting in, I asked them was there any chance of a lift to the docks as they were headed in that direction.

The sergeant said, 'You can fuckin' walk,' and they took off and left me there.

The Avonmouth cops were definitely the worst I came across anywhere and much worse than the police on Liverpool, London or Birkenhead docks.

My Barbara Windsor lookalike had a regular boyfriend in a German coaster which ran to Avonmouth regularly and when he appeared on the scene, I was on the outer, so I moved on to another girl who drank in the Royal. She was a prostitute, but she never told me and I never let on that I knew.

When I got my sub on Thursdays, she never had to pay for a

thing all weekend, but when I ran out of cash in the early part of the week, she always covered me until sub time came around again.

I knew she was on the game as she always had money, despite not having a job and was always disappearing at short notice or not being able to meet me from time to time.

It didn't worry me, as we were not going to be in Avonmouth for ever and she was attractive enough and a good laugh, but she and all her mates were terrified of the cops.

One day, Tony, Alan and I obtained a visitor's pass from the mate and brought our women aboard the *Westmorland* but had to have them ashore by 22:00 when the pass expired.

After a few beers and time in the bunk, we took them ashore but were running a bit late and it had gone 22:00. We didn't think it mattered but the women were in a right state and refused to go through the gate with the cops on duty, as they reckoned that the police would give them a hard time and make things tough for them.

Despite our protests, they headed off across a 200-metre stretch of wasteland, which was shoulder high in weeds and full of potholes and piles of debris. The women were in high heels, tights and skirts, so it was a bit of a mission getting across the patch of wasteland to where we came out at the Avonmouth railway station, which was closed for the night. We climbed up to the platform, down onto the railway track and across to the other platform, which we mounted, before coming to a wall about 10 feet high which dropped into the street.

Alan and I straddled the wall and lowered the women to Tony in the street, one by one, before jumping down to join them.

While all of this was going on, not a single car or person had passed by, which just demonstrated how dead Avonmouth was at night.

The women had obviously done this before as they were familiar with the route, but they still suffered with laddered tights and dirty shoes, and we were all somewhat dishevelled and out of breath.

Once in the street, we split up and went our separate ways to take the women home, but when we arrived at my girlfriend's place, her landlord refused to let me in, which I wasn't in the least surprised about, but she kicked up a bit of a fuss.

The landlord was adamant, so she took me up the road and up an alleyway to a patch of vacant land surrounded by ancient terraced houses on all sides. It was pitch-black but I could make out a single-decker bus parked in the centre of the lot and she led me to the front door of the bus, which she pushed open very quietly.

She told me to go down to the back of the bus and wait for her on the back seat, while she squatted down by the front wheel to take a pee. The bus was obviously one of the places she used to entertain her clients when she had nowhere else to go.

I headed off in the dark down the aisle towards the rear of the bus and was almost there when the floor disappeared and I found myself straddling the drive-shaft with badly scraped shins.

I hauled myself out as silently as I could and lay on the back seat in agony and trying to get rid of the pain in my legs.

As I lay there, I could see her silhouetted against the windscreen making her way down the aisle and assumed that she knew about the missing inspection cover over the driveshaft, but it turned out that she didn't, as her head suddenly dropped out of sight and I found her straddling the shaft with badly bruised and scraped inner thighs.

As I was struggling to pull her out of the space, a spotlight was suddenly turned on from the upper window of one of the houses and the light slowly panned over the bus while we both lay very still on the floor of the bus until it went out.

We swiftly exited the bus, and as there was now no chance of sex, I escorted her home, bid her goodnight and hobbled off in the direction of the dock gate.

At the gate, I showed the cop on duty my seaman's card and headed off to the *Westmorland* where I found a bicycle standing at the bottom of the gangway.

It was now after 02:00 and as I climbed aboard, I came across a policeman with the bosun, who were looking for the three women who had been aboard and had not exited the gate.

The cop had woken the bosun and made him look for the women with him and when they saw me, they demanded to know where the women were.

I told them we had taken the women ashore through the gate before 22:00 and I had just returned from ashore. The cop accused me of lying but I told him to telephone his mate on the gate who would confirm that I had just passed through the gate a matter of minutes ago returning from town, so I had to have gone ashore earlier.

It felt great putting one over on the cops, but we knew they would be gunning for us in future and we would need to keep out of trouble.

I apologised to the bosun for his disturbed night, but he blamed the cops for not doing their job properly and wasn't blaming us, so that was a let off.

A few nights later, Alan, the Geordie steward, was walking his girl through Avonmouth Park and came across an unlocked groundsman's shed, so they both slipped inside for some privacy. He told her to get her gear off, which she did, literally, and stripped off naked. Suddenly, the door swung open and two policemen walked in to investigate what was going on.

They both shone their torches on Alan's girl and told her to get dressed but wouldn't turn their torches off and give her some privacy and thought it was a huge joke watching her put her clothes back on.

Alan got a bit agitated, but managed to control himself and in the end, they got off with a warning, but his girl was so upset that he had to take her home and when he met up with us in the pub he was still fuming at the cops.

We moved into the dry-dock for repair work and maintenance to be carried out, so had to use the shoreside toilets, of which there were crew, officers and ladies. The ladies' toilets were kept locked and a key was kept in the officers' recreation room for the use of the 2nd engineer's wife, who was a Kiwi and a really lovely lady, who we all thought the world of.

We three stewards had just returned from a lunchtime session in the Royal and had commenced work when the 2nd steward, accompanied by the 2nd engineer's wife, approached us and asked us if we knew where the key to the ladies' toilets was.

Unfortunately, we had reached that stage of inebriation where even the most innocuous of comments were found to be hilariously funny and at the mention of the ladies' toilet key, we just cracked up.

The more we tried to get serious, the more we fell about laughing and I'm sure the 2nd steward thought we had hidden the key as a joke and was getting seriously pissed off with us.

I suggested to the 2nd steward that he take the lady down to the officers' toilets and stand guard outside while we searched for the key, which he did but we couldn't locate the key.

Eventually, the key was found and it turned out that one of the officers had moved it, not being aware of what it was for, but the 2nd steward wasn't terribly impressed with our childish behaviour, which he claimed had embarrassed him, and he gave us shit for quite some time afterwards.

We apologised to the 2nd's wife for the way we had reacted, but she was okay with us and could see the funny side, which she used to joke about.

I was in the Royal one afternoon when I bumped into one of the ex-Blue Funnel boy ratings I had coasted with, who was now cook/steward in one of Everards coasters berthed across the dock from us.

He invited me back to the coaster for a look round and a few drinks, which I accepted. I found myself sitting in his cabin, drinking Bacardi out of a baked-bean tin, as he had no glasses or cups, while he puffed away on a joint of cannabis and got high.

I accompanied him to the galley where he was preparing dinner for the rest of the crew, which consisted of 'bangers and mash'. He put the sausages and mash on the plates and then loaded the plates into a warming cabinet with wire shelves.

Unfortunately, the weight of all the plates was too much for the shelf to bear and as he opened the cabinet to put the final plate in, the shelf buckled and all the dinners came sliding out of the cabinet to smash on the galley deck, which didn't look as though it had been scrubbed in a month of Sundays.

He then found some unbroken plates and proceeded to slop the mashed potato and sausages off the filthy deck and back onto the plates, picking out the shards of broken crockery in the process, and put the plates back into the cabinet.

He then went ashore, back to the Royal, while I returned to the *Westmorland* on the other side of the dock.

That incident cured me of any romantic notions I may have entertained about life on 'rock-dodgers'.

Following a further visit to the dry-dock, our time in

Avonmouth finally came to an end and we departed for Southampton.

Leaving our berth, we passed close alongside a Blue Funnel ship on the berth ahead of us and I spotted Brian Stewart, one of the guys I had been trapped in the Bitter Lakes with aboard *Melampus*.

He had been made up to 2nd steward and we had a swift, shouted conversation until we were out of earshot.

I think the Royal was sad to see us go, as we had certainly put some money across the bar and in the jukebox, but the women were all excited at the recent news that one of the shipping companies was looking for female crew for one of its cruise ships, instead of the regular male crew, and the girls were all busy putting their CVs together.

If one of the criteria for the job was screwing the passengers, then they were all guaranteed a berth.

From Avonmouth, we sailed around to Southampton where we berthed for a couple of days and where I managed to pick up a Maltese girl and bring her back to the ship, but the mate caught me taking her ashore next morning and gave me a talking-to.

He wasn't so much concerned about me having a woman aboard as me taking her ashore while the dockers were working.

It was a pleasure sailing into and out of Southampton as so much was going on and there was so much to see, with it being the height of summer and beautiful weather.

During our time in Avonmouth, Tony had experienced some type of family emergency and had had to pay off and was replaced by an assistant steward named Don, a Londoner, so we no longer had access to Tony's collection of artistic photos and particularly of the very photogenic Horse, which was a shame.

In London, we came across a pub, the Windsor Castle on Paddington Road, which was a bit of a hike from the Royal Albert

Dock but put on a Music Hall show of old Victorian and Edwardian songs from the Boer War era, such as 'Goodbye Dolly Gray' and 'Soldiers of the Queen', and as the place was fairly popular, we made it our regular hangout.

It made a bit of a change from the Steps and the Connaught, and it attracted quite a few women who seemed to enjoy the atmosphere and the sing-along, although we never had any luck with any of them, sad to say.

The Royal Docks were still fairly busy in the early seventies, with a steady coming and going of all the major shipping lines, such as, Port boats, Star boats, Shaw Savill, NZSC, Glen boats, P&O cargo ships and the odd Blue Funnel ship, and it was great to experience the hustle and bustle of such a busy waterfront. It was an experience that was becoming increasingly rare at most of the other British ports.

We departed the Royal Docks, bound for Wellington, New Zealand via Curaçao, for bunkers and the Panama Canal.

Geordie Alan was messman, Don was tiger and I was officers'/engineers' steward, with Billy Battson still chief steward, Brian Epps 2nd steward and Norman Constantine, a Scouse guy living in Bebington, as chief cook.

Alan was being paid an allowance to look after four dogs which were being shipped out to New Zealand and Danny, the motorman, was looking after a couple of pedigree cats.

John North was no longer in the *Westmorland* and the new skipper had his wife and two young children with him, which pissed Don, the tiger, off, as it appeared he didn't like kids and was always moaning about them, but they seemed pretty polite and well behaved to me.

CHAPTER 23

THE VOYAGE OUT TO WELLINGTON WAS UNEVENTFUL AND WE tied up at a berth adjacent to the inter-island ferry, so we had the pleasure of waving to all the women passengers aboard the ferries as they arrived and departed.

We managed to arrange a few dates, as the ship-girls were regular users of the ferries, and we caught up with some of them in the local bars and hotels.

After discharging cargo, much to our disappointment, we were moved from this prime position over to a 'lay-by' berth to wait for a cargo to become available and ended up being on 'lay-by' for 10 days.

My girlfriend from the previous trip in *Dorset*, Maryanne, was no longer working at the Purple Onion and rumour had it that she was coasting one of the Shaw Savill boats, but there was plenty of activity in the *Westmorland* crew bar every night and no shortage of women.

One evening, Alan and I returned early from ashore, before the bar had got going, to find the only occupants were Danny, the motorman and a young woman, who was cowering in the corner and very relieved to see us, when we came aboard.

Danny's grandfather had served in the Dorset Regiment on the Western Front during the First World War and had filled Danny's head with all sorts of lurid tales of his experiences in the trenches and also his life as a ploughman behind a horse-drawn plough after the war.

When Danny got pissed, which was a regular occurrence, he would sometimes disappear into this fantasy land of fighting in the trenches or following the plough, and he did it with all the actions, which could be a bit disconcerting when you came across it for the first time.

Every so often, Danny would start chucking grenades around and bayoneting German soldiers, accompanied by all the appropriate sounds of explosions and people being stabbed in the guts.

Either that, or he was guiding his pair of Shire horses, each by name, attached to the plough, around the bar while he ploughed up the deck in regulation furrows.

When Alan and I arrived back aboard, Danny was back in the trenches and the poor girl was terrified, wondering what the hell was going on. She had come aboard with her girlfriend and one of the crew and been left in the bar while her mate and the crew member had retired to his cabin.

She had been having a normal conversation with Danny when he suddenly turned into this raving maniac and then we had turned up.

Alan managed to calm her down and reassure her and even ended up taking her to bed.

The crew bar was pumping in Wellington, as there were not many 'home-boats' in and the officers and engineers were regular welcome visitors and added to the atmosphere.

The mate was not much of a drinker, but didn't mind the women being on board, provided that they were ashore during inspections and woe betide anyone caught with a woman in his cabin when he was doing the rounds.

One evening, the 2nd engineer had picked up a woman in the crew bar and she had spent the night in his cabin, but just before inspection, he had insisted that she leave his cabin and return to the crew deck.

All the women had gone ashore for the day, while inspection played out, with the exception of this girl, who was found crying in the crew alleyway by one of the ABs as the inspection party made its rounds.

He hid her in one of the cubicles in the crew heads, but when the mate demanded to know who was in there, the game was up.

She was distraught and embarrassed, but did not dob in the 2nd engineer, so the mate assumed that she was with a member of the crew and was highly pissed off.

After inspection the chief steward rounded up all the catering crowd and began to lecture us on having women aboard during inspection and advised us that the mate would be 'gunning' for us on future inspections, so we had better watch out.

At that point, we put the boss straight and told him to make sure that the mate was put in the picture and informed of what had taken place between the 2nd engineer and this girl, which the boss did do and we never saw the 2nd in the crew bar again.

Had the 2nd kept the girl in his cabin for the inspection, it was likely that the mate wouldn't have said a word, as there was one rule for the upper deck and another rule for the lower deck, but as the 2nd was a married man, he was probably too embarrassed to let the mate find a woman in his room.

Eventually, we sailed down to Lyttelton and commenced loading a part cargo. It was winter and Lyttelton was pretty cold which led to a bout of colds and flu that laid a few of us low for a day or so and was one of the only times I can ever recall being hit with the flu during my time at sea.

The British Hotel was our regular watering hole but there was much more action in the *Westmorland* crew bar, so on some nights we didn't bother going ashore.

On one night, just before our visit to Lyttelton came to an end, the nightwatchman came across a young woman sheltering from the wind and rain on the wharf, while waiting for the inter-island ferry from Wellington to berth.

She was waiting for her brother, who was bringing her three-year-old daughter back from a visit to Hamilton and they were on the ferry which was due in later that night. He invited her up to the crew bar to keep warm and dry and left her there.

I was in the bar having a quiet drink and had left my spectacles in my cabin but couldn't be bothered going back to get them, so everything was a bit of a blur.

I had the feeling that this woman was staring at me but being short-sighted, her face was out of focus and I just ignored her and got on with drinking.

The bar became packed out and I decided to turn in for the night, so just slipped away.

A day or so later, we sailed into Dunedin and that night, on a run ashore, I walked into the European Hotel on the Octagon in the city centre. As I walked through the door, a woman approached me and said, 'Hi, you're off the *Westmorland*, aren't you? Do you remember me from the other night?'

Well, I had to say no, I didn't remember her, as I had never seen her before in my life, but we soon established that the reason I hadn't recognised her was because I hadn't been wearing my specs, and she let me off.

She was with a big group of her girlfriends, so I arranged to meet her the following lunchtime in a pub just outside the wharf, and that was how I met my future wife, Maggie. One afternoon she brought her daughter, Lisa, aboard who was celebrating her fourth birthday and the assistant cook baked her a small birthday cake. She was a cute little girl who soon became a firm favourite of the crew and they spent time entertaining her. By the time we departed Dunedin, Maggie and I were in a steady relationship and looking forward to catching up again next time I was in New Zealand.

The next port of call was Napier, in the North Island, where I came across Maryanne, the stripper from the Purple Onion club in Wellington, in the Copacabana Bar.

She was with some guy off one of the Shaw Savill boats, which was tied up across the dock opposite the *Westmorland* and although I still had feelings for her, I was happy to see that she was doing fine and still had a great outlook on life.

She did come over to the *Westmorland* a couple of times to have a few drinks, and although, one afternoon, returning from a session in the Copacabana, we both ended up swimming fully clothed in the ocean, until the cops turned up and told us to get out of the water as it was too dangerous for swimming, we remained just good mates.

During our time in Napier, the deckies had been busy painting the superstructure and funnel and the funnel in particular was a work of art, with its distinctive Federal markings on candy apple red background.

During our final night in Napier, the Shaw Savill crowd snuck aboard and threw buckets of black paint all over the newly painted funnel and superstructure, leaving it in a right mess, which severely pissed off the Old Man, the mate and the bosun.

This type of activity was quite common, between ships on the coast, and crews were forever painting witty and amusing slogans on the sides of other ships in port but chucking buckets of paint over new paintwork was simply mindless vandalism.

When we looked across at the old 'rust-bucket' on the berth across from us, we could fully understand their envy and jealousy, as no amount of paint and effort was ever going to improve the looks of that old tub.

When we pulled off the wharf that morning, there was none of the usual banter and joking between crews, as normally happens at such times, and most of their crew were noticeably absent from being out on deck, a sure sign that they realised that they had overstepped the mark and we slipped out to sea in total silence.

As we sailed up the Waitemata Harbour, into Auckland the next morning, people on passing boats were doing a double-take at the sight of our funnel, and quite a few altered course to check us out and have a closer look.

The poor old nightwatchman copped a load of flak over not detecting the Shaw Savill crowd, but he was probably in the crew bar when they snuck aboard, so he possibly deserved it.

Earlier in the voyage, Ken had written to me and told me that he was planning on getting married and wanted me to be his best man. The timing of the wedding was based on the estimated return of the *Westmorland* to the UK but departing Auckland, bound for Liverpool, we were well behind the original schedule, and I wasn't going to be able to make the wedding.

I sent them a telegram of congratulations a few days short of the UK and was disappointed not to have made Ken's big day, but his wife probably heaved a huge sigh of relief.

The second morning I was home, a policewoman knocked at the door and when I answered it, she handed me a summons to appear in Holyhead court to answer a paternity suit against me.

My girlfriend from the rail ferry *Hibernia* had not been joking when she had told me she was pregnant, and a couple of years later had decided to do something about it.

Mum was not very happy about it and was pissed off that I had never informed her that I was a father, although, at that time, I was not sure that I was.

A week or so later, I caught the train to Holyhead and after a couple of pints in the Edinburgh Castle to steady my nerves, made my way to the courthouse, where I was approached by my ex-girlfriend's solicitor, who asked me where my solicitor was.

When I told him that I did not need a solicitor, as I either was the baby's father, or I was not the baby's father and the court would decide that, he must have thought he had a right one here, that's how naive I was.

When we were on the ferries, we had both had multiple partners and although I had no problem supporting the baby if the baby was mine, I did not want to end up supporting someone else's baby, so I just needed a blood test to prove paternity, which I assumed the court would order me to have.

After hanging around the court for an hour or two, I was again approached by her solicitor, who advised me that, due to the backlog of cases, my case had been adjourned and the court would be back in touch to notify me of a new date for my appearance.

I caught the train back to Chester and called into the Dee Miller for a few pints, where no-one would believe that the case had been adjourned and just assumed that I was too embarrassed to admit that I was the father of the baby. Even Mum found it hard to believe and thought I was hiding something.

While on leave, I introduced Dennis, the manager of the Dee Miller, to Ken and his new wife, Gaynor.

Dennis had offered to help them try to get a position as pub managers and eventually they ended up managing the Beehive pub on Hoole Road, Chester for a number of years and then moved on to The Bull at Clotton, just outside Chester on the road to Crewe.

Meanwhile, I had been contacted by the office and instructed to rejoin the *Westmorland* in the Royal Docks, London.

Maggie, the girl I had met in Dunedin, telephoned me a number of times from New Zealand, while I was on leave and reversing the charges each time. She always seemed to call me just after she had come home from the pub, so the conversations tended to be somewhat disjointed and drawn out, which ran up the telephone bill.

She was now living with her sister in Auckland but told me that she would keep an eye on the shipping news and meet me in Wellington when *Westmorland* arrived.

Dad had no idea that the telephone calls from New Zealand were collect calls, so on the day I left home to rejoin *Westmorland*, I felt a little guilty and told him. I gave him some money towards the cost of his telephone bill but I don't think the amount would have gone far towards covering the true cost of the calls and he never had me on about it.

I had still not heard anything from the courts, so decided to join the *Westmorland* and deal with the issue when it came up, as I could not afford to remain home without a ship for much longer.

I caught the train to Euston and then on to Plaistow in the East End and caught a cab to the Albert Dock.

The catering crowd had all decided to return, so the faces were all familiar and we soon settled down again and enjoyed some good runs ashore around the East End pubs.

We were working by for about a week prior to sailing day and I had completely forgotten about the Holyhead court amid all the hustle and bustle of getting ready to go deep sea, until sailing day finally came around and we were due to depart the Royal Docks at 17:00.

Just after lunch, Mr Larsen, the catering superintendent dashed on board and told me that I had to go ashore to the office and contact my father urgently. The super, who assumed that it was a family medical emergency, told me that he would arrange transport home for me and also arrange for a replacement steward to take my place.

I hurried ashore to the office and telephoned my father, who informed me that the clerk of the Holyhead court had been in touch, demanding to know why I had not fronted up to my rescheduled court appearance. I hadn't received notification of a rescheduled date prior to rejoining *Westmorland* and Dad said that no official-looking letters had arrived for me so I told him not to worry about it and to telephone the court to tell them I had sailed and I would deal with it when I came home.

I returned to the ship and told Mr Larsen it was a false alarm and nothing to worry about and he could cancel my replacement. He gave me a bit of a funny look but I didn't go into any further detail and left it at that.

At 17:00, we locked out into the Thames bound for Le Havre, just across the Channel, to pick up a deck-cargo of 34 pedigree Charolais cattle destined for New Zealand.

The following afternoon, I arranged to meet the lads in a bar, but first had to go to the local post office to change some English pounds into French francs. When I gave the old lady behind the counter my pounds, she didn't go into the till but picked up some franc coins from a shelf behind her, which she gave to me.

When I got back to the bar, I put these francs on the bar to pay for a round of drinks, but the barman burst out laughing and refused to accept them, as they were occupation francs and worthless.

Alan picked up the bar-tab, but I didn't have time to go looking for the post office again and confront the old lady, and I found it hard to believe that someone would deliberately do such a thing in such a blatant manner. I just had to accept that some French people still hate the English enough to do such a thing.

We departed Le Havre with inboard-facing crates, containing the cattle, down each side of the after-deck and a couple of Kiwi stockmen in the supernumerary cabin, aboard to look after the cattle.

Fortunately, the weather remained fine and the seas calm, for the entire trip out to Wellington and the livestock soon lost their novelty.

The stockmen did a good job of looking after the cattle and cleaning the after-deck, so there was not so much of a stink as we had at first feared.

We arrived in Curaçao for bunkers in the early evening and as the time to take on oil was usually about six hours, we had time for a run ashore.

I had heard lots of tales about Campo Alegre, the legendary open-air brothel on the island, but had never visited the place, mainly because the timing was not right, but this trip we had the whole evening ahead of us.

The place was a cross between Butlins holiday camp and Stalag Luft 13, with guards on the gate, and you had to pay admission to get in and then negotiate with the women inside for sex.

It was rumoured to have been opened by the tanker companies, whose ships were regular visitors to the island for the oil produced there but, in fact, it had been opened by the government, to combat the prostitution problem in Willemstad.

The place was situated a few kilometres out of the town and the girls were all foreigners from the surrounding countries, such as Venezuela, Cuba, Colombia and elsewhere. They were issued with a three-month visa and rented a place in the compound where they serviced their clients. Regular medical check-ups were mandatory and the use of condoms compulsory.

Although I had heard plenty about the place, I had half assumed it was a bit of a mythical place and the stories made up by sex-starved seamen, so when four of us jumped out of the cab that took us there and lined up to pay our admission, I was amazed to find it exactly as described.

Once through the gate, we made our way to the busy open-air bar, where we bought a bottle of rum, a bucket of ice and some Coca-Cola and settled down at one of the tables, where we were instantly joined by a few of the women.

Most of them were very attractive, with stunning figures, and there was a constant coming and going from the bar as the girls took their clients to the rented rooms for sex and then back to the bar.

Most of the tables were occupied by seamen from the ships in port and although the atmosphere was raucous and rowdy, it felt perfectly safe and we were a fairly relaxed group as we made our way back to the ship in time for sailing.

One evening, mid-Pacific, I wandered down the alleyway to the crew bar, only to find it totally deserted. I grabbed a cold can of beer and was returning to my cabin, when I heard sounds coming from one of the deckies' cabins and knocked on the door. When the door opened slightly, to let me in, I found three or four of the lads with towels stuffed around the door, smoking dope and giggling like a bunch of schoolgirls.

I was a non-smoker, so had never tried dope and much preferred alcohol, but dope was rapidly becoming the drug of choice and was having a major impact on social life aboard ship.

With alcohol, you could consume four or five cans before you began to feel the effects and you became a bloody nuisance, but with dope you could be coherent one minute and talking complete shit the next, so dope smoking and beer drinking were never compatible.

I tended to drink in my cabin for most of the voyage out to Wellington and the crew bar was never the social hub at sea that it had been in the past, unfortunately.

CHAPTER 24

WHEN WE FINALLY ARRIVED IN WELLINGTON, WE HAD TO anchor off Soames Island, the quarantine station in the middle of Wellington Harbour, to unload the cattle.

After being a month out from the UK, it was pretty frustrating to be swinging on the hook, so close to land, looking at the bright lights, and not being allowed a run ashore.

The following morning a large pontoon was towed out and made fast to the *Westmorland*. The cattle crates were lowered onto the pontoon by the ships gear, one at a time and a Royal New Zealand Airforce Iroquois helicopter lifted the crates from the pontoon and ferried them across to the quarantine island. The helicopter ferried a few crates from the barge but then started lifting them directly from the deck of the *Westmorland*, as it was faster that way.

The operation took most of the day to complete but by late afternoon we were tied up alongside and looking forward to a night on the town.

I met Maggie in the Royal Oak and at the end of the night

carried her bag aboard *Westmorland* and she made herself at home in my cabin.

A number of other women had also met the ship to be with members of the crew and the crew bar was soon pumping, as was the officers' bar.

The following day, the local paper, the *Dominion*, printed a cartoon showing the *Westmorland* tied up to the quay and a little old lady on the wharf surrounded by three burly policemen, with the caption, 'But I only shouted bull-ship, officer'.

This was in reference to the Germaine Greer court case taking place in Auckland at that time, where she had been accused of using the words 'fuck' and 'bullshit' in public. She got off on the 'bullshit' charge but was found guilty on the 'fuck' charge.

How times have changed.

From Wellington, we sailed down to Dunedin where Maggie went ashore to stay with her ex-mother-in-law, who was looking after her daughter.

She rejoined the ship shortly before we departed Dunedin for Bluff and the issue of women on board was now fairly relaxed provided that they weren't anywhere to be seen during inspection. A number of crew girlfriends, including officers, were aboard for the entire coastal trip and the atmosphere was totally relaxed.

After discharging the last of the cargo in bluff, we then moved onto a lay-by berth to await a cargo for the homeward trip.

While we were there, the *Melbourne Star*, one of the Blue Star boats, arrived and tied up on the opposite side of the harbour from *Westmorland*.

That night, a group of us, including Maggie, decided to go across for a visit and see if we knew anyone on board. When we got there, we found that the catering crowd were European and the deck crowd West Indian and I got the shock of my life when I found out that Mick, my mate from Blue Funnel, was chief cook.

When I came across him in the crew bar, he was dancing closely with one of the deck-crowd to a slow, romantic song and wearing full make-up.

I don't know which of us was embarrassed the most, Mick for being seen wearing the make-up, or me, for finally having to acknowledge something I'd been trying to ignore.

We had a long conversation reminiscing about old times, but his boyfriend wasn't too happy about me monopolising him and Maggie wasn't too keen on the situation either, so we finally headed back to the *Westmorland* and, sadly, that was the last time I came across Mick.

One of the ABs had picked a woman up in one of the pubs, brought her back to the ship and she had stayed the night. Unfortunately, she had omitted to tell him that she was married to one of the Bluff wharfies and next morning this guy turned up with a few of his mates, to sort the AB out.

It turned into a Mexican standoff between the wharfies and the crew of the *Westmorland* and the upshot was that we had to be careful when drinking in the local watering holes and most of our socialising was done aboard ship.

It wasn't worth the time and effort to travel into Invercargill, which was a few kilometres, and a few dollars, away in a taxi, as there wasn't much doing there either.

Mick Jagger famously remarked on the Stones visit there that 'Invercargill was the arsehole of the world'. He may well have added 'that Bluff was the turd hanging out of it', as it definitely had nothing going for it back in the day.

There was a freezing works and an aluminium smelter there, which were the main sources of employment, but the town was bleak and depressing and the weather cold and miserable for the entire time we were there.

Eventually, we were directed to sail up the coast to Timaru, to pick up a few hundred tons of cargo and then we would be returning to Bluff, to go under the all-weather meat loaders for a full load of frozen meat, which would take a week or so.

The thought of returning to Bluff for any length of time was disheartening and added to the thought of the long haul back to the UK with the social side of being at sea now much more oriented towards the dope smokers, and the beer drinkers now being in the minority. I was beginning to think more and more of a way out.

Time was running out for me, as even at the tender age of 23, I was one of the older members of the crew and even some of the new 2nd stewards were younger than me. Promotion was highly unlikely, due to some of my disciplinary issues in the past, and it didn't appear that there was much future left for me at sea.

The promotion aspect did not concern me, as I had never aspired to making chief steward, due to them being seen as neither officer nor crew, particularly in Blue Funnel, where they were seen as petty officers, despite the importance of the position.

I just didn't feel like spending the rest of my time at sea being ordered about by people who were younger than me. I didn't want to become one of those lonely old guys that you came across on every ship who had left it too late and only had the ship and the alcohol to look forward to.

It may have seemed like a romantic lifestyle when you were young and had it all before you, but the reality was that the sea was a young person's game and only emphasised the idiosyncrasies of the older generation.

I had rarely come across anyone over the age of 30 who was happy and contented with a life at sea and even the mates were breaking their necks to find employment as shore-side surveyors once they had put in some time at sea.

So, it wasn't too surprising, when Maggie raised the subject of me jumping ship, or 'skinning out' as it was known, that I began to give the idea some serious consideration.

Maggie was a very attractive lady, with a strong personality, and I was smitten with her, to such a degree that the thought of skinning out to be with her was beginning to seem like a viable and desirable proposition.

Although she got on with very few women, blokes were attracted to her like flies and she was always the centre of attention, so I felt particularly proud to have been singled out by her as a love interest.

Unfortunately, it would take me a few years to realise that I would never possess a sufficiently strong enough character to handle Maggie and it was a long and sometimes bitter road we travelled, until we both finally realised that we were not compatible, although I think that Maggie had figured that out way before I ever did. But that was all in the future and for the moment I was totally in love with her.

We were only going to be in Timaru for a few days before returning to Bluff, so if I was going to skin out, I was going to have to get organised.

I 'subbed' as much of my wages as I was permitted and borrowed $50 from Alan, who we had let into our plan. $50 was a lot of money at the time and poor old Alan probably thought he was never going to see it again, but he quite willingly lent it to me and as soon as I was in a position to repay it, I sent him a cheque for the $50 plus some extra for interest and a drink.

I packed my suitcase and took it ashore to the old Hydro Hotel, where they agreed to keep it for me until I could pick it up. People who saw me leave the ship with the suitcase assumed that it was Maggie's and that I was taking her to the station.

I worked through the following day and straight after dinner said goodbye to Alan and then Maggie and I went ashore to the

Hydro to pick up my case and then headed to the railway station, where we caught the train to Christchurch.

In Christchurch, we booked into the cheapest hotel we could find for the night and when I woke up in the morning, it was to a sense of unease and a feeling of 'what the hell have I done?' and if I could have returned to the *Westmorland*, I would have done but it was too late now.

I found it weird that I had skinned out of the *Westmorland*, which was the happiest ship I had ever sailed in but had stuck it out in the *Dorset*, which was definitely the worst ship I had sailed in.

I finally put the difference down to meeting Maggie.

We caught a taxi out to the airport and flew, via Wellington, to Hamilton in the North Island, where Maggie's family lived in the suburb of Melville.

There was some sort of family gathering going on, so I met most of her family, but we did not let on that I had just jumped ship and instead came up with some story about me signing off and being in New Zealand legitimately.

The following day we caught the Road Services bus to Auckland and moved into Maggie's sister's flat out in the suburb of Manurewa in South Auckland.

Maggie's sister was pregnant and had recently married the 2nd mate of a Dutch Straats boat who was currently back in the Netherlands and preparing to emigrate to New Zealand, so we had to be out of the flat before he returned.

I also had to find a job, as the money we had was not going to go far and although I had not had a drink since leaving the ship, there were still plenty of other living costs.

Fortunately, there was plenty of work available if you weren't too fussy and the local paper, the *New Zealand Herald*, had several pages of situations vacant, requiring unskilled labour.

I caught the bus along Great South Road to the suburb of Otahuhu, which was an industrial area with plenty of factories and workshops looking for labour. I called at a leather factory I had seen advertised in the paper and had an interview, while Maggie and her sister went to the local cemetery to visit their father's grave.

The gentleman doing the interview advised me that I had the job and asked me if I could begin work the following Monday, to which I replied in the affirmative.

As I was leaving his office, he asked me why a person like me was seeking work in a leather factory and said, 'You're not a ship deserter, are you?'

I hastily assured him that I wasn't and left but there was no way I was going back there, job or no job, if he had seen through me that easily.

I was later to find out that the workforce was full of jumped seamen, but most of them jumped in Australia and then came across the Tasman to enter New Zealand legally and vice versa, seamen who jumped in New Zealand flew across to Australia.

However, I still needed a job, so I walked further up Great South Road into the next suburb of Penrose, which was even more industrialised than Otahuhu, and managed to secure a job in a factory making cardboard boxes.

The work wasn't very challenging, in fact it was mind-numbingly boring, but at least I now had some money coming in while I looked around for something better with more money.

While we were staying at Maggie's sister's, I had telephoned home and spoken to my parents, who were not in the least impressed with my decision to leave the *Westmorland*, and my mother, in particular, had not held back and had given me a right earful.

The company had contacted her to let them know that I had

deserted the ship and I assured her that I was fine and things would be okay.

One part of me was feeling guilty for what I had put my parents through, but another part of me needed the excitement of being in a strange country and making a go of things.

The novelty of coming home after a trip to sea was beginning to wear off and after a day or so of catching up with family, my mind had more and more been out of the UK and overseas, whether it was Japan or New Zealand, and although I could see that there wasn't much future for me at sea, I did not look forward to settling down in the UK.

I asked Dad to close down my bank account and send the money out to me, which wasn't much, as I had left my pay-off in *Westmorland* in the ship, apart from what I had managed to sub, and I had loaned Ken and his wife a few hundred pounds to enable them to move into their cottage in Holyhead, but the balance would hopefully help us get somewhere decent to live.

Maggie had found a job in a shop in Otahuhu and had then located a two-bedroom, furnished flat which was light and airy, clean and well maintained.

The rent was at the top end of our budget, but it was only a short walk to the shopping centre in Otahuhu and on the main bus route to Auckland city or South Auckland, so it was a handy location and only took me about 10 minutes to get to work.

When we had been in the flat a few weeks and were beginning to get ourselves sorted, Maggie flew down to Dunedin to pick up her daughter, Lisa, who was four years of age and being looked after by Maggie's ex-mother-in-law, with whom she maintained a good relationship.

Lisa was too young for school, so we paid one of the neighbours to look after her during the day while we were at work.

Money was still an issue as neither of us was well paid, but we weren't drinking during the week and only very occasionally went out socialising, so we were managing.

I detested my job and was always on the look-out for alternative employment, but with no skills, I could only look out for other factory jobs and they all paid about the same amount.

There wasn't a single day that I did not wish I was back in the *Westmorland*, but I had made the decision to skin out so I had to live with it.

Maggie's eldest brother, Michael, had run away to sea in a Norwegian tanker when he was 16 and had then worked for the Union Shipping Company on the Kiwi and Aussie coasts. He had then got a job at one of the local freezing works and put himself through flying school and had gone on to become an airline pilot.

Maggie's younger brother, Alex, was following in his footsteps and worked at the same freezing works, while he put himself through flying school and would go on to become an airline pilot.

You certainly couldn't call them underachievers.

I had been at the cardboard-box making factory for about five months and even working as much overtime as I could, I was still on lousy money. One weekend, Alex told me to line up at the freezing works first thing Monday morning, as it was the beginning of the lamb and beef season and the works was taking on more hands for the summer season.

The freezing works was Westfield Freezing Works, which was situated in Otahuhu and was owned by the Vestey family, the well-known British family who also owned the Blue Star Shipping Co.

I duly joined the line at 07:00 on the Monday morning and found that it stretched right across the yard and there were literally hundreds of people lined up, mainly Māori and Polynesians and I was one of the few European faces in the queue.

I began to sense that it was a hopeless exercise, as most of the people that I spoke to had previous experience and had worked at the freezing works in prior seasons, so they weren't going to take on someone with absolutely no experience. I was just about to give up and carry on to work at the box factory, when Alex, Maggie's brother, turned up and pulled me out of the line.

Alex was a leading hand on the beef floor and he led me through the works and up to the beef floor, where he introduced me to his foreman. He told his boss that I was an experienced knife-hand and recommended me for the position, so his boss agreed to give me a start.

I was shown to a locker to store my things in and given a set of white overalls, an apron and a pouch containing a knife and steel, and a chain-mail hand guard for my left hand and then taken to the beef-floor to begin work.

Alex showed me to the head-chain, where to my horror, a line of skinned calf heads were coming at me at a steady pace down the chain, and he then demonstrated how to detach the cheeks on either side of the skull and leave them hanging down and then how to cut through the base of the chin to drop the tongue out of the skull. This was called 'tongue and cheeking' and was the final stage of the beef chain and the last step in breaking down the beef carcass.

I was now a C-grade butcher on the very lowest rung of the beef-chain ladder.

I was in a state of shock, at the sights and the sounds around me, which were like scenes from hell. If you couldn't stand the sight of blood, which I definitely couldn't, this was not the place for you.

I had developed tunnel vision with the shock but managed to follow the job Alex was showing me until he decided that I had the hang of it and left me to my own devices.

I only had a vague idea of how to sharpen my knife on the steel and wished that I had paid more attention to galley-work when I had the opportunity, so I was sawing at the meat instead of slicing it, which only made the job that more difficult.

I was having a job to keep up with the chain, despite it only going at about half speed but, fortunately, with so many new people starting, there were lots of stoppages, which enabled me to catch up.

I had no stomach for lunch on that first day and just ate an apple to keep me going but only nibbled at the bits my hands hadn't touched, as the thought of consuming anything I touched, despite scrubbing my hands, was just too much.

I managed to make it through the first week okay but watching the cattle being driven up the race and then stunned and bled was pretty traumatic and the season was only just beginning and had not yet moved into top gear.

On the plus side, I was now earning reasonable money and with two hours' overtime each day on the clean-up and work available every Saturday morning, the financial pressure was easing.

One morning, one of the foremen came to do some work on the chain alongside me and asked to borrow my knife to cut part of a carcass away. I lent him my knife, but it was so blunt and would not cut properly that he handed it back and said, 'What the fuck's that?'

I made the excuse that I had just run it over some teeth and had not yet resharpened it, but he borrowed another knife and after that humiliation, I was determined to learn how to sharpen a knife properly and have the sharpest knife on the floor.

I spent every break and most of my lunchtime at the whetstone, watching guys sharpen their knives and learning the technique and I also invested in a custom-made steel, which one of the guys made for me.

With my new-found confidence and sharp knife, I began to move up the head-chain, until I could carry out every operation from start to finish.

It was still a shit job, but the chain kept you so busy that the day soon went by and as the speed of the chain increased as the season advanced, time just flew by.

Maggie and I could afford to go out a little more often, now that I was on better money, so we caught the bus into the city on either a Friday or a Saturday night to go to the movies or drinking and dancing.

Getting the bus back to Otahuhu last thing at night could be a little hairy though, due to all the drunks who congregated at the bus station and fights were forever breaking out, so we invested in a little Ford Anglia to avoid the buses.

I couldn't get my driving licence as I was going under an assumed name, so Maggie drove everywhere and enjoyed it.

Drink driving wasn't quite the big issue that it is now so you could have a few drinks before you were over the limit and Maggie didn't drink much anyway.

Being one of very few 'Poms' in the works, I used to cop a fair amount of flak from time to time, but most of it was pretty good-natured and taken in fun.

However, things got rather ugly in December 1972, when the All Blacks prop, Keith Murdoch, got sent home from tour after punching a security guard at a hotel in Cardiff, following the Welsh test.

The New Zealand media were up in arms about this, as the All Blacks were untouchable and could do no wrong, so one of the radio talk-back hosts in Auckland began a 'punch-a-Pom-a-day' campaign, which began to gain some traction.

I was okay on the beef-chain, as I was part of the team and just got slagged off with a lot of banter, but one Saturday morning, on overtime, I was sent to the mutton-chain, to load the chillers with carcasses. The guys there had soon picked up on my accent and were hurling mutton carcasses down the line without warning me and if one of those had collected me, it would have been 'goodnight nurse'.

I spent the entire morning looking over my shoulder and dodging carcasses and was never more relieved to get to the end of the shift. I must have lost pounds in weight with all the ducking and diving.

CHAPTER 25

Eventually, the killing season began to wind down, and the foremen and leading hands began to appear with sheaves of coloured forms, which they began to hand out. If you received one of these, it meant you didn't come into work the following day and had to reapply at the start of the next season in the spring.

Every morning, there were fewer and fewer faces appearing on the floor and I was frantically searching through the *Herald* every morning for my next job, which I knew would be nowhere near as remunerative as my current job, but at least I now had the experience and stood a good chance of being re-employed in the new season.

Over the course of the next few days, the number of coloured slips being handed out slowed down and then stopped altogether. Alex had been transferred to another department and no longer knew what was happening on the beef-floor, but I couldn't believe that I had not been laid off and thought that there must have been some mistake and I had been overlooked.

After about a week or so, when I realised that I had been kept on permanently, I plucked up the courage to approach the foreman and ask him why I had been retained, when guys who were much more experienced and skilled knife-hands than I was had been let go.

His reply to me was that 'You might be a useless Pommie prick but at least you turn up for work every morning and you do the overtime. Those other guys might be good with a knife but if they don't turn up for work every Monday and Friday, they're no fuckin' use to anyone.'

So, it was only my lack of absenteeism that had kept me in the game and I tucked that bit of knowledge away for future reference, and just thanked my lucky stars that no matter how depressed and fed up I had been, I had still managed to make it into work every morning.

The money wasn't quite as good during the off-season and we had a few early finishes due to lack of stock, but compared to my previous job, I was still earning almost twice as much.

I was still only drinking mainly at weekends, with the odd session on pay-day, when we called into the Criterion Hotel in Otahuhu or the Otahuhu Workingmen's Club, but I was too scared to go home to Maggie with a seriously depleted wage packet, so resisted the urge to stay too late.

When we went into Auckland city, socialising, we usually kept away from the wharf to avoid me being picked up by the police, but one weekend, the *Westmorland* arrived in port and I decided to take a chance and pay a visit to catch up with any of the lads who were still aboard.

I apologised to Billy Battson, the boss, for jumping and caught up with Geordie Alan and Norman, the cook and bumped into the chief electrician, Ian McLean, who told me that I was the last person he thought would have jumped ship. He also told me that the mates and engineers had not realised just how good I was at my job, until they had to put up with the blokes who came after me.

I was chuffed with that comment and still think it's the best compliment I have ever had.

I tended to steer clear of the seamen's bars in Auckland, partly because of the danger of being recognised and picked up but mainly because I no longer felt part of the scene, now that I was no longer at sea.

As spring came around again, the killing season started to pick up and the beef-chain got busier.

I moved up from C-grade butcher to B-grade butcher, which meant quite a hefty increase in pay and as I was still doing as much overtime as I could get, it meant that we were now fairly well off financially and money worries were a thing of the past, especially as Maggie now had a well-paying job in the offices of a local civil engineering company.

I could now carry out most of the work involved in butchering the beef carcasses coming down the chain, but the job I had made my own was removing the heads from the carcass at the beginning of the head-chain. I could take the head off a huge Angus bull in less than 20 seconds and when the chain was flat out and we were processing 600 head of cattle per day, I was proud of the fact that I never had to stop the chain for any cock-ups.

There was a bit of a knack in locating the exact spot on the neck of the carcass, where you had to make the first cut in order to expose the joint, so that you could begin the process of removing the head. If you missed the joint, it made it very difficult to remove and you invariably had to stop the chain to complete the operation.

I was amazed at the number of blokes that I had to train up who just couldn't get it right and I put it down to my crap training. But even when someone else took over training they still couldn't

get it, so in the end the foremen just left me on the job for most of
the season, which suited me, as I quite enjoyed it.

At last I had discovered something that I was really good at,
but it was a pity that I did not intend cutting cows' heads off for
the rest of my life.

I was now beginning to realise that there was not much chance
of obtaining a good job with prospects while I was going under an
assumed name and to be successful in acquiring a position with a
future would entail background checks.

I was also frustrated at not being able to gain a driver's licence.

Despite the money at the freezing works being excellent, the
thought of doing that job for the rest of my life was more than
depressing and I knew that I would have to find some way of
sorting things out and making a fresh start.

We had been saving hard and now had enough money to fly
Maggie and Lisa to the UK so we decided that I would give myself
up to the authorities, pay the fines and accept deportation and
then we would return to New Zealand after a couple of years and
start again.

We decided to get married and then I would commence the
process of giving myself up and being deported and Maggie and
Lisa could fly to the UK to be with me.

Dave Smith, the AB from the *Westmorland*, had jumped ship
and was living in Ponsonby, so he agreed to be my best man.

I had arranged a few days off from work and on Friday, 2
November 1973 we got married at the Auckland registry office in
High Street in front of some of Maggie's family and a few friends,
and then we crossed the road to the Hotel De Brett for a few
drinks and then back to the flat in Otahuhu for a party.

Maggie went back with some of the girls in the party in her
girlfriend's car, while I jumped in with Dave, my best man, for the
drive back to Otahuhu.

Dave was a huge bloke and well over 6 ft in height but had bought a tiny little clapped-out Fiat Bambina and looked ridiculous hunched over the steering wheel of such a small car, but we drove through town and then onto the motorway headed south. Things were fine as long as we were on the flat or going downhill but the minute we hit any type of incline the seriously underpowered car really began to struggle and was almost down to walking speed at times. I was trying to slide down out of sight in my seat while Dave copped all sorts of abuse from passing motorists and to make matters worse, it was approaching rush-hour and the motorway was busy.

How we were never pulled over by the cops I will never know, but we eventually made it home with me silently vowing never to accept a lift from Dave again, but Dave was probably thinking it was payback for the time I left him with the girl who had her period in Liverpool.

On the evening of Monday, 5 November, Maggie dropped me off outside the Otahuhu police station, not expecting to see me again for a few days, and I walked up to the desk, produced my British Seaman's ID card and advised the officer on duty that I was a jumped seaman.

He was somewhat taken aback and at first did not know what to do with me, but then he arrested me and escorted me to a cell, while he figured out what to do with me.

On the way to the cell, we had to pass through the canteen, where a group of policemen were playing cards at one of the tables.

The constable escorting me shouted out to one of the policemen playing cards, 'Hey Bob, I've got one of your compatriots here who's jumped ship.'

The policeman replied, 'How the hell do you think the rest of us got here.'

After about 20 minutes in the cell, the same police officer came and released me, told me to present myself to the sergeant of the Wharf Police in Auckland, the following morning, and then sent me home.

Maggie got a bit of a shock when I walked in the door, as we had been expecting that I would be held in custody, so it was a relief to be able to sleep in my own bed that night.

The next morning, I caught the bus into the city and walked along Quay Street to the Wharf Police station and introduced myself to the sergeant, who was expecting me. He told me that they had no record of me leaving the *Westmorland* and had not been looking for me so I hadn't needed to be living under an assumed name.

He was a really nice guy and advised me that I would have to appear in court on a ship desertion charge, I would be fined and automatically sentenced to deportation, but if I appealed the deportation, the police would not object and I would be allowed to stay.

However, by this time Maggie had her heart set on a visit to the UK and I really needed to go home and make my peace with Mum and Dad, so we decided not to appeal the deportation.

A few weeks later, I received my summons to appear in the Auckland District Court on a charge of ship desertion and received a fine of $60 and was sentenced to be deported. I paid the fine by cheque and was released to await deportation.

I hadn't told anyone at work about what was happening and just carried on as normal, but the weeks and then the months slipped by, without me hearing anything about my deportation, so I decided to contact the wharf police and find out what was going on.

When I spoke to the sergeant, he was surprised to hear from me and had assumed that I had appealed the deportation.

When I explained that I really needed to go home and clear a few things up, he advised me that he would start the process immediately and that I would hear from them in due course.

A few days later, I was contacted on the telephone by a representative of P&O Shipping Co. who asked me whether I would be interested in working my passage home in one of their cargo ships and I immediately jumped at the chance, as the idea of being paid on my way back to the UK seemed like a good idea to me.

He asked me to come into the office later in the week and I gave immediate notice at the freezing works, and it was with some relief that I walked out of the gate for the final time. It had been fantastic money, but it was a terrible job and I had seen some horrific sights during my time there, so I left with few regrets.

It was Friday morning when I attended the P&O agent's offices in Auckland and almost fell over when they told me which ship I would be joining.

It was the *Westmorland* and I would be flying down to Timaru, via Christchurch, on Sunday afternoon to join *Westmorland* first thing Monday morning. They sent me down to the Wharf medical centre for a medical check-up and a smallpox vaccination and when I returned to the office, they gave me an airline ticket and sent me on my way.

The most difficult job was finding a pair of blues to go with my white jackets for uniform, as the shops closed on Saturdays and all the big stores were shut.

I managed to locate a uniform supplier who had a pair that had been made for someone else but never picked up and he offered to alter them for me if I came into town for a fitting and have them ready for me on the Sunday morning.

It was a bit of a scramble, but I managed to pick them up before being taken out to the airport by Maggie, where I said my goodbyes to her and Lisa, before boarding the plane. They would be flying over to the UK in a few weeks' time to coincide with my scheduled arrival in the UK.

Changing flights at Christchurch, I went to the gate when my flight was called, to see a sleek, modern aircraft sitting there and when I asked the security guy on the gate if that was the Timaru flight he replied in the negative and pointed to an old, clapped out DC-3 sitting on the tarmac and said, 'No mate. That's your flight over there.'

Upon boarding the plane, I had to haul myself up a steep incline to my seat at the front of the cabin and once we took off, I could not put my feet on the deck, due to the heat radiating from the engine.

The plane flew at a couple of thousand feet following the main highway all the way down to Timaru, which mercifully wasn't too far, as it was the most uncomfortable flight I have ever been on.

The shipping agent picked me up at Timaru airport and booked me into the Grand Hydro hotel, which was the same hotel I had left my bags the night before skinning out of the *Westmorland*.

He told me that he would pick me up first thing in the morning to take me down to the wharf to join the ship and then left me to my own devices.

The following morning, just after breakfast, the agent picked me up in his car and drove me down to the wharf, where we watched *Westmorland* slip through the breakwater and come alongside at the very same berth she had been on when I left her two-and-a-half years earlier, which was quite an amazing coincidence.

The only faces that I recognised from the past were Geordie Alan, who was still crew messman, and the motorman, Danny, from Dorset.

MV Westmorland (Credit: Chris Howell)

I signed on immediately and began work straight away as saloon steward and it felt as though I had never left her, as I was soon into the old routine.

A number of the mates and engineers had their wives with them for the trip, as did the 2nd steward, an old Cockney bloke, who was on his last trip to sea and had been permitted to take his wife along for his final voyage before retiring.

After a few days, we departed Timaru for New Plymouth but upon turning to the following morning we found ourselves sheltering from a westerly gale in Golden Bay, off Nelson, as the anchorage off New Plymouth was fully exposed to the gale and we were unable to enter the port.

Eventually the gale died away and we proceeded to New Plymouth, where we tied up alongside on the main wharf.

I was attempting to be as frugal as possible and save all my pay for arrival in the UK, so I was avoiding the bars up town and just visited the Seamen's Mission.

I was also trying to stay clear of the crew bar in the *Westmorland* and avoiding the ship-girls, now that I was married and was looking forward to finally leaving the coast and getting away deep sea.

While we were in New Plymouth, one of *Westmorland's* sisters, the *Tongariro*, tied up on the wharf opposite us and the captain of *Westmorland* told me that he had invited her captain over for lunch and would like me to remain on duty after the main lunch to wait on himself and his guest.

When they both arrived in the saloon for lunch, I was mortified, as the captain of *Tongariro* turned out to have been the captain of *Westmorland* when I jumped ship and he wasn't too pleased to see me.

He never acknowledged me, or spoke to me, during the entire meal, apart from placing his lunch order, while the captain of the *Westmorland* sat there with a huge grin on his face, thoroughly enjoying my discomfiture and thinking it was a huge joke. I was very relieved when lunch was finally over.

I telephoned Maggie almost every day, and she was getting concerned at the length of time *Westmorland* was remaining on the Kiwi coast, as we had been under the impression that she would be departing for the UK from Timaru and with Maggie due to fly to the UK in a couple of weeks, there was no way that I would be home in time to meet her off the flight from New Zealand.

We eventually departed New Plymouth but were bound westabout to the UK via South Africa and were scheduled to call into Cape Town to pick up a few hundred tons of cargo for delivery to Le Havre in France, so arrival in the UK was falling further and further behind schedule.

The weather crossing the Australian Bight was extremely rough with very heavy seas, which slowed us down quite a bit, but once into the southern Indian Ocean, conditions improved somewhat and weren't quite as bad.

As we were approaching the Cape, in the vicinity of Port Elizabeth, the engine stopped, as they hadn't yet resolved the problem which had plagued the ship for years and we illuminated the light signal indicating we were not under control.

A Russian freighter altered course to offer assistance and circled us a couple of times before being advised that we did not require help and that the problem would soon be resolved and that she could resume her course.

Fortunately, the seas were moderate and no cause for concern and although the ship was wallowing somewhat, conditions weren't too bad and after about an hour, we were under way again.

I was just thankful that the incident had not occurred in the Great Australian Bight, a couple of weeks earlier, as we would definitely have been in trouble had it done so, given the conditions we had experienced there.

When we arrived in Cape Town, it was the middle of the rainy season and despite only having to load a few hundred tons of frozen fish, the hatch-covers were rarely off, due to the heavy rain, and loading was a very slow process indeed. It reminded me of the trip when we had visited in the *Dorset* and the conditions were similar, with cargo being unable to be worked for days on end.

I had to go ashore the first day in Cape Town to get my glasses fixed, as I had broken them while we were at sea and the 'chippie' had managed to fix them temporarily, but they required a professional repair. Alan and I caught a cab into town, and I dropped my 'specs' at the optometrist and then headed to a nearby hotel for a beer.

While we were there, a group of businessmen walked in, accompanied by a woman, and they sat at the table next to us.

After a short while the woman picked up on our accents and

invited herself to our table for a chat, wanting to know where we were from and what we were doing. We had a good laugh with her and a few more drinks, when the barman approached us and told us that Alan and I had to leave as the 'suits' on the next table had complained about us using the 'f-bomb' in conversation and objected to it.

The woman did not mind and had in fact been using the word in conversation, but the guys on the next table were determined we had to go, so after directing a few choice expletives their way and telling the barman he could stick his hotel up his arse, we said goodbye to the woman and left.

I called into the optometrists to pick up my specs, which were looking like new, and they refused to accept payment for the repairs, so one bad experience had been offset by one good one, so I thanked the shop assistant profusely and we caught a cab back to the ship.

All the way back to the port, the cab driver had been trying to convince us to let him take us on a tour of Cape Town, for free, as he wanted to show us the sights. He finally convinced us that he was genuine and as we had had a few beers, we agreed to go with him just as we were approaching the dock gates, so he swung the cab around, turned off the meter and we headed back into the city.

The first thing he did was pick up his girlfriend, who got into the front seat with him and they had a long conversation in Afrikaans, which Alan and I could obviously not understand, and then he headed to a huge mansion house surrounded by a wall, where his girlfriend disappeared inside through a back door and then reappeared a few minutes later with a couple of young Coloured girls in tow.

The two girls climbed into the back seat with us so that the four of us were crammed in the back and barely able to move and then he headed off to park up in some secluded, tree-covered area where he proceeded to have sex with his girlfriend in the front seat, while exhorting Alan and me to have our way with the two girls in the back.

Even if the girls had been willing, and we weren't totally sure that they were, it would have been impossible to indulge in sex, due to the fact that we were crammed into a confined area and unable to move and it was absolutely pissing down with rain outside so getting among the trees was totally out of the question.

Alan and I just sat in the back, wondering what the hell we had got ourselves into and regretting the fact that we had not headed back to the ship when we had the chance.

All the while this had been going on, the taxi driver's dispatcher had been calling him on the radio in a monotonous Afrikaans voice, which he had just been ignoring but which was beginning to get on our nerves.

While he was having it off in the front seat he just kept telling us, 'You do your shaggings in the back man' in his Afrikaans accent.

He and his girl weren't in the least bit embarrassed to be doing it in front of total strangers and they were like a couple of rabbits going at it, despite her being one of the plainest women I had seen for some time. The two girls in the back with us just took the whole thing in their stride, laughing and talking in some South African dialect as though what was going on in the front seat was completely normal.

We eventually managed to convince him to drop us off at the port and thanked the girls for their company, which under different circumstances might have been appreciated a little more, and he departed with the sound of his dispatcher on the radio still trying to contact him.

Dinner was well over by the time we got back aboard *Westmorland*, but the chief steward wasn't too fazed, as he told us that he was half expecting us not to turn to and didn't even log us or give us a telling off. We didn't bother trying to explain what had happened to us as no-one would have believed it. I found it to be one of the weirdest experiences ever, but when Alan and I caught up many years later, he could remember every detail and we had a great laugh about it.

Eventually, despite many rain interruptions, we managed to complete loading the cargo of frozen fish and finally departed Cape Town for Le Havre.

The weather up the West African coast was fine and hot and over the following couple of weeks I managed to acquire quite a good tan as we steamed north.

Even the Bay of Biscay was calm for my final crossing and the weather continued fine with perfectly blue skies as we approached Le Havre, our final port before arriving in the UK.

Once we were alongside, a fleet of huge Spanish refrigerated, articulated trucks arrived over the next couple of days to take away the cargo of frozen fish, which was obviously destined for somewhere in Spain.

I was busting a gut to get home to the UK as Maggie and Lisa had arrived a couple of weeks ahead of me and were living with my family, so I was constantly going out on deck to check on the discharging of cargo and how it was progressing. This became a bit of a joke with the French dockers, who started taking the piss out of me, but as I couldn't understand a word they were saying, it didn't worry me too much.

And so we departed Le Havre for Avonmouth in the Bristol Channel, where we arrived the following day in glorious weather to find Maggie waiting on the quay for *Westmorland* to berth.

Ken and his wife, Gaynor, had driven her down to meet me and as soon as I had Customs clearance, I dashed down the gangway to the cheers of the wives on board *Westmorland* and embraced her.

I noticed that she didn't seem quite so excited to see me as I was to see her but let that go.

That night, a crowd of us had dinner in Avonmouth but I couldn't wait to get to bed and wasn't really interested in dining and the next day we paid off.

I had an interview with one of the catering officials prior to leaving *Westmorland* who was making noises about me possibly being allowed to continue at sea despite having jumped ship, but as I knew that there was no way that Maggie would agree to that, I did not follow up on it and let it go.

I left the ship and Ken drove us up the M6 to Chester, where I had to face the wrath of my mother over my decision to desert *Westmorland* on the other side of the world.

CHAPTER 26

MY PAY-OFF FROM WESTMORLAND WASN'T GOING TO LAST forever, as Maggie had already racked up a few bills, so my main priority was to look for a job. Vauxhall Motors in Ellesmere Port were recruiting so I attended an interview one morning. The gentleman interviewing me enquired what my previous occupation had been and when I replied, 'Merchant Navy,' he implied that working on an assembly-line in a factory would be too boring for me after a life at sea, but I managed to convince him that I really needed the job and would stick it out if he gave me a chance. He eventually relented and told me that I would be notified by letter in due course, when I would commence work.

In the meantime, I still needed to earn money so I applied for an advertised position as a knife-hand at an abattoir on the local industrial estate and with my experience at the freezing works in Auckland behind me, I was taken on. The comparison between this place and Westfield was beyond belief, as there was no automation whatsoever and carcasses were manhandled around the chain from station to station.

They were processing between eight and 10 head of cattle per day and the procedure was very labour intensive, so when I informed them that back in New Zealand, at the height of the killing season, we had been processing 600 head of cattle per day on one chain, they would not believe me and thought I was bullshitting them.

I was there for about two weeks when one evening, Maggie came to pick me up and told me that the letter from Vauxhall's had arrived and I was due to start work the following Monday, so I quit on the spot and vowed that that would be the last time I ever worked in a slaughterhouse!

Vauxhall's assembly line was a bit of a shock to the system to begin with as, although it didn't appear at first sight to be running too fast, if you weren't up to speed you soon found yourself falling further and further behind your station. My first job on the line was attaching drill clamps to the boot-lids and drilling the holes to attach the make and model insignia. Fortunately, drill-bits were not rationed, as for the first few weeks there I was breaking off a drill-bit every couple of vehicles I worked on.

If anyone who owned a 75/76 Vauxhall Viva or Chevette ever wondered what was causing that annoying little rattle in the boot-lid, well now they know!

Eventually, we bought a house in Little Sutton, a village just outside Ellesmere Port, and we spent the next 18 months doing it up before selling it in late 1977. By this time, Maggie was homesick for New Zealand and I was actually missing the place as well, so we decided to call it a day and return.

Mum and Dad weren't too happy at the decision, but we flew out to New Zealand on 7 January 1978.

I commenced working for Nissan at their car-plant in Wiri, South Auckland but eventually successfully applied for an advertised position as 2nd steward at the Royal New Zealand Yacht Squadron, Westhaven, Auckland and so commenced my 40-year association with clubs in New Zealand.

Jumping ship out of *Westmorland* had traumatised me far more than I realised and I missed my life at sea far more than I ever thought I would. I had never been the life and soul of the party and without the stimulus of alcohol, I reverted to my introverted self with very little conversation. Maggie very soon realised that I was not the person she thought she knew when she first met me in *Westmorland*.

Although I regretted jumping ship almost from the very moment I did it, the likelihood of me ever residing permanently in New Zealand had I not skinned out would have been extremely remote. It took me quite some time to accept that it was probably for the best, as the British Merchant Navy, as I knew it, ceased to exist only a relatively short while later.

Sometime during the 1980s my father sent me a newspaper cutting from the *Liverpool Echo* announcing the sale of the last Blue Funnel ship owned by Holts. Containerisation had finally taken over and most of the famous old shipping companies that I had grown up with had fallen by the wayside, leaving only the huge container conglomerates crewed by Middle and Far Eastern seamen. Had I hung in there, I would have eventually ended up having to make a career switch much later in life than I did, and I can't imagine that my life would have been as interesting and as successful as it has turned out to be.

Growing up, the last thing I had ever intended was to go to sea in the Merchant Navy as a steward, but apart from the initial period of settling in and getting over my homesickness, it turned out to be the most amazing experience I could ever have imagined and I sailed with people who I will never forget. The catering department at sea turned out not to be the lowly, last resort I had imagined but a vibrant, mostly humorous environment that taught me the value of hard work and how to look after myself, full of the most amazing characters you could ever wish to meet.

GLOSSARY

A/S. Assistant steward.

AB. Able bodied seaman.

Board of Trade Sports. Lifeboat drill.

Boss. Chief steward.

Bosun. Senior Petty Officer in charge of the deck ratings.

Bunkering. Taking on fuel oil.

Chippy. Ship's carpenter.

Coasting. A voyage to ports within the UK, Ireland and Europe, e.g. Hamburg, Amsterdam.

Deep-sea. A voyage to ports outside UK, Ireland and Europe.

Dhobi. Laundry.

Donkey-man. Engine-room petty officer.

EDH. Efficient deck hand.

Foc'sle. Raised deck at bow of ship.

Gash-bucket. Bin for food waste.

Geordie. Native of Tyne-side, Northumberland

Heads. Toilets.

Home boats. Name given to British ships in New Zealand due to large percentage of the population being of British descent. Term no longer in use.

JOS. Junior ordinary seaman.

Lamps, lampy. Lamp trimmer, the Bosun's right hand man.

Locking in, out. Entering into or departing docks through a system of locks.

Mama-san. Woman in charge of bar girls.

Mates. Navigating officers.

Monkey-island. Small platform above bridge for lookout.

Motorman. Engine-room rating.

OS. Ordinary seaman

Poop. raised deck at stern of ship.

Roads. Sheltered area outside a port where ships anchor.

Rock Dodger. Small coastal vessel.

Rosie. Rubbish bin.

Saloon. Dining room.

Saloon Bobby. Steward in charge of the saloon.

Sarnie. Merseyside term for sandwich.

Scouser. Native of Liverpool.

Shelties. Native of Shetland Islands

Skinning out. Jumping ship. Term used mainly on the Australian and New Zealand coast.

Soogee. Solution containing caustic soda for washing down paintwork and woodwork.

STD. Sexually transmitted disease.

Stornowegians. Natives of Stornoway in the Outer Hebrides.

The Clap. Venereal disease.

The Mate. Chief navigating officer.

Tiger. Captain's steward.

Windy hammer. Pneumatic hammer for removing rust.

ABOUT THE AUTHOR

Philip Saul was born in Chester in the UK. In 1964, he joined the Merseyside shipping company Blue Funnel Line as a catering boy and spent most of the next decade at sea in the British Merchant Navy. He jumped ship in New Zealand and spent two years working in the freezing industry under an assumed name before being arrested, fined and deported.

He emigrated to New Zealand in 1978 with his wife and daughter, working in the hospitality industry and eventually beginning a 40-year association with Clubs New Zealand, thirty-three of which were spent as General Manager of the Howick Club Inc. Philip is now retired and lives with his wife in Tauranga, Bay of Plenty, New Zealand.

Contact: elizabeth.st.publishing@gmail.com

ACKNOWLEDGMENTS

I'd like to acknowledge the generous assistance I received in the early stages of this book from my brother-in-law, Les Jones. For assistance later in the project, my thanks go to Martin Taylor and Brian O'Flaherty. Lastly, a special thanks to my wife Sharon for her encouragement and support, ensuring that this book, long in gestation, finally reached publication.

CPSIA information can be obtained
at www.ICGtesting.com
Printed in the USA
LVHW080843150922
728282LV00003B/6